PHENOMENOLOGY AND ESCHATOLOGY

This book brings together a world-renowned collection of philosophers and theologians to explore the ways in which the resurgence of eschatological thought in contemporary theology and the continued relevance of phenomenology in philosophy can illuminate each other. Through a series of phenomenological analyses of key eschatological concepts and detailed readings in some of the key figures of both disciplines, this text reveals that phenomenology and eschatology cannot be fully understood without each other: without eschatology, phenomenology would not have developed the ethical and futural aspects that characterize it today; without phenomenology, eschatology would remain relegated to the sidelines of serious theological discourse. Along the way, such diverse themes as time, death, parousia, and the call are re-examined and redefined.

Containing new contributions from Jean-Yves Lacoste, Claude Romano, Richard Kearney, Kevin Hart and others, this book is necessary reading for anyone interested in the intersection of contemporary philosophy and theology.

ASHGATE NEW CRITICAL THINKING IN RELIGION, THEOLOGY AND BIBLICAL STUDIES

The *Ashgate New Critical Thinking in Religion, Theology and Biblical Studies* series brings high quality research monograph publishing back into focus for authors, international libraries, and student, academic and research readers. Headed by an international editorial advisory board of acclaimed scholars spanning the breadth of religious studies, theology and biblical studies, this open-ended monograph series presents cutting-edge research from both established and new authors in the field. With specialist focus yet clear contextual presentation of contemporary research, books in the series take research into important new directions and open the field to new critical debate within the discipline, in areas of related study, and in key areas for contemporary society.

Other Titles in the Series:

Exodus Church and Civil Society
Public Theology and Social Theory in the Work of Jürgen Moltmann
Scott R. Paeth

Eucharistic Sacramentality in an Ecumenical Context
The Anglican Epiclesis
David J. Kennedy

Phenomenology and Eschatology
Not Yet in the Now

Edited by

NEAL DeROO
Boston College, USA

JOHN PANTELEIMON MANOUSSAKIS
College of the Holy Cross, USA

ASHGATE

Published by
Ashgate Publishing Limited
Wey Court East
Union Road
Farnham
Surrey, GU9 7PT
England

Ashgate Publishing Company
Suite 420
101 Cherry Street
Burlington
VT 05401-4405
USA

www.ashgate.com

British Library Cataloguing in Publication Data
Phenomenology and eschatology: not yet in the now. – (Ashgate new critical thinking in religion, theology and biblical studies)
1. Eschatology 2. Phenomenological theology
I. DeRoo, Neal II. Manoussakis, John Panteleimon
236

Library of Congress Cataloging-in-Publication Data
DeRoo, Neal, 1951–
Phenomenology and eschatology: not yet in the now / Neal DeRoo and John Panteleimon Manoussakis.
p. cm. – (Ashgate new critical thinking in religion, theology, and biblical studies)
ISBN 978-0-7546-6701-8 (hardcover: alk. paper)
1. Phenomenology. 2. Eschatology. 3. Philosophy and religion. I. Manoussakis, John Panteleimon. II. Title.
B829.5.D435 2008
236.01–dc22

2008037175

ISBN 978-0-7546-6701-8

Mixed Sources
Product group from well-managed forests and other controlled sources
www.fsc.org Cert no. SA-COC-1565
© 1996 Forest Stewardship Council
FSC

Printed and bound in Great Britain by
MPG Books Ltd, Bodmin, Cornwall.

Contents

Notes on Contributors

Jeffrey Bloechl is Associate Professor of Philosophy at Boston College. He has lectured and taught widely in contemporary European philosophy and philosophy of religion, with a particular interest in the relations of phenomenology and psychoanalysis to Christian thought. He is also the series editor of *Levinas Studies: An Annual Review* (Duquesne University Press) and, with Kevin Hart, of *Thresholds in Philosophy and Theology* (University of Notre Dame Press).

Neal DeRoo is Teaching Fellow in the Department of Philosophy at Boston College. He is the co-editor of *The Logic of Incarnation: James K.A. Smith's Critique of Postmodern Religion* (Pickwick Publications, 2009), and has lectured worldwide on topics ranging from Husserl to Derrida and psychoanalysis. In addition, he has contributed to *The Heythrop Journal*, *Essays in Philosophy*, and other journals.

Jeffrey Hanson received his Ph.D. from Fordham University and is currently adjunct assistant professor of philosophy at Boston College.

Kevin Hart is Edwin B. Kyle Professor of Christian Studies and Professor of Religious Studies in the Department of Religious Studies at the University of Virginia, where he also holds professorships in the Department of English and the Department of French. He is the co-editor of the *Thresholds in Philosophy and Theology* series for University of Notre Dame Press. His most recent books include *The Dark Gaze: Maurice Blanchot and the Sacred* (Chicago University Press, 2004)*, Counter-Experiences: Reading Jean-Luc Marion* (University of Notre Dame Press, 2007) and, with Michael A. Signer, *The Exorbitant: Emmanuel Levinas between Jews and Christians* (Fordham University Press, 2009). His poetry is gathered in *Flame Tree: Selected Poems* (Bloodaxe Books, 2004), and *Young Rain* (Australia: Giramondo Press, 2008; United Kingdom: Bloodaxe Press, 2009; and United States: Notre Dame University Press, 2009).

Richard Kearney is Charles B. Seelig Professor in Philosophy at Boston College. He is the author of numerous works in philosophy and religion, including *Poétique du Possible* (Beauchesne, 1984), *The Wake of Imagination* (Hutchinson and Routledge, 1988), *On Stories* (Routledge, 2001), *The God Who May Be: A Hermeneutics of Religion* (Indiana University Press, 2001), *Strangers, Gods and Monsters: Interpreting Otherness* (Routledge, 2002), and *Anatheism: Returning to God After God* (forthcoming from Columbia University Press). He is the co-editor of the *Thinking in Action* series (Routledge, Taylor and Francis), and his works have been translated into 15 languages. He is also a published novelist, with *Sam's Fall* (1995) and *Walking at Sea Level* (1997), and poet, with *Angel of Patrick's Hill* (1991).

Douglas H. Knight teaches Christian theology in London. He is the author of *The Eschatological Economy: Time and the Hospitality of God* (Eerdmans, 2006) and editor of *The Theology of John Zizioulas: Personhood and the Church* (Ashgate, 2007) and *John Zizioulas, Lectures on Christian Dogmatics* (T&T Clark 2008).

Jean-Yves Lacoste is Professor of Philosophy at the Institut Catholique de Paris. He is the author of the hugely influential *Experience and the Absolute: Disputed Questions on the Humanity of Man* (English translation by Fordham University Press, 2004), *Note sur le Temps: Essai sur les raisons de la mémoire et de l'espérance* (Presses Universitaires France, 1990), *Présence et Parousie* (English translation forthcoming from Notre Dame University Press) and *La phénoménalité de Dieu* (Paris, 2008). He is also the editor of the *Encyclopedia of Christian Theology* (English translation by Routledge, 2004).

John Panteleimon Manoussakis is visiting Assistant Professor of Philosophy at the College of the Holy Cross. He is the author of *God After Metaphysics: A Theological Aesthetic* (Indiana University Press, 2007). He edited *After God: Richard Kearney and the Theological Turn in Continental Philosophy* (Fordham University Press, 2005), and is the co-editor of *Heidegger and the Greeks: Interpretive Essays* (Indiana University Press, 2006) and *Traversing the Imaginary: Richard Kearney and the Postmodern Challenge* (Northwestern University Press, 2007).

Jean-Luc Marion is Professor of Philosophy at the University of Paris IV (Sorbonne) and the John Nuveen Professor at the University of Chicago Divinity School, Department of Philosophy, and the Committee on Social Thought. Some of his early works include a trilogy on Descartes: *Sur l'ontologie grise de Descartes* (J. Vrin,1975), *Sur la théologie blanche de Descartes* (Presses Universitaires France, 1981) and *Sur le prisme métaphysique de Descartes* (Presses Universitaires France, 1986). He became known in the English-speaking philosophical world through the translation of his groundbreaking work *God Without Being* (University of Chicago, 1991). His phenomenological work includes the trilogy *Reduction and Givenness: Investigations of Husserl, Heidegger and Phenomenology* (English translation by Northwestern University Press, 1998), *Being Given: Toward a Phenomenology of Givenness* (English translation by Stanford University Press, 2002) and *In Excess: Studies in Saturated Phenomena* (English translation by Fordham University Press, 2004). His most recent works to appear in English are *The Erotic Phenomenon* (University of Chicago Press, 2008) and *The Visible and the Revealed* (Fordham University Press, 2008).

Ilias Papagiannopoulos is teaching political philosophy and history of ideas at the Panteion University for Social and Political Sciences in Athens. He has also lectured at the University of Innsbruck (Austria) and was a research fellow at the Greek Academy for Sciences and Arts under the supervision of John Zizioulas. He has published, in Greek, *After the Stage. An essay on Herman Melville's Moby-Dick* (2000), and *Beyond Absence. An essay on the person, on the track of Sophocles' Oedipus Rex* (2005).

Claude Romano is Associate Professor in Philosophy at the University of Paris-Sorbonne. He is the author of several works in phenomenology, including *L'événement et le monde* (Presses Universitaires de France, 1998), *L'événement et le temps* (Presses Universitaires de France, 1999), *Il y a* (Presses Universitaires de France, 2003), and *Le chant de la vie. Phénoménologie de Faulkner* (Gallimard, 2005). He is also the co-editor of *Le néant. Contribution à une histoire du non-être dans la philosophie occidentale* (Presses Universitaires de France, 2006), and served as the editor of the French journal *Philosophie* from 1994–2003. His works that have been translated into English include *Event and World* (Fordham, 2008), *Event and Time* (Fordham, forthcoming), and *There Is* (Fordham, forthcoming).

Judith E. Tonning teaches Systematic Theology in the Theology Faculty at Oxford University, where she is currently completing her DPhil. She is the General Editor of *The C.S. Lewis Chronicle*, and has published on eschatology in relation to Heidegger, Stanley Cavell, and Shakespeare in journals such as *The Heythrop Journal*, *Literature and Theology*, and *The Glass*.

Acknowledgments

We would like to thank the American College of Greece and its President, Dr. John Bailey, for graciously hosting the conference on "Phenomenology and Eschatology" — the fifth of its kind — in the summer of 2006. A number of the essays published in this volume were originally presented during that conference. We would also like to thank Sarah Lloyd, Anne Keirby and everyone at Ashgate for their wonderful patience and assistance in bringing this book to completion.

John Panteleimon Manoussakis would also like to thank the American College of Greece, its executive Vice-President Nick Jiavaras and the indispensable Ms. Anna Fotinou for their generous hospitality during the summer of 2008, during which he was able to complete his editorial work on this volume.

Neal DeRoo would like to thank the Social Sciences and Humanities Research Council of Canada (SSHRC), whose grant made possible the editorial and translation work that he did on this volume between the summer of 2007 and the summer of 2008.

Introduction

What does eschatology, the study of the last things, have to do with phenomenology, the study of the things themselves? What does Freiburg have to do with Patmos? The key to unraveling this question lies in properly understanding the question. First, we must get a handle on these slippery concepts called "eschatology" and "phenomenology." Only then can one begin to understand the conjunction between them in the title of this volume, "Phenomenology and Eschatology."

Introducing Eschatology and Phenomenology

So, what is eschatology, and what is phenomenology? Let us take them in turn, beginning with the end.[1] *Eschaton* is the Greek word for end, and eschatology has traditionally been understood as the study of the end times. Most manuals of doctrines have treated the end times in light of four major "last things": resurrection, judgment, heaven and hell.[2] The task of eschatology has traditionally been to elucidate these last things on the basis of scriptures and the tradition. For centuries, much of this study crystallized around interpretations of the Biblical book of *Revelation*, which was understood as a view of the future *eschaton* revealed to John on the island of Patmos. Like the book of *Revelation*, eschatology was usually something of an afterthought added to the end of a systematic study of theology,[3]

---

[1]   Anyone looking for a more comprehensive account of these terms should consult, in addition to the works cited throughout this introduction: Brian Hebblethwaite, *The Christian Hope* (Basingstoke: Marshall, Morgan & Scott, 1984), and Herbert Spiegelberg, *The Phenomenological Movement: A Historical Introduction*, 2 volumes (The Hague: Martinus Nijhoff, 1965).

[2]   Cf. David Fergusson, "Eschatology," in *The Cambridge Companion to Christian Doctrine*, ed. Colin E. Gunton (Cambridge: Cambridge University Press, 1997), 226–44; 226. In *The Reality After Death*, the second Vatican council affirmed eight eschatological realities which flesh out these four major last things; cf. *The Reality after Death* in *Vatican Council II: More Post Conciliar Documents* ed. Austin Flannery (Collegeville: Liturgical, 1982), 500–504; and Peter C. Phan, "Contemporary Context and Issues in Eschatology," *Theological Studies* 55 (1994), 507–36.

[3]   Jurgen Moltmann makes this claim in his *Theology of Hope: On the Ground and the Implications of a Christian Eschatology*, trans. James W. Leitch (New York and Evanston: Harper & Row, 1967). For example, the term "eschatology" was apparently coined by Abraham Calovius in 1677, when he used the term *Eschatologia Sacra* as a general heading at the end of his twelve-volume dogmatics. The term "eschatology" did not gain widespread use in German theology until well into the nineteenth century; cf. Erwin

"the final piece in the jigsaw of Christian belief, [which] could be set out largely in isolation from the exposition of other doctrines."[4]

This notion of eschatology changed in the twentieth century. Johannes Weiss, Karl Barth, and Jurgen Moltmann, in Protestant circles, Karl Rahner in Catholicism, and John Zizioulas in Greek Orthodoxy have all made eschatology central to Christianity.[5] This "eschatological turn" in twentieth century theology[6] emphasizes that the *eschaton* has real consequences, here and now, for theology, creation and the church. Despite a multitude of differences, one can see the seed of an essential relation between eschatology and the structure of creation emerging in these various accounts. In speaking of the early twentieth-century fascination with eschatology under the guise of the "kingdom of God," Christofer Frey writes that each "interpretation of the Kingdom of God includes *a priori assumptions of reality and history*."[7] These *a priori* assumptions "frame the horizon of possibilities"[8] of ethics, ecclesiology, biblical exegesis, and more. The influence and importance of the *eschaton*, then, is not solely futural, but works retroactively to condition the present and the past. If the kingdom of God is "not-yet" fully here, it is also "already" here. It is one of the hallmarks of twentieth-century theology to take seriously this "already — but not yet" character of eschatology. In doing so, eschatology takes a central role in any theological system: as the end which retroactively conditions the present and past, eschatology affects all aspects of a systematic theology. To do theology, one must now take eschatology seriously.[9]

Phenomenology is widely said to have begun with the work of Edmund Husserl.[10] While already nascent in his *Logical Investigations* (1900/1901), phenomenology emerges explicitly in Husserl's *Ideas towards a Pure Phenomenology and*

Fahlbusch, "Eschatologie," *Evangelisches Kirchenlexikon*, ed. E. Fahlbusch et al., 5 vols. (Göttingen: Vandenhoeck & Ruprecht, 1986–97), vol. 1, p. 1107.

   4   Fergusson, "Eschatology," 226.

   5   Cf. Johannes Weiss, *Die Predigt Jesu Vom Reiches Gottes* (1892); in English as *Jesus' Proclamation of the Kingdom of God* (Philadelphia: Fortress Press, 1971); Karl Barth, *Der Römerbrief* (1921), trans. Edward C. Hoskyns as *The Epistle to the Romans* (London, Oxford, New York: Oxford University Press, 1933); Jurgen Moltmann, *Theology of Hope*; originally published in Germany in 1964; Karl Rahner, *Foundations of Christian Faith: An Introduction to the Idea of Christianity*, trans. William V. Dych (New York: Crossroads, 1982); John Zizioulas, *Being as Communion: Studies in Personhood and the Church* (Crestwook, NY: St. Vladimir's Seminary Press, 1985).

   6   Fergusson, "Eschatology," 226.

   7   Christofer Frey, "Eschatology and Ethics: Their Relation in Recent Continental Protestantism," in *Eschatology in the Bible and in Jewish and Christian Tradition*, ed. Henning Graf Reventlow (Sheffield: Sheffield Academic, 1997), 62–74; 65.

   8   Ibid.

   9   Further examples of twentieth-century theologians who take eschatology seriously include Wolfhart Pannenberg and Rudolf Bultmann; cf. Frey, 66 ff.

   10   Thus separating "phenomenology" as a philosophical method from earlier philosophical uses of that term, most notably in Hegel.

Phenomenological Philosophy (1913). As was the case with eschatology, there are multiple meanings associated with the term phenomenology, and multiple strands of it as well (one often reads of Husserlian phenomenology, Heideggerian phenomenology, Sartrian phenomenology, etc.), so that determining exactly what defines phenomenology is a difficult task.[11] At the very least, phenomenology takes as its motto a return "to the things themselves" (*zu den Sachen selbst*). To do so, Husserlian phenomenology focuses on consciousness, and more specifically, on one's own consciousness, on the first-person perspective. Rather than some banal relativism, such a move is meant to ground phenomenology as a rigorous science;[12] by focusing on our own consciousness of phenomena, we can better understand the world around us, because, as the phenomenological notion of "intentionality" states, all consciousness is consciousness *of*, and therefore our consciousness connects us to (or constitutes)[13] the world around us.[14] By examining one's own consciousness, one retains the centrifugal force that is primary in our experience of the world: my experience of the world is always *my* experience of *my* world, that is, of the world as I live in it, act in it, influence it, am influenced by it, etc. Without keeping this central insight in mind, science risks losing its attachment to the world in which we live, conforming the world to abstractions rather than employing abstractions to help us understand the world.[15]

---

[11] This task is made infinitely more difficult by the fact that the most famous first generation disciple of Husserl, Martin Heidegger, is also the proponent of the main phenomenological rival to Husserlian phenomenology, i.e., Heideggerian phenomenology. Hence, from almost its earliest stages, phenomenology is torn in two.

[12] Cf., for example, Husserl's "Philosophie als strenge Wissenschaft," *Logos*, I (1910–11), 289–341, trans. Quentin Lauer as "Philosophy as a Rigorous Science", in Edmund Husserl, *Phenomenology and the Crisis of Philosophy* (New York: Harper & Row, 1965), 71–147.

[13] The notion of "constitution" in phenomenology is complex, and even Husserl seems to be ambiguous on exactly what it means. The reader interested in knowing more about constitution and how it functions to "connect" us to the world, should consult Robert Sokolowski, *The Formation of Husserl's Concept of Constitution* (The Hague: Martinus Nijhoff, 1970).

[14] As Michel Henry states, "Phenomenology is the science of phenomena *in their reality*. Its object is not the ensemble of phenomena with their structures and, as a result, with their specific domains, but the essence of the phenomenon as such"; Michel Henry, "The Essence of Manifestation", trans. Girard Etzkorn (The Hague: Martinus Nijhoff, 1973), 53. Husserl elaborates on the subtle critique of science mentioned here in *The Crisis of European Sciences and Transcendental Phenomenology*, trans. David Carr (Evanston: Northwestern University Press, 1970).

[15] For a more in-depth investigation into the relationship between science and phenomenology, consult Marvin Farber, *The Foundation of Phenomenology: Edmund Husserl and the Quest for a Rigorous Science of Philosophy*, 3rd edition (Albany, NY: State University of New York Press, 1943).

The relationship of the individual to the world is central to all phenomenologies, due to its reciprocal nature: on the one hand, the world I see is always *my* world, that is, the world I constitute, and on the other hand, the individual that I am is always part of, that is, constituted by, the world. This reciprocal relationship between world and consciousness is discussed under many rubrics, including the Husserlian "life-world,"[16] and Heideggerian "thrownness."[17] This focus on the individual's relation to the world led Sartre from his early phenomenological works[18] to his later "existentialist" writings.[19] Gadamer, too, was undoubtedly influenced by the phenomenological movement with his notion of "horizons."[20] This idea of the life-world as constitutive of the individual is one of the major themes in twentieth-century Continental philosophy, and has its roots in phenomenology.

Though certain themes, such as the life-world, that have come to gain prominence in Continental philosophy find their provenance in phenomenology, this does not entail that all the philosophies that employ these themes (e.g., existentialism, hermeneutics, deconstruction, etc.) are phenomenological. There is something specific to the work of, e.g., Husserl, Merleau-Ponty, and Jean-Luc Marion (to name a few), that sets them apart as distinctly "phenomenological." Precisely what this "something" is, however, is a matter of debate in phenomenological circles. While some will argue that phenomenology has strict methodological controls, and is therefore defined principally by that methodology, others seem to include the study of figures who have practiced phenomenology within the field of phenomenology.[21] Phenomenology, like eschatology, is a broad field of study, including many disparate figures and ideas within itself, while still maintaining

---

[16]   Husserl discusses his notion of the *lebenswelt* especially in the Fifth of the *Cartesian Mediations*, trans. Dorothy Cairns (The Hague: Martinus Nijhoff, 1950) and in *Ideas Pertaining to a Pure Phenomenology and to a Phenomenological Philosophy, Second Book: Studies in the Phenomenology of Constitution,* trans. Richard Rojcewicz and André Schuwer (The Hague, Netherlands: Kluwer Academic, 1989).

[17]   Cf. Division I of *Being and Time.*

[18]   Most notably, *The Transcendence of the Ego* (1936), trans. Forest Williams and Robert Kirkpatrick (1957) and *The Imaginary* (1940), trans. Jonathan Webber (London and New York: Routledge, 2004).

[19]   Including most of his plays and novels, as well as 1946's *L'Existensialism est un humanisme.* Sartre's magnum opus, *Being and Nothingness*, occupies a somewhat ambiguous space in between phenomenology (hence it's subtitle: "Essai d'ontologie phénoménologique") and existentialism.

[20]   Hans-Georg Gadamer, *Truth and Method*, trans. Joel Weinsheimer and Donald G. Marshall (London and New York: Continuum, 2004).

[21]   Dominique Janicaud would be one proponent of the former (cf. his concerns in "The Theological Turn in French Phenomenology", trans. Bernard G. Prusak in Janicaud et al., *Phenomenology and the "Theological Turn": The French Debate* (New York: Fordham University Press, 2000), and Richard Kearney (cf. his contributions to *After God: Richard Kearney and the Religious Turn in Continental Philosophy*, ed. J.P. Manoussakis (New York: Fordham University Press, 2006) and Dan Zahavi (cf. *Husserl's Phenomenology*

certain overarching themes. This broad nature is both evidence of its fecundity, and what makes it so difficult to define.

Problems in Phenomenology and Eschatology

Eschatology and phenomenology, then, while structurally similar, would seem to have little to do with each other except for a shared period of intellectual popularity (and that not even in the same discipline). One deals with the end times, the other with things as they appear to me here and now; one searches Scripture and tradition for answers, the other searches for answers within one's own consciousness or experience of the world.[22]

There is, however, one particularly fruitful area of overlap between eschatology and phenomenology. It concerns the question of time. For eschatology, the importance of this cannot be overstated: if one wants to recover the importance of the *eschaton* for the present and the past, as much of twentieth-century eschatology wants to do, then one must first tackle the issue of how we can conceive of a future time as being in any way effective for previous times. This seems to go against common sense notions of time as a line that moves from the past into the future, and not the other way around.

This issue shows itself in eschatological discourse in the debate between futuristic and realized eschatologies. In futuristic eschatology, the *eschaton* foretold by the Scripture is yet to take place: eschatological events are still in the future, and the best we can do is to try to predict when they might occur. This has been by far the dominant position throughout the Christian traditions. Realized eschatology, on the other hand, claims that the eschatological passages in the Bible were fulfilled already in Jesus' time; the *eschaton*, such as it is, is in the past. The sharp temporal distinction between past and future necessitates the sharp distinction between futuristic and realized eschatology: if things can only happen in the future or in the past or in the present, then the *eschaton*, discussed in the Bible, must refer either to future or past events, that is, events that have already occurred or that remain yet to occur.

(Stanford: Stanford University Press, 2003) are perhaps proponents of the latter view of phenomenology.

[22]   This emphasis on the first-person perspective – on *my* experience or *my* consciousness – is challenged, but not, I think, immediately done away with by the work of thinkers such as Emmanuel Levinas and Jean-Luc Marion. The focus on the Other that dominates in the work of these thinkers, I would argue, is meant to further clarify the nature of the self: I am not my own, but am hostage to the other (Levinas), am called by the other (Marion). The complex relationship between subjectivity and otherness introduced by Levinas, Marion, and others like them is hotly contested: it is either one of the most fruitful areas of current phenomenological research, or an abandonment of phenomenology altogether. Both sides of this debate are given voice in Janicaud et al., *Phenomenology and the "Theological Turn"*.

A way around this disjunction is suggested in the idea of an inaugurated eschatology. It suggests that the death and Resurrection of Christ have inaugurated the *eschaton*, but that some events (the Second coming, the resurrection of the dead, etc.) remain yet to come in the future. In this way, the *eschaton* is understood as having already begun, but not yet being finished: as being already (here), but not yet (fully here). One problem with this view, however, is that it needs to answer how the *eschaton* can hold together, e.g., the life of Christ told in the Gospel narratives and the Second Coming foretold there. At stake is whether the *eschaton* is still occurring, that is, whether we live in the eschatological age, or whether it has been interrupted, like a play taking a very long intermission between Acts I and II. Further, if the *eschaton* is on-going, then one must question the role of humanity in the events of the *eschaton*, whether we actively participate in these events, or whether, rather, they are merely things that happen to us, outside of our control.[23] And again, if we are involved, to what extent are our actions shaped by the coming events, that is, the future coming of Christ and the resulting full presence (*parousia*) of God with us in the world? If present actions are shaped by the future events, then the issue of how the future can be effective in the past and present remains pressing: without a revised notion of temporality, even an inaugurated eschatology is at a loss to explain the efficacy of future eschatological events for present and past events.

What is needed, then, is a notion of time that can take seriously the "already, but not yet" character of much of twentieth-century eschatology. Such a notion of time is a prevalent theme in phenomenology. Heidegger, for example, speaks of the future's determining of the past through his notions of "anticipatory resoluteness" and "projection," which leaves Dasein "essentially ahead of itself."[24] Phenomenology's reception in France only enhanced this thematic. While criticizing Heidegger for over-emphasizing the future, Sartre himself held that the future creates meaning for the past.[25] This entails that a person, in her freedom, is essentially a projection of what she is not yet, and hence she escapes her essence as expressed in her past.[26] If both Heidegger and Sartre emphasize the future,

---

[23]   Richard Kearney's notion of a "micro-eschatology" seeks to answer this question directly; cf. Richard Kearney, "Epiphanies of the Everyday: Toward a Micro-Eschatology", in *After God*, 3–20.

[24]   Heidegger, *Being and Time*, §79 (German, p. 406).

[25]   Cf. J.P. Sartre, *L'Être et le néant: Essai d'ontologie phénoménologique* (Paris: Gallimard, 1943), trans. Hazel E. Barnes as *Being and Nothingness: A Phenomenological Essay on Ontology* (New York, London, Toronto, Sydney: Washington Square Press, 1992). Sartre's most explicit critique of Heidegger's focus on the future occurs on p. 451 of the French edition. His discussion of temporality occurs throughout, but especially in chapter two of Part Two.

[26]   *L'Être et le néant*, 515.

Merleau-Ponty notes that the future must always be embedded in the present.[27] This does not, however, reduce the future to the present. Rather, it breaks up the finality of both future and present via the "ecstatic" character of subjectivity,[28] which enables the subject to be a temporal being, that is, a being that can reach beyond the mere present into the past and future.[29]

This notion of temporality is rooted in Husserl's discussions of the internal time-consciousness (*Zeitbewusstein*) of the subject. Through lectures over the course of several years, Husserl developed this idea of consciousness' awareness of time, and especially of the self-awareness of the internal time of the constituting ego.[30] These published lectures provide the theory of temporality that undergirds all of the notions of the efficacy of the future in the present and past that occur in the work of later phenomenological thinkers. Husserl's essential finding in this work is that our consciousness of time is inherently trinitary: in perceiving the present, we also retain the immediate past as it "runs-off" into the past (retention), and we anticipate the immediate future (protention). By opening up subjectivity essentially to the future, Husserl is able to emphasize the anticipatory, and hence future-oriented, movement of all consciousness. Unfortunately, Husserl does not discuss the idea of protention at length within the pages of *On the phenomenology of the consciousness of internal time*, except to state that protention works like retention, except in the other direction.[31] This has lead to a great deal of confusion regarding how this future-oriented temporality functions.[32]

---

[27]   Maurice Merleau-Ponty, *Phenomenology of Perception*, trans. Colin Smith (New York and London: Routledge, 1962; reprint, 2002); cf. especially Part III, Chapter 2, "Temporality."

[28]   Ibid., 487 ff.

[29]   Jacques Derrida, with his notion of the messianic, would also seem to fall into this line of thought (cf. *the Specters of Marx: the State of the Debt, the Work of Mourning,* and *the New International,* trans. Peggy Kamuf [New York and London: Routledge, 1994]). His inclusion within the tradition of phenomenology is a matter of great debate, and so I have left discussion of him within this context to a minimum.

[30]   Husserl, *On the phenomenology of the Consciousness of Internal Time (1893–1917)* trans. John Barnett Brough (Dordrecht, Boston, London: Kluwer Academic, 1991). All citations are from the German version, found in Volume X of the *Husserliana* series. Hereafter cited as Hua X.

[31]   Hua X, 75. Husserl makes similar claims in §77 and §81 of *Ideas: General Introduction to Pure Phenomenology*, trans. W.R. Boyce Gibson (New York: Collier, 1962). This work is a translation of *Ideen zu einer Phänomenologie und phänomenologischen Philosophie*, the two books of which appears as Band III/1 and Band V of the Husserliana series.

[32]   Some of this confusion has hopefully been remedied by the relatively recent publication of some of Husserl's work from the years 1917–18, while he was in Bernau. Formerly accessible only in the Husserl archives (where they were known as the "L" manuscripts), they were published in the Husserliana series in 2001; cf. Edmund Husserl, *Die Bernauer Manuskripte über das Zeitbewusstsein (1917/1918)* Husserliana Band XXXIII, R.

Husserl's theory of internal time-consciousness undergirds the theme of temporality in phenomenology. By providing a notion of time that incorporates the past and future into the present, this phenomenological conception of time is able to support notions of temporality that see the future as efficacious in the present and the past. This would suggest that such a notion of temporality might be able to provide assistance to theologians working in the realm of eschatology, in terms of the problem outlined above.

(How) Can Phenomenology and Eschatology Help Each Other?

In discussing the problem of time, in both its eschatological and phenomenological guises, we have seen that both disciplines seek to make the future causally efficacious in the present. Eschatology seems to know why it should do so, but is not yet sure how. Phenomenology suggests precisely how this could work. Husserl describes his theory of time-consciousness in terms of "the transformation of the now into the no-longer—and, in the other direction, of the not-yet into the now."[33] This last phrase, the not-yet into the now, directly parallels the major theme in twentieth-century eschatology that sought to understand the power of the future (the not-yet) to act in the present (the now). The problem that remains, then, as the title of this book suggests, is to explain how the "not-yet into the now" of Husserlian protention can be understood, and can help us understand, the power of the not-yet to act in the now that characterizes eschatology. This is but one step in a more general project: the project of relating phenomenology to eschatology. What is at stake in this larger project, as has already been suggested by the previous discussion of temporality, is an examination of both phenomenology and eschatology. Holding these two together seems to promise a new understanding of each of these disciplines. The efforts in this volume aim at just such an understanding.

The first part of the book, "Phenomenology of Eschatology," seeks to begin the process of understanding phenomenology and eschatology together by examining phenomenologically certain key eschatological concepts. In the first essay, "The

---

Bernet, and D. Lohmar Hrsg (Dordrecht/Boston/London: Kluwer Academic, 2001). Husserl discusses futurity and protention in much more detail in this work than he did in Hua X. As such, a renewed interest in Husserl's concept of the future has emerged. For more on Husserl's theory of time, cf. Toine Kortooms, *Phenomenology of Time: Edmund Husserl's Analysis of Time-Consciousness* (Dordrecht/Boston/London: Kluwer Academic, 2002). For more on Husserl's concept of the future, in general, and of protention, more specifically, cf. James R. Mensch, "Husserl's Concept of the Future," *Husserl Studies* 16 (1999), 41–64, and Lanei Rodemeyer, "Developments in the Theory of Time-Consciousness: An Analysis of Protention", in *The New Husserl: A Critical Reader* edited by Donn Welton (Bloomington and Indianapolis: Indiana University Press, 2003), 125–54, respectively.

[33]   Hua X, 76–7.

Phenomenality of Anticipation," Jean-Yves Lacoste offers a sustained discussion of experiences both everyday (such as waiting for a friend's visit, or listening to "The Art of the Fugue") and more rigorously phenomenological (such as the experience of enjoyment/*jouissance*), in order to highlight the key modalities of anticipation and its manifestation in our conscious experience. In doing so, he distinguishes anticipation from non-anticipatory modes of givenness, and suggests that anticipation is a fundamental structure, not just of eschatological experience, but of our consciousness *per se*.

The next essay, "Awaiting" by Claude Romano, analyzes the phenomenon of awaiting both in its own right, and as it relates to Husserl's accounts of protention and anticipation. The rigorous investigations undergone in this chapter distinguish between awaiting as a permanent disposition of consciousness and awaiting as a consciously adopted existential posture. In so doing, they unearth a surprising connection between language and awaiting, a connection that has serious philosophical implications for a phenomenology of time and its relationship to the novelty of the event: one can only experience the novelty of the new in light of the more primordial expectation of a consciousness that is always stretched out before itself into the future.

Both of these first two essays, then, in analyzing eschatology from a phenomenological point of view, reveal that key eschatological concepts such as awaiting and anticipation are characteristic of human experience of the world in general. Hence, eschatology seems to play some fundamental role in structures of human experience and behaviour. But is the reverse also true: can the understanding of structures of human experience and behaviour provided by phenomenology also shape how we understand eschatology? The papers from the second part of the book, "Phenomenological Eschatology," suggest precisely this.

Richard Kearney's "Sacramental Imagination and Eschatology" uses the phenomenology of Maurice Merleau-Ponty as a starting point to launch a re-evaluation of the nature and substance of eschatology, recasting it in terms of our everyday experience rather than as a grand narrative of the end-of-times utopia. By focusing on the "flesh," in its multiple phenomenological layers, Kearney is able to show that the mundane world is infused with divine depth. This is made possible in part by the development of a "sacramental" imagination of the things to come.

The necessity of the imagination for both eschatology and phenomenology is the end point of John Panteleimon Manoussakis's "The Promise of the New and the Tyranny of the Same." Beginning with phenomenology's re-evaluation of the post-Cartesian epistemological priority of the past over the future, Manoussakis goes on to show the significant repercussions this new account of temporality has for eschatology and liturgy. Here, Kearney's philosophy of ethics and imagination is brought together with the rigorous theological and Eucharistic resources of Lacoste and Marion to show, among other things, the importance of the distinction between fantasy and imagination, and the privileged place of the latter, in eschatology. What emerges from this sustained interaction between phenomenology and eschatology is a philosophical and intellectual justification for eschatology to again assert its rightful place in theological discourse.

The last paper in Section II, Douglas Knight's "John Zizioulas on Eschatology and Persons," uses the work of the Orthodox theologian John Zizioulas to show that persons are necessarily plural beings who include and represent the entire world of relationships. Grounding this conception of personhood in the trinity, Knight goes on to show that, apart from God's empersoning power, the human is a tragic individual rather than a person. Humanity is then called to bring freedom to creation by freely choosing to participate in the life of God. By using this concept of the person to re-imagine the eschaton, Knight is then able to reconceive sin, creation, and Christology through this analysis of human personhood and freedom.

At this point, the book will have shown that a phenomenological analysis of key eschatological terms reveals that these terms are characteristic of human experience in general, and that this has enabled eschatology to be re-thought by way of resources taken from the phenomenological tradition. The third section of the book, "Eschatological Phenomenology," endeavors to show that the influence of phenomenology on eschatology is not a one-way street: not only do certain eschatological concepts shape human experience, but eschatology itself plays a major role in the constitution and self-understanding of phenomenology.

Ilias Papagiannopoulos's "The Eschatology of the Self and the Birth of the Being-With; or, on Tragedy" takes up the themes of tragedy and personhood from the previous paper, but employs them in the other direction, if you will: rather than using phenomenology to reconceive eschatology, Papagiannopoulos here uses eschatological resources to reevaluate the idea of the person, showing that the relationship between selfhood and experience in phenomenology has a necessarily eschatological core. Using a sustained analysis of the "tragic" character of Oedipus to illustrate its claims narratively, this paper challenges the standard metaphysical accounts of selfhood, finitude and negations, showing that the eschatological orientation of otherness as a call to or upon the self affects our understanding of the self's relationship with itself, with others, and with phenomenology.

Continuing the analysis of the eschatological constitution of phenomenology, the next paper, Jeffrey Bloechl's "Being and the Promise," demonstrates that an "eschatology of being" makes phenomenology possible by way of a call that issues from beyond our world. Tracing this call through Heidegger's later work, this chapter demonstrates that the "this-worldliness" of human existence is justified only by appeal to conditions that transcend it, thus placing a certain "faith" at the heart of phenomenological thinking. This "eschatology of being," and the notion of faith that derives from it, are then contrasted with the notion of a promise that grounds faith and leads to an "eschatology of love," which enables us to re-evaluate, among other things, the importance of incarnation and embodiment for both religion and phenomenology.

To bolster the arguments for the eschatological nature of phenomenology, the book next moves on to a study of the role of eschatology in the work of some key figures in the history of phenomenology. This section, entitled "Phenomenology and Eschatology: Historical Confluences," suggests that the work of Heidegger and Henry, specifically, is fundamentally shaped by those thinkers' implicit and explicit interactions with eschatology. Given the immense influence of these thinkers on later strands of phenomenological thought, this section helps to reinforce the arguments of the previous section of the book that phenomenology cannot be properly understood without also understanding eschatology.

Judith Tonning, in her "'*Hineingehalten in die Nacht*': Heidegger's Early Appropriation of Christian Eschatology," continues and deepens the examination of the profound influence of eschatology had on Heidegger's work that was begun in Jeffrey Bloechl's paper. Tonning shows that Christian eschatology was a key factor in the formation of such key Heideggerian concepts as facticity, attunement, care [*Sorge*], being-unto-death, angst, and others. This discussion poses serious problems for a thinker who wants to distinguish sharply between philosophy and theology, as Heidegger does in his infamous 1928 lecture "Phenomenology and Theology."

Though Henry did not seek to distinguish so sharply between philosophy and theology, Jeff Hanson's "Phenomenology and Eschatology in Michel Henry" clearly shows that one of the fundamental distinctions that Henry does want to make, namely that between the "truth of the world" and the "truth of life," cannot easily be accommodated to the eschatology that emerges from Henry's work. Hanson shows that a certain "realized eschatology," which he traces through Henry's work, suggests that phenomenology is always "too late" for Henry, and that this has serious ramifications for Henry's notion of truth.

Staying with Michel Henry, Kevin Hart, in his "'Without World': The Eschatology of Michel Henry," discusses how an understanding of Henry's implicit eschatology also affects Henry's conception of philosophy, arguing that only a phenomenology with an adequate understanding of intentionality and counter-intentionality can provide the ground for a Christian philosophy in any meaningful sense, like the one that Henry supports in *I am the Truth: Toward a Philosophy of Christianity*.

The book then closes with an appendix, Jean-Luc Marion's "The Present and the Gift," which provides a classic example of the inter-penetrating influences of phenomenology and eschatology in Marion's account of "Eucharistic ontology." Through this careful study, which is at once an eschatological analysis of phenomenology and a phenomenological analysis of eschatology, Marion uses the Eucharist to develop a reinterpretation of both eschatology and phenomenology, further demonstrating that these two fields can be most fruitfully understood when one holds them together.

The argument of this book, then, is that the disciplines of eschatology and phenomenology overlap in a fundamental and meaningful way. In rigorously pursuing this line of examination, the studies presented here have opened up questions of temporality, ontology, ethics, and much more. Through these openings, we can begin to see eschatology and phenomenology flow together.

So what does eschatology have to do with phenomenology? In answering this, we have been forced to acknowledge that phenomenology is no longer the sole property of Freiburg, and eschatology has left the island of Patmos. Where they go from here, only the future will tell ...

PART I

Phenomenology of Eschatology

Chapter 1

The Phenomenality of Anticipation

Jean-Yves Lacoste

To ensure the accuracy of our investigation into anticipation, let us specify at the outset that we are dealing with a double phenomenon. On the one hand, anticipation is the gesture of a consciousness that ensures the coherence and sense of its present experience by relating this experience to a pre-experience of what is not yet here but will, in time, realize what is already here. Just as the pre-perception by which the already played notes permit us to foresee the notes that will be played, so it is too with those who know what they wait for and "rehearse," by anticipation, what will (certainly, maybe, etc.) come. On the other hand, all that is given to us inchoately, in the mode of a hint or promise, makes use of anticipation, for example the short visit that anticipates the long day that I will spend with a friend the next month. The two aspects of the double phenomenon are evidently related in that they reveal to us that the only present is a living present, because it shelters a quasi-experience of the future, because its signification is suspended to a future that is pre-given in the here and now. For our investigation into anticipation to be as clear and accurate as possible, then, pre-experience and pre-givenness must be the phenomena first named.

How does the act of anticipation manifest itself to itself as such? How does pre-givenness distinguish itself from a givenness that is not part of any promise, but rather is its own beginning and its own end? We propose some answers.

Anticipation and Repetition

To put it plainly: each mode of being has its own mode of appearing. Number is not given to intuition in the same way as the book lying on the table or the work of art are given to the intuition, and number does not appear in the same way to the one who uses it in a simple and utilitarian calculus (counting apples, to use Wittgenstein's example) as it appears to a mathematician who demonstrates the cardinality of the continuum. The book does not appear to its reader as it appears to the one who sees just a book among many, and, *a fortiori*, to the one who sees a mere object on the table. The work of art does not appear in the same way to the one who rejoices in its presence as it appears to the technician who restores it. There is a good reason for this: rare are the beings that possess only one mode of being, and still rarer are the consciousnesses that, *vis-à-vis* some particular being, possess only one possible mode of intentionality. There are multiple modes of being, then, and therefore multiple modes of appearing, and multiple receptions in consciousness.

The work of art, for example, is also an object, like any other thing that can be taken in hand, reducible to its representability. The text presents itself to be read but also to be seen: there would not be a text if there were not a book, paper, ink, and binding (or computer screen). And because the work of art possesses a physical reality (sonorous material, cloth, paint, etc.), this material may be perceived in an autonomous way: for example, when we are interested in quality typography or in the sound of the piano.

Interested in the modes of being and of appearing, we are thus led straightaway to recognize an irreducible plurality. The way in which the ego appears to itself, for example in the phenomenon of awakening, has nothing in common with the way in which a number falls under intuition — except that in both cases a mode of consciousness is in play, and that there is no consciousness, at least no awakened consciousness, to which anything would appear that would not do so in an act of intuition, that is, that would be consciousness without being conscious of what it is. And between the way in which I perceive a book as a book and the way in which I perceive it as an object, the same irreducibility exists: the book is both, yet I cannot interest myself in one without disinteresting myself in the other; the two modalities of intuition are both valid, but are mutually exclusive.

The discussion so far, however, suffers from a lacuna: for it has not taken into account the *temporal* character of all appearances. "To appear" in effect must be understood as an event. Somebody that I did not see a few seconds ago now crosses the street. Something comes back to memory, and that it comes back means that it was absent from my field of consciousness before its return. And if one can legitimately say that there are phenomena that are perpetually given — if one can say that the phenomenon of the world co-appears with every appearance, that the ego co-appears to itself with every appearance — it must be the case, then, that we always deal, in the first place, with something that appears to us now, whose appearance lasts more or less time, and completes itself in a disappearance. So conceived, the event entails that being is given to us.

That which is given to us can be available to us, as the book lying on the table, or not available to us, as the passer-by who crossed the street and who I will not see again. The event, therefore, can possess the character of repeatability (I could always re-open the book to the same page, grab it in the same way, etc.) as well as that of unrepeatability. But there is much yet to be said about repetition. Opening the book to this page right now, and re-opening it tomorrow to the same page, are not identical experiences. I shall not be the same tomorrow, and therefore I will open the book again — precisely *again*, already knowing what it says, and reading the page with the power of anticipating what the next page will say. I will open it again, on the other hand, because tomorrow I shall not be identical to what I am today: my humor, or my attention, or the purpose of my gesture (to re-read the book, or to try to prove that an event can be repeated) might not be the same.

Thus, the opposition of the available and the unavailable, and that of the object and the event, do not hold, and ought to be measured against the immutable temporal structures implied in all perception. It is in the grasping of a spatial or temporal object that retention and protention are always at work. On the other hand, we can always remember the book as well as the sound, the state of the thing as well as the event, and this remembering itself has the quality of the event. Furthermore, we can confer a quasi-presence on what has not yet been presented to us by the senses, as when protention permits us a pre-experience of the notes that have not yet been played, but of which our memory or our musical culture permit us to know, and to foresee, that they will be played in a future instant. This does not entail that all appearance necessarily has a future and appears with a right to own it, and therefore, that no event is ever really closed. What appears might re-appear thanks to memory — but what we remember has its own proper phenomenality, and therefore re-appears to us as past, and thus as already realized. That which is past, insofar as it is passed, has said its final word, has already been realized.

We don't need to be taught that an event can belong simultaneously to our past and, by its *Wirkungsgeschichte* (history of reception), to our present. Whether represented in memory or present through the causality that it still exercises, the past defines itself as that which has disappeared but has left traces. There are multiple traces, in consciousness or outside of it: I remember a final visit to a now-deceased friend, and an object lying above a pedestal table is the trace of a gift that was given to me. What disappears is not absorbed into some nothingness. However, there remain phenomena that are antithetical to those of the trace or of the *Wirkungsgeschichte*: first, the phenomena of forgetting (Nietzsche was the first to recognize its positive meaning — a consciousness incapable of forgetting would be a monstrous consciousness), the phenomenon of the erased traces, of a past that has become useless, without effect, *wirkungslos*, and that only a genealogical analysis would allow to re-appear. What has appeared or arrived, and what appears or arrives now, can do so only in passing (and primarily, for us, by passing in consciousness), and therefore holds no future for us. In examining disappearance, then, we see that what has disappeared may have disappeared entirely. The play of appearance and disappearance, in all its modes, is a game with which we are familiar from time immemorial. The play of re-appearance, in both memory and imagination, is a game in which we (almost) always already have taken part.

This seems to pose a question. Every appearing is an event; hearing a car pass under my window is a micro-event. Every appearing, on the other hand, is tied to a disappearing: either because my work absorbs me enough that I cease to perceive the noise, or because the noise ends. One can say, then, with all the "appearances" of philosophical good sense, that the present event will (immediately, tomorrow, etc.) be a past event and perhaps even a forgotten event. Given all this, of which event can we say that we have witnessed it fully, in such a way that something appeared, as if out of nowhere, and then disappeared into nothingness?

The frontiers of an event are difficult to trace. When does an encounter begin and end? When does a concert begin and end? In this case, it is easy to distinguish. It is primarily with these types of events, those with clear contours, that our consciousness can anticipate what will come, experience what comes, and keep the memory of what came and be influenced by it. For example, a ritual (whether religious or not) is achieved by the scrupulous respect paid to the gestures and to the speech acts that constitute that ritual, and necessarily includes its first and last word or gesture. (Besides, one hesitates to speak of an event *à propos* of that which thereby possesses the quality of previsibility and repeatability: a process is not an event.) There is nothing vague about hearing a musical piece (which is different from going to a concert): there is a first and a last chord. Here, we are still in the domain of the repeatable and, even if we do not know the piece that well, in the domain of the expectable (*prévisible*). When the priest sings the dismissal, when the last chord is played, or when the neurotic has made all the ritualistic gestures that precede his going to bed, an event has taken place and a totality has appeared and been constituted. We can certainly keep this event in memory and allow what has disappeared to re-appear a little. Tomorrow, we can meticulously repeat the gestures done today. But, and this is a major point, what has taken place, has taken place in its entirety. A ritual, a text, a musical piece, a painting, etc., in the event where they appear to us, manifest all that can be manifested. Certainly, we may listen distractedly, not be as engaged as we ought to be, or enact the gestures of the ritual absent-mindedly, but this matters little: the event will not thereby possess less clear and distinct limits. Repetition, or rather quasi-repetition (to re-read, to participate in the ritual again) is always possible.

In the case of neurotic rituals, the neurotic person will attain a pathological perfection: exactly the same gestures, at exactly the same moment, in exactly the same order, etc. However, repetition is nothing more than repetition. It is repetition only in so far as it comes "again" and counts as an additional event, and yet we desire repetition in order to achieve the same pleasure, to better perceive what we have already perceived, or to obey the rules of behavior that we have given to ourselves. In any case, an axiom should govern the intelligence of repetition: the same might be given to us, but we will not be the same. The same score will be played, but the attention that we pay to it today will not be the same as that which we paid to it the first time — the first notes played, today, permit a pre-experience of what will be played, an anticipation that was not in our power the first time that we heard the score. The same gestures will be posed, but today we will be affected by the memory of the previous day, while yesterday we were forced to wait unknowingly for what was to come. In talking of the event, we are speaking first of appearance (and the reception that we reserve today for what appears to us is only vaguely reiterable tomorrow), and secondly, of the object as given to us. It has disappeared from the field of sensory perception or the fields of memory or imagination (for there are also events in memory and in imagination). The event of appearing is closed, as when I leave a museum room and lose interest in one work and become interested in another, with the evident reservation that the contemplation of the first painting will probably accompany the contemplation of the second and will pre-determine it in some way.

Nevertheless, talking in terms of events, we must guard against believing that the life of consciousness is a sequence of discreet acts. On the contrary, one thing is certain: all the micro or meso-events that we have mentioned are taken, in so far as they befall us, that is, in so far as they are objects of experience, and of our experience, as part of a larger event, namely the event of our presence in the word between birth and death. The concert, the visit that I receive, the regret that I feel when the visitor leaves me, etc. — none of this is dissociable from this larger event, as if we started to exist whenever a new episode begins. An event, in any way in which I am implicated in it, whether as a spectator or an actor, is always individualized: I am not present in the same way when I am an actor as I am when I am a spectator, when I perceive as when I wait and imagine.

Two points remain true, in any case, for all experience: if the event is thought from the life of consciousness, and if consciousness is that of an *existant*, of a *Dasein*, nothing happens without the dimension of the future being perpetually open; on the other hand, this opening forces one to concede a certain primacy to non-experience. If we must use experimentation to generate the example of what is to come, this surely shows a poor relation to the future. We can project, master, etc., the behavior of certain objects in certain circumstances (equally, we can project and master the behavior of the human being in certain conditions), but if we think existence as the deployment of a unique event in which the *existant*, the existing being, comes to itself within the event of its birth and death, then these relations of projection and mastery erase themselves before a definitive overhanging of the past and the present by the future. We can attempt to exist from an absolute future — Heidegger's anticipatory resoluteness is the model of such an attempt. However, the attempt is bound to fail for the following reason, which is itself Heideggerian: the possible — and thus the future — is taken as higher than the real (speaking here of a present or a past real that has not fallen into oblivion). Between the present of the decision and the realization of our highest possibility, what is not yet does not cease to prove the excess of experience in relation to non-experience.

The link between experience and non-experience, between what happened, the happening, and the non-happening, is the point of departure of any investigation into anticipation. Only absolute knowledge, if its concept resisted reality, would be an experience that could not be suspected of containing any non-experience. Now, one of the essential traits of consciousness is what Husserl named its narrowness, which we here take the liberty of understanding in the broadest way possible. To narrow consciousness only a region of being appears, primarily because it has an intuition of something. Consciousness is narrow, also, because it can perceive, remember, or imagine, but it cannot perceive, remember, and imagine simultaneously. Whoever talks of the "experience of consciousness" and refuses to give to these words the sense that Hegel gives them, must therefore say that all experience, the most rudimentary and the most rich, is intrinsically limited, and that human experience is in fact impossible unless it possesses limits and obeys them (any other type of consciousness would certainly be an angelic consciousness). Further, the concept of an experience that is only experience, not bordered by any non-experience, cannot, *a prima vista*, be rationally formed.

All experience is therefore obviously partial. We see the façade of the house, and symbolic perception allows us to say that we see a house, but we do not perceive it adequately as a totality. The following example will illustrate our point even better. We hear *The Art of the Fugue* under the direction of Scherchen, and the piece appears in this one particular way through the mediation of a very particular musical and orchestral aesthetic, very different from, for example, the later interpretation of the Juilliard quartet. Each interpretation makes the same piece appear, but according to distinctly different perspectives. Scherchen's interpretation, when it appears to us as a source of joy, surely offers us a full experience from which nothing is missing, and to which we already ascribe the word enjoyment (*jouissance*).[1] However curiosity, which is never too far away, tempts us to listen to other interpretations. And if we give in to this temptation, we easily discover that every interpretation is partial, that every experience that we have suffers from a deficit: we cannot simultaneously understand all existing interpretations and, even less, all possible interpretations; there is, then, no experience that is not related, in every occasion, to non-experience.

Certainly, there are phenomena that give themselves completely once and for all and also repeat themselves identically: strict repetition is possible in a domain that we have already evoked, namely the domain of experimentation (with the condition that we bracket the moods of the experimenter). But what is given, and the reception that we reserve for it, are different, regardless of the name we give to this reception, be it perception, intelligence, or interpretation. And if we can be completely finished with something (and be capable of forgetting it—remembrance does not guarantee repetition, on the contrary), the richest experiences are probably those unachieved, and perhaps unachievable, those where the thing is always given to us in the mode of renewal or in the mode of a putting-into-perspective, where no perspective can fully satisfy us because we know that there are other perspectives. Here, the musical example remains good, and permits us to go farther. On the one hand, the plurality of interpretations is normally valid: the most scrupulous philological fidelity cannot teach us how to play *The Art of the Fugue* infallibly. On the other hand, this plurality is unmistakably given to consciousness. Whoever knows only Scherchen's interpretation, or only the Juilliard interpretation, does not know the piece as well as somebody familiar with both ways of playing Bach's score, which are as different from each other as possible. And, in the end, we know

---

[1]   TN: Enjoyment (*jouissance*) has a particular philosophical meaning here: the experience of one totally absorbed in his pleasure. Leaving *jouissance* untranslated would arouse too many psychoanalytic overtones that are not present in the French. Hence, we will translate it throughout as "enjoyment," though the reader must be sure to keep in mind the philosophical sense of this term, alongside its standard meaning.

that the final interpretation will never be given and we should unconditionally admit that others will come who will show us something in the piece that Scherchen, the Juilliard quartet, and others, have not yet shown us. The idea, then, of the most faithful of all interpretations, which will give us the piece in all its truth and will not call for any other future interpretation, is a pseudo-idea.

Though this idea has been dismissed, we must still maintain that the musical piece (or the painting, the literary work, etc.) hides nothing of itself from us. It is fully given and available to us, as long as one knows how to read, to see, and to decipher the music. It is precisely present to us, which means that it does not content itself with being here, but offers itself to us as given to affection[2] (and to be experienced even when nobody is here to experience it). However, as it appears here and now, the work is presented to me only partially. The adequate perception (that which would be caused by the totality of what is given) is forbidden to us.

All perception, even if it lingers in enjoying what is given to it, calls for a new perception, just as every interpretation calls for a new interpretation. We can speak of acquired knowledge: we certainly know *The Art of the Fugue*. However, we cannot speak of comprehensive knowledge. And we can even add that what now provokes our joy, that of which we would like to have full knowledge, might possibly bore us tomorrow.

Anticipation and Enjoyment

The concept of enjoyment, then, enters directly into the discussion. Presence, in its rigorous sense — an appearance given to affection — evokes enjoyment merely as a mode of feeling (alongside theoretical interest and sympathy), but also of fear and distaste. In any case, we enjoy the pleasure that some particular presence offers us in a way that takes hold of our consciousness, and that in a certain sense we become one with what we enjoy. Enjoyment is not punctual: without the work of retention and protention, and more broadly, without the work of memory and anticipation (a parallel that permits us to begin to circumscribe what anticipation means as a product of consciousness), a work of art could not appear to us purely and simply, could not make itself present. Even a painting is an event whose appearance can only be lived in the course of time.

Obviously, every appearance does not generate joy. Actually, it is precisely this mixture of joy and pleasure that merits the name of enjoyment. We will hear or see some artwork again, but we will understand it differently, for example, with the goal of criticizing our previous experiences. However, knowing here does not forbid the presence of enjoyment from being sufficient unto itself, that is, not suffering any lack. The moment that I rejoice in a presence, nothing other than this presence appears to me. Certainly there are margins to all experience: we see the painting and also its frame; we listen to the score and also see the orchestra that

---

2   TN: "given to affection" translates "*donnant à sentir*."

plays it; we read the text and also see a book. Even still, it remains true that the concept of enjoyment is that of an experience that marginalizes all co-experience, and that has its first property, in the exact sense of the word, in satiating us.

Enjoyment does not exclude protention, but its logic excludes anticipation: what provokes enjoyment is not the pre-givenness of something that will be more present in some future moment; the presence of enjoyment does not anticipate a future that will give us more joy. If, by any chance, we lack something when we are looking at or listening to a work of art, we would not let that which we lack appear as such, or the work of art would not be able to appear: for example, a worry will prevent the work of art from being purely received, and could perhaps even marginalize the artwork, since our experience will be primarily focused on the worry, and only secondarily on the marginal perception of the work of art.

Now, the phenomenon of enjoyment is that of plenitude. Nothing is lacking from its presence. This does not entail that enjoyment is *ipso facto* the highest or the final experience: we can enjoy multiple presences, but they do not all present the same thing to us. On the other hand, it is possible for us to be fully and solely invested in a presence — in this experience we do not feel any non-experience. We do not enjoy the whole, but always only something particular. But the fulfilled consciousness, together with the body, seems to employ the entirety of their aptitude in the experience of enjoyment. Hegel's critique therefore applies to enjoyment: as an immediacy, enjoyment has no place in the work of reason or its products. However, this critique has an involuntarily positive side. In fact, doesn't enjoyment transcend all mediation and all distancing, and doesn't it seem to be bracketed in the common order of experience? We enjoy presence: that is, we enjoy phenomena that we experience by letting ourselves be affected by them. What is content with merely being here, on the one hand, is not present and we cannot enjoy its being-here, by simple definition: we can only notice it, represent it, etc. On the other hand, there is room in the realm of experience for presences that we do not enjoy, those which scare us, make us anxious or make us suffer in any way.

The link between presence and enjoyment, in any case, is remarkable in that it causes us to think or experience a displacement of our daily relation to time. This displacement is totally precarious. We can conceive of a perpetual joy, but not of a perpetual enjoyment. Hegel would seem correct, then: such an experience would perpetually separate us from reason. It would also abolish the unavoidable plurality that is the distinctive mark of the appearing and receiving of phenomena. The event of existing would thereby be reduced to a unique experience that abolishes the proliferation of the modes of appearing and letting appear. The idea of an uninterrupted enjoyment that only death could interrupt is as counter-intuitive as it is counter-experiential, and has no place in the logic of being-in-the-world, where enjoyment intervenes only sporadically and feebly. Evoking it only grants plausibility to the eminently fleeting and provisional character of a pure presence that remembers no past and waits for no future. The proper temporality of enjoyment, then, is either a provisional suspension of being-in-the-world or a poor experience of the world. Enjoyment assures the primacy of a pure presence, a present without residue. It is used solely to serve my pleasure. Care for the other, if it finds any place here, is reduced to its simplest expression. Enjoyment is evidently mine.

But enjoyment does not involve us as existing-beings. It only puts into play a minimal form of existence, the same way in which idle talk, curiosity, and other phenomena can serve as paradoxical revelations of existence, the fact of facts. Enjoyment matters only because of the gap that it introduces. In the presence of enjoyment, I exist otherwise than in the presence of care, of fear, etc., of all that is constituted by denying the centrality of presence. Enjoyment is a stranger in the world. It conceals from us more than it reveals. This oblique veiling and unveiling, as we have already noticed, exists only in a precarious way, at the limits of a givenness which is no pre-givenness, in an experience that is not a pre-experience. And since we are put entirely into the service of enjoyment — even if, as we have already said, it also has its margins — it is only after the fact that we describe it and attempt to think of it as one thinks of a pure past. And in this after-the-fact, two consequences become clear. The first is the totally-past character of the event: I enjoyed it, and that is the end of my enjoyment; no memory will return it to me, though I desire its reiteration. The second is the impossibility of this reiteration.

Without some experience that would validate it, we cannot venture to say that the same gift is given to us again and that we receive it identically. This is equally true if we take, for example, "objective" experience, which deals with beings that are here without being given to affection.[3] Even here, it is still necessary to admit that we do not perceive a cube today as we perceived it yesterday, because between yesterday and today we have become different, or simply because a perception, for merely organic reasons, cannot be identically repeated. Enjoyment is without past or future. The work of art is certainly in our disposition, the lover is almost in our disposition, the landscape is in our disposition, but nothing guarantees repetition. We enjoy always once and for all, and this *ephapax*, this once-and-for-all, announces nothing. No enjoyment has as its function to give us a foretaste of an even greater enjoyment. If its object disappears, or if we cease enjoying its gift, we are left with only our memories and our desires. The place of dreams is certainly inscribed in the experience of the one who knows enjoyment: the dream that the thing or the person will still be present for us tomorrow, or the dream that we will be fully devoted to it. But in the present of enjoyment, we cannot identify any promise.

Between birth and death, our existence is shaped as an event. To such an event, it belongs to be partly expectable and controllable: I can decide to go tomorrow and visit the museum where that painting seduced me. The same painting will be there, but will I be the same? Will another painting call irresistibly for my attention? The centrality of presence always imposes itself exclusively. There is no

---

[3]   TN: here, "given to affection" translates "donner à l'affection," rather than "donner à sentir."

eschatology of enjoyment (that is, of an enjoyment whose present instance will be but the penultimate, and will present itself as such) or, what amounts to the same thing, all enjoyment is its own end. The presence that is given to us can very well be taken from us once and for all, and, supposing that it is somehow given to us again, we can show ourselves incapable of receiving it again as it is.

Anticipation and Parousia

While we cannot bet on the re-appearance, nor even describe it rigorously, a concept permits us to go farther than the *aporias* of enjoyment: fidelity. Speaking of enjoyment, it would surely be imprecise to use the lexicon of love, if for no other reason than that we can love while feeling only an absence, or because we can love without something being given to affection (*donner à sentir*). The phenomena of fidelity, love, and enjoyment have, however, something in common: our desire for permanence. If it is true that enjoyment is experienced only in the interim, it is also true that, in willing the repetition — and we often will it — we make an act of fidelity. This allows another concept to enter the scene, the concept of hope. The reasons for hope are as faint as they are real. They are real, because what has provoked our enjoyment has not necessarily disappeared forever and therefore might re-appear. However, they are faint, for we cannot swear that we will receive this re-appearance in the same way that we received the first appearance. We cannot count on the repetition and yet we wait incessantly for it. Now, using the language of fidelity and hope, and using it legitimately (it may happen that we are faithful to what was given to us, and it may happen that our hope in a re-appearance is fulfilled) allows us to include a relation with the future that is suddenly and absolutely imposed in the aftermath of enjoyment. The disappearance does not promise us any re-appearance, unless we leave the realm of existence for that of the mechanical.

But when a presence that we enjoyed erases itself, the hope of a new givenness of that same presence is a logical response (there are surely others, e.g., resignation and oblivion) that we can attribute to its disappearance. Fidelity and hope are related in this way. Our fidelity is proven wherever we pursue a repetition or, perhaps, a re-appearance that offers us even more. And hope is related to fidelity in so far as fidelity refuses all satisfaction, refuses ever being bored by what it enjoys and, perhaps, deciphers promises in what appears and then disappears.

There is no mystery in what we have just acknowledged. The work of art, e.g., the painting, promises us beauty and goodness, because it is here today, because it will be here again tomorrow and will be made present (though it is us who must receive its presence). And not only do we have the right to hope that it will be here tomorrow to be given to affection, but we even have the reasonable right to hope, to the full extent of our fidelity and desire, that we will make present our consideration of it. It occurs to us to encounter the absolutely unrepeatable, which comes, evokes our enjoyment, and disappears forever (although we can remain faithful to it in the element of memory). And when what has provoked our enjoyment has disappeared, it also occurs to us that we have to recognize that that presence has sufficed and that we now desire other presences: fidelity does not necessarily follow the event where a presence has contributed to our joy. Fidelity, then, does not break the enclosure of the presence of enjoyment. It comes after enjoyment and wants to live before a repeated enjoyment. Its principal accomplishment is re-introducing the phenomenon of enjoyment into a temporality that is not concentrated solely in the present.

In order to continue, we must indicate the conceptual weight of what often has no weight in the current language: absence. In common usage, what is not here is absent. And, because there are only a few things here, the field of absence, in its trivial sense, is evidently immense. Now, as much as presence defines itself by affection — by what is given to affection and what I experience — do we not need to say that something might not be here anymore, but that its not-being-here can affect us? In doing so, do we grasp a more rigorous definition of absence? Not being here is certainly not sufficient for being absent. I can, for example, remember what I did one hour ago (I left my house, I drank a cup of coffee, etc.) without anything in this past possessing the quality of absence. In the same way, remembering does not confer presence to what is remembered, for memory can put into presence what it remembers only if what is remembered is given to affection.

Absence, defined in this way, is given to affection. More precisely, it is given to affection in that it is given to suffer, in one mode or another. We would not speak of absence à propos of something that made us suffer and is no longer here: once accomplished, the toothache is not "absent"; once he has left his victim in peace, the torturer is not "absent." What is absent lacks, or creates a defect. The experience of absence is, therefore, made present in a presence that is antithetical to the presence of enjoyment. And this presence, then, can have hope or waiting as its characteristic tonality. It does not always have this tonality, for we can attribute to absence the quality of what occurred only in passing — of the unrepeatable *par excellence*. But it can often have it. And when what was given to us disappears and its disappearance hurts us, it is possible that we might feel ourselves (though is it not certain that we would know this) as the recipients of a promise that promises us a re-appearance.

We now (finally) cease to treat the problem of anticipation only obliquely. Rare are the appearances that, between retention and protention, do not engage any future, as brief as that future may be. Consciousness is instinctively protentional. There is also an art of pre-experience: for example, the art of the musician who deduces from a measure the measure that will follow. But when what appeared has disappeared and its absence seems to us to cover up the promise of a re-appearance (the friend takes leave and promises that he will come back) and perhaps of an appearance even more present, we are facing another problem, our problem at last: the problem of the intrinsic phenomenality of what has not emptied its being in its being-present but which is given to us to anticipate a future presence that will be even fuller. Can what is present to us be so only in the mode of the beginning or the hint? Does this mode give itself to us in the same way that it appears to us?

To respond directly: anticipation can only appear to us in a non-parousiac mode. By parousia, we mean a double phenomenon: a total presence indissociable from a definitive presence. Two important points must be noted:

1. The musical piece, like all works of art, conceals nothing of itself from us (i.e., there is no hidden side to the work of art); but it is also always partial and never fully realized in perception. The mediation of the interpreter and the partiality of our perceptions carry out the same function: they manifest that the work of art is here completely (at least, completely within some particular duration), but that this being-here cannot be identified with a complete presence. A new interpretation, a new look, a new reading, will let appear what has not yet appeared — even though it was "here." There are two reasons for this. On the one hand, we always receive what is given to us in parts; on the other hand, what is given cannot be received in one glance or one sole reading. Repetitions, variations in interpretation, and different perspectives of reading, all prove to us that a fully available being-here must not be too quickly identified with a parousia-like presence. And if we want to understand what parousia, defined in this way, has or does not have to do with the logic of enjoyment, it is necessary, first of all, not to hasten to attribute the quality of the parousia to what delights us, and to specify that that which causes us joy, within the limits of the world, is evidently present but is not all-present. It is not necessary for a presence to be total for it to delight us. And, if it can happen that anything or anyone that delighted us yesterday bores us today (as the angels themselves, according to Origen, were capable of being bored by the presence of God),[4] likewise it is from common experience that we learn that the work of art is almost incomprehensible and it only presents itself to us in a fragmented mode. The conjunction of a thing's complete appearance with a consciousness that receives completely what appears to it occurs only as an exception, if it occurs at all.

2. Every logic of appearance, as we have already said, calls for the deployment of a logic of disappearance; in other words, there can be no continuing presence without our self-presence — which clearly tells us that nothing in the time of the world gives itself definitively to affection. It is necessary to add here that my self-presence is certainly not parousia-like, since it has a history, and no privileged episode in this history permits me to grasp or

---

[4]   Editor's Note: Origen believed that those souls of humans and angels who "fell" away from God did so as a result of experiencing boredom or satiation (*koros*). Thus, he derives the Greek word "soul" (*psyche*) from the verb "to grow cold" (*psychestai*). See, *De Principiis*, II, viii, 3.

to feel myself in my totality, and that if such an episode must occur, this experience would not be definitive.

It is unhelpful, then, to render an account of enjoyment by appealing to parousia. Since we enjoy what impresses itself on the affection of a self-enclosed presence, the question of omni-presence is not to be posed. Enjoyment disguises itself as the last word of experience, but this last word is precarious; and we know very well that we know little of how to enjoy it. And if all presence must include an absence, either because things themselves are absent, or because I am absent, it is obvious that nothing is absolutely present to us. The idea of a parousia that would be granted to us and then withdrawn from us is the same idea as the presences that we already enjoy. Enjoyment has to do with presence, which is not to be taken lightly. But, taking these words seriously, we see that enjoyment has nothing to do with parousia. There is only partial and provisional presence.

Anticipation shows itself to us, then, as an essentially non-parousia-like phenomenon. Let us clarify this further. According to the definition of anticipation, its experience cannot enclose itself without losing its sense. A text that clearly shows this is the gospel story of the Transfiguration (Mt. 17:1–8.). Blinded by the glory of Christ transfigured, the disciples believed they were witnessing the end of history — the end of their own history and of the history of Israel in the clear and distinct manifestation of the Messiah. The tents that Peter wanted to erect are a final resting place, not the dwelling places of nomads. The Transfiguration resembles the occupation of the temple of Jerusalem by the divine Shekinah. And if the disciples were right in interpreting the scene in this way (though in a confused manner, as the text of the gospel tells us), there would be nothing left for them to see — they would have seen it all. What was given to them would have been given definitively. Now, not all has been seen, and the episode only anticipates what is still to be seen, the highest phenomenon given in history, the appearance of the risen Christ. There is more. To the disciples who have seen his glory in advance, Christ enjoins silence. Reduced to itself, in fact, the episode of the Transfiguration would be largely incoherent: the last word — parousia — would have been given, but it would have been given only provisionally, and history would continue.

Now, and according to Christ's warnings, anticipation receives its meaning from what it anticipates. It is interpretable only from the end. And this end itself will be given in a non-parousia-like presence, since the Risen One will be elevated and will remain present only in the evidently non-parousiac mode of the sacrament. This synopsis leads to four conclusions. The first is that parousia, strictly understood, probably has no place in the world. We exist in the element of the provisional, which is the element of always-partial presences. This partiality is due either to the appearance of things, or to our interest in things, or to both at the same time. The second is that all enjoyment, if it is not recognized as a limited experience, can lead us to incarnate an "unhappy" consciousness, a consciousness muted by the desire for parousia but that only experiences non-parousia-like presences. Men and things are in our disposition, almost every being can be made present, numerous things evoke our enjoyment, and if we can be satisfied with the partial and the provisory, we still also want the whole and the definitive — and in wanting it, we will be necessarily frustrated. The third is that the desire for parousia does not prove that it is given to us in some particular phenomenon, since we licitly speak of anticipations only from realizations that do not have the character of parousia (I wait for a friend and then my friend's visit comes). Parousia ought to be thought of as transcending all experience realized within the limits of the world, and therefore having nothing in common with the phenomenon of presence, nothing in common with the experiences which reveal that presence is merely presence. Moreover, since there are limits, nothing can be concluded regarding the possible existence of a transcendence of these limits. The stories of the Transfiguration can be read as stories anticipating the appearances of Easter — but, as we have already said, the Paschal appearances offer only a provisional experience. A last conclusion: if realization alone reveals that something was given in the mode of anticipation, anticipation's proper phenomenality can only be that of the unrealized. Now, can the unrealized appear to us as such? Might the gap that separates presence and parousia appear in the very experience of presence? That is what remains to be discussed.

The Provisional and the Unrealized

It is necessary to speak here of a final word — of eschaton — and of what does nothing but announce it or hint at it (at all that is not pre-given or pre-experienced). Moreover, certainly nothing is easier, once introduced to the concept of the unrealized, than placing oneself under the protection of an eschatology that one conceives of as a utopia, as the accomplishment of history or as the perfection of a logic of experience. It is worth saying again what we see now and have seen already from the start: if all experience has the character of the once-and-for-all (i.e., nothing will restore to me the present moment exactly as I now perceive it), then all experience also possesses the character of the fragmentary and the precarious. Only the ego is (almost) present to itself — which does not mean, moreover, that it is identically present to itself, nor, *a fortiori*, that it is never in a full mode that it could not exceed. And when we interest ourselves above all in phenomena that are given to affection (when we interest ourselves in the general logic of presence), then we see that these necessarily have features of a game of appearance, disappearance, and re-appearance in which nothing permits us to wait for a full givenness — a parousia.

What is only a being-here is fully given in many cases, but it is not present because of that. Presence is a fragmentary appearance, to which a fragmentary enjoyment might correspond. The reception that we reserve for a presence can, certainly, ignore this double fragmentary character. We can find satisfaction, in the full sense of the term, with the Juilliard interpretation of *The Art of the Fugue*, and therefore take joy [*jouir*] in it. We can also, because we are familiar with other interpretations, know that each interpretation is a perspective on the piece, and that we will never have the adequate interpretation that would give us all of what the score can give us. The intervention of the concept of adequate interpretation, like that of full givenness, is a properly eschatological experience (and a regional eschatology, of a last word or experience that would only be the last word or experience of some particular thing, this would not be less of an eschatology). As played here and now, within the limits of a dated musical aesthetic (to have a great orchestra playing *The Art of Fugue*, or to have it played by a chamber orchestra, or to use instruments of the epoch, etc.), the piece is evidently present to us, it evokes our pleasure, but we still know that all is not given to us and we have the means, in our pleasure, to critique this — not to disavow it, but to comprehend that it was not a final experience. The idea of a final experience can certainly be cited, and it might occur to us to believe that some interpretation is (almost) the final one, that it gives us the work in its flesh and bones, in its completeness. This idea arises as impossible, as that which is impossible within the limits of the world. In the world, there could not be a final interpretation, as there could not be a final experience, because the concept is related to an infinite task — the work overflows all interpretation — and the interpretations contradict each other as much as they mutually enrich each other. It is therefore necessary for us to accept this contradiction, and to accept it knowing that it cannot be mediated. A final interpretation or final appearance: these things are only dreams.

But a dream is not nothing. A dream is nothing less than a dream, and does not stop carrying out a heuristic function, much like a utopia. It denounces, primarily, the proper un-realization of all lived experience in the time of awakening. If other experiences are possible (and real) which manifest the same thing to us, then these experiences are a matter of presence and not of parousia. By forcing us to remain within the language of un-realization, the eschatological dream forces us to go back over every experience, as best we can, with the power of being unsatisfied: of perceiving it as unaccomplished. And it is at this point that, refusing anything to do with enjoying what is given to us, we can receive what is given as anticipation: receive it as the pre-givenness of what cannot be fully and definitively given in the time of the world.

The space between pre-givenness and a givenness that remains impossible in the here and now can be occupied by fidelity, waiting, and perhaps by hope. The logic of the dream is, in part, that of desire, and to relate it to waiting is legitimate. Waiting matters to us here because it uses anticipation, and because this anticipation can be either frustrated (the friend that I wait for will not come) or satisfied. Nothing is more banal, then, than the realization of an anticipation, and nothing is more banal than the distinction of their proper phenomenalities. We find ourselves in the element of imagination, inevitably free to construct a scenario, but the sound of the doorbell brings us back to the world of perception, and what we perceive — the friend at the door — vividly realizes what we had blurrily anticipated.

No confusion is possible, then, between anticipation and realization. The experience of waiting is not one of enjoyment: this preserves the certainty of waiting. We must clarify this further. The friend will not be present to us in a parousia-like mode (one of the problems of intersubjectivity is that we are never completely and definitively present to one another). This visit will certainly not have the character of a final experience: not only will there probably be other visits, other words exchanged; not only is the present experience suspended to an undetermined future, but, in addition to all that, every visit will simultaneously be experience and pre-experience; we enjoy a presence, this presence is removed from us, we can only restore it in the order of memory and wait for it to be returned in the order of perception and interlocution. And yet, between the waiting and the visit, what is anticipated finds itself realized, and maybe fully realized: perhaps we have waited for nothing except that. And in the majority of our lived experiences, we experience anticipation in a modest way, just as in an unnoticeable way our aptitudes for protention permit us to hear Bach's prelude and not an incoherent sequence of sounds.

That being said, let us confess, if we must, that we have just separated the final word — the eschaton, in its full sense — from the realization, and that we were right to do so. In speaking of realization, we do not retain the language of the end, but that of an end, one among many, and there is no more common experience than the play of waiting and realization. Of course, not everything finds its realization, and there is nothing but realization to "put an end" to anticipation: the one who waits can be frustrated and the promise not kept, and in this case, the pre-experience will not be followed by any experience. Nothing is more common than to dream of an end that realizes all waiting and all anticipation. But whatever use the dream of the end may seem to have for us, in fact, it enables us to understand the logic of the ends (plural), of regional eschatologies. If it translates our desires, the dream speaks of us, and that is already enough.

But if it translates only our desires, who will authorize us to speak of realization? The answer is simple: the concept of anticipation can only be elucidated via some realization. The experience of a consciousness that lives only in the mode of anticipation would be either a monstrous, indescribable experience, or an illogical one. And if we admit that the logic of the end is not that of the multiplicity of ends, and, on the other hand, that "end" is not always the synonym of realization, nothing remains except the need to outline a response to our question — how does anticipation appear as such? — supposing that only the logic of the end can permit us to take just measure of the regional eschatologies.

We can form more hypotheses. It is primarily, as we suggested, anticipations that are realized. But it is high time to be evidently true: if we wish to remain in the language of the end, we dwell in the domain of the unrealized — after all, Jesus' disciples still had something to wait for even after his resurrection — or we should concede that the end is in possession of death (ours, the universe's) and only of death. The logic of anticipation is calmly inscribed in the logic of experience: even if anticipation is thwarted, which often happens, we perfectly accommodate this. As soon as we investigate the final word — about the "final end" — in the limits of the world, however, we are forced to admit, on the one hand, that in this limit the final word belongs to death, and that, logically, the final anticipation is Heidegger's "anticipatory resoluteness," or any other way of making our death our own.

This being admitted, is there a space for a logic of the parousia? We have all the means to doubt this and to suppose that the gap between presence and parousia remains necessarily insurmountable. The taming of our death is possible, although doing so will diminish the realm of the unrealized. Partial perceptions always anticipate a fully adequate perception that will never take place (this, moreover, hardly discomforts us). No experience is comprehensive. No presence is to be confused with a parousia. Enjoyment is mistaken when it believes it is in total possession of its object.

This entails the conclusion that either anticipation appears as such when it knows its realization (I know that I anticipated Pierre's visit when Pierre shows himself at the door's threshold), or it appears as such when it stumbles into the essentially unrealized character of existence. A change of emphasis must be noted. Anticipation is (pre-)experience and (pre-)givenness. To expand: on the one hand, it is experience and givenness, and on the other, it is pre-experience and pre-givenness. The distinctions matter. Anticipation certainly has an experiential reality similar to anything else that is experienced in consciousness, and the event of anticipatory signification is given to us with as much reality as everything else: pre-experience is an experience and pre-givenness a givenness. On the other hand, however, pre-experience and pre-givenness have the character of a preamble and of an announcement — and if they do not seem to match up to this character, we will have to conclude that we are mistaken concerning their appearance.

In the episode of the Transfiguration, the disciples had the experience of givenness, but they did not perceive that the event was an investment of the present by the future, ultimately by an absolute future. The event is reduced to its presence, and this presence becomes incomprehensible. Anticipation, certainly, does not have as its exclusive function to frustrate us: it can be joyful. Still, we do not perceive it as such if we do not perceive the gap that separates the pre-experience from the experience and the pre-givenness from the givenness, and if this gap does not provoke a waiting and, perhaps, a hoping, a hope. Does this gap force itself upon us? Surely not; at least, not always, since we can render autonomous and self-sufficient what by definition should not be: turn the occasion of enjoyment into the occasion of waiting, or believe that the end has come when what is given is only a precursory sign. To believe that this is the end (of some particular waiting) is perfectly licit when it is effectively finished, and there is nothing left other than receiving a presence or keeping it in memory. Even if the instant of the encounter lives in the trace of memory and that trace renders it richer than it was, we cannot deny that it is no longer present but deferred, put back into presence. Nothing is more banal than that the musical phrase is realized in conformity with our anticipations. But the problem occurs when we enjoy what is not given to our enjoyment but is given only to revive our waiting. Anticipation is exemplarily what we do not have the right to enjoy, except in exercising the right to distance ourselves from this enjoyment.

Thirdly, would eschatological anticipation not be the anticipation *par excellence*, which reveals to us what is enjoyable in all pre-givenness and in all pre-experience? We can respond affirmatively. First affirmation: when we speak of the end, it is at a distance from us and may be inaccessible. Second affirmation: it can cause us to pre-see or pre-feel in our presence. Third affirmation, if we speak here from the restricted but rigorously prepared terrain of theology: we are right to anticipate the end. The experience of the end is prohibited from us; the pre-experiences, on the other hand, are not. Everyone says that man does not know God in history as man will know God eschatologically: this would only be because the eschaton is the abolishment of all sacramental economy. Within the limits of the world, waiting, eschatological desire, can take the characteristics of pre-eschatological experiences, which only know how to be pre-eschatological, and do not overflow the limits of being-in-the-world.

Similarly, and using the same example, the sacrament does not realize the eschaton, but is a pre-givenness. Hegel was partially wrong, then: the sacramental economy is not an economy of enjoyment, because nothing realizes the experience of a sacramental presence without learning that this experience is not that of the parousia — and it is urgently necessary for the one who does not know this to learn it.

On the one hand, we can only anticipate: our relation to God within the time of the world is waiting for a definitive relation that can only have a place beyond the world. On the other hand, the gifts made to us are the anticipation of a gift that they promise to us, but which dwells in a withdrawal. It is of anticipations other than those of the absolute future. To give the final word to eschatological anticipation permits us, as we supposed, to take the true measure of what it means to anticipate.

To summarize: the logic of anticipation is, in the first place, antithetical of that of enjoyment: if we enjoy only the pre-appearance of the future in the present, we prove that the proper phenomenality of anticipation eludes us. Secondly, a consciousness that would not anticipate is evidently an unthinkable consciousness: to let the future appear in our presence is an exercise in which we perpetually indulge ourselves, and with ease, be it in the spontaneous order of protention, or in the wanted, desired, or imagined order of anticipation in the strict sense. Thirdly, the last anticipation — the one that gives us more, and more to desire — is the anticipation of an absolute future. We want to enjoy a parousia, but not even the beings that show themselves fully can be the object of a complete and definitive apprehension. We want to enjoy, but we ought not to forget that if enjoyment totally absorbs us, it seizes upon a presence that is not parousia-like because it is a presence.

The question that occupied us, "what is the mode of appearing proper to anticipation?" is now easy to answer. On the one hand, anticipation appears as having the character of a non-realization: it does not put the end in our disposition. On the other hand, anticipation appears to us as being nothing but anticipation, in two ways: because its experience is inchoative, and because the gift accompanies itself with a promise and with a future revival of experience. And all discourse on anticipation, to conclude, must be maintained within the horizon of the end. The end may take place: the event that we have anticipated has taken place in conformity with our anticipation. It may not take place: the eschaton is at a distance. The problem of pre-givenness and of pre-experience ends up being related to the problem of the promise. The eschatological anticipation does not appear to us as such except by virtue of eschatological promises. But is it not also because Pierre had promised his visit, that the few lines through which he transmits his promise permit us to anticipate his visit?

Translated by Ronald Mendoza-De Jesús and Neal DeRoo

Chapter 2
Awaiting

Claude Romano

"Ce que je suis" est une attente permanente, générale …
[…] Nous vivons dans une préparation ou disposition perpétuelle
(P. Valéry, *Cahiers, I,* p. 270)

The title of this volume, "Phenomenology and Eschatology," invites us to meditate upon the problem of expectation. I will respond to this solicitation with means that are strictly philosophical. It is not my place to say if the reflections which follow may be of value for theology. Rather, they go right to the heart of the matter on essential problems from the point of view of a phenomenology of time.

What can awaiting teach us about phenomenology? What can phenomenology teach us about awaiting? In the chiasm of these questions, something, already, becomes clear regarding the stakes of a phenomenology of awaiting. A phenomenology of awaiting is also and at the same time a phenomenology of time. The phenomenological enterprise is that of a description of our experience in its lively sense of appearance. And appearance as such, the phenomenality of phenomena, has for its essential character *novelty*. That which appears, that of which I have an experience, is always in a certain sense unexpected, surprising. The dimension of surprise inherent in all apparition is not merely a contingent aspect of the phenomenality of phenomena; it is rather in some sense consubstantial with this phenomenality. Even for a thing which rests in itself, which lets itself be identified and perused, to appear is to announce itself in a manner each time original and, consequently, unforeseeable. In the movement of living perception, our habitual and tired looking relates to those things to which we are most acclimated only in discovering them afresh in a new light. To see something again is to see it, only now, for the first time. This first time is of all times; it confers upon the present its irreducible sense. *A fortiori,* the same holds for changes which take place contrary to our expectations and which thwart our predictions: the problem of their initial upsurge into our view, an upsurge which they alone initiate, is that of the phenomenalization of phenomena, and thus of the temporalization of time.

Such considerations are, however, too general to provide a solid starting point for a phenomenology of time which would refuse to see in the novelty of phenomena anything other than their perishable part. In effect, such an approach relies upon an insufficient comprehension of awaiting and of its different modalities. What is awaiting? What is the unexpected? These are the questions — as simple as they are difficult — that we must take as our starting point.

Expecting

Awaiting is lodged in the heart of our existence not as a contingent attitude that we could or could not adopt, but rather as a permanent disposition. This disposition, this aptitude for anticipation, is at work in all perception, in all behavior, in all speech: I am already at the end of the sentence when I begin to pronounce its first words. This style of anticipation differs from awaiting by virtue of which we are turned and directed toward the future, and to which a certain event, if it takes place, would correspond: it is a perpetual resource of our being.

The French distinguish between two possible constructions of the verb 'awaiting' or 'waiting' (attendre): one can *s'attendre à* someone/something; one can *attendre* someone/something. According to the first sense of the word, 'awaiting' [*s'attendre à*] means "to expect" or "*anticipate*" or "*foresee*." Such a fore-sight or anticipation is present in all actual perception. According to the classical Husserlian example, to perceive a cube is to await, in the sense of "to expect" [*s'attendre à*], from the very first, its hidden faces, in the event of rotating it, according to a typical configuration and style. In the second sense, *attendre* is close to waiting in view of something, to watch out for, to get ready for it. Awaiting thus designates a particular attitude, an *existentiell* posture that one adopts from time to time, and of which it would be absurd to affirm that one adopts it permanently. If it is true that I may not perceive a cube without expecting to perceive its hidden sides in a manner prescribed by the nature of this object, it would be false to conclude from this that as soon as I perceive a cube, I am placed in a situation of *awaiting*, I adopt a particular attitude with regard to it, or with regard to the horizons which envelope it. Otherwise, awaiting would abound. It would have neither beginning nor end. It would be in each instant, each perception, each gesture. If it is true that, when we perceive, we expect what the course of experience unfolds continually in a characteristic style, it is not true that, from the first instant we open our eyes, we're in the middle of awaiting.

For the moment, let us stick to the first kind of awaiting. We shall designate it by the term "anticipation." How do we account for this from the phenomenological point of view? Let us return to Husserl: "Seeing, perceiving, is essentially having-something-itself (*Selbsthaben*) and at the same time having-something-in-advance (*Vor-haben*), meaning-something-in-advance (*Vor-meinen*)." To understand this, two Husserlian concepts can serve as our guide: (1) that of *appresentation*, that is to say an empty intending which, understood in the framework of a doctrine of the intentionality of consciousness, is related to aspects of the object which are not given in flesh and blood, which are not presented intuitively in the present perception, but which constitute the internal or external horizon of an object; and (2) that of *protention*, that is to say an intending of the future as future, which is related to contents not yet given — for example, the hyletic *datum* of a sound to come which clings to sounds already heard, and which blends together with them in the unity of a melody. What is common to appresentation and protention is their intuitive vacuity. However, if protention is a modality of appresentation, all appresentation, inversely, is not a protention.[1] For example, there exist empty intendings which are directed not toward the *actually* invisible (or the actually imperceptible), i.e. toward potentialities implied in the actualities of consciousness, sketching the horizons of a possible fulfillment, but rather toward the *absolutely* invisible or imperceptible, such as that which is analyzed in the Fifth *Cartesian Meditation*, where the consciousness of the other, the *alter ego*, is *appresented* — without ever being able to be presented — on the basis of its givenness as flesh. Moreover, it is fitting to specify that empty anticipation of protention differs in principle from that of awaiting, in the eyes of Husserl, since whereas waiting is an occasional lived experience, all consciousness is at each instant protential, the protention belongs to its immanent temporal constitution. Do these descriptions allow us to specify the nature and the status of these anticipations that accompany, for example, all perception in each of its constitutive moments? Certainly not. For, whatever relation holds between protention and appresentation, the two being generally intertwined in the teleological process of perception, they both raise the same kind of problem.

In effect, what defines these two modalities of the empty intending of consciousness is that they are simultaneously determined and undetermined. The appresentation which, in the actual perception of a cube, is related to its hidden sides, must intend them at the same time as sides to a large extent determined, susceptible to presenting themselves in a determined mode, with edges at right angles to each other, identical proportions, etc., and in a manner relatively undetermined: nothing, in the present appearance of the cube, allows us, for example, to anticipate the color of its other, hidden surfaces. But can we account for this determination *and* for this indetermination, in thinking appresentation in the manner of an *object-consciousness*? What must we understand, in effect, by "object-consciousness"? The object — be it sensible or ideal — is for Husserl a given, at least potentially so. But all that which is given to a consciousness possesses a certain intuitive fullness. If the object is a potential given, it must already be determined in the consciousness which intends it. And yet, this object is intended *emptily*, that is to say in the absence of such-and-such a determination. But how can the same consciousness be at once both determined and vague? How can it be saturated by the same object as that which it intends and intend it in an "empty" manner? For it is required by Husserl's entire conceptual framework that one may speak here of the same object: it is *the same* object which must be emptily

---

[1] Nor, *a fortiori*, awaiting: cf. Husserl, *Logical Investigations*, VI, §10, trans. J.N. Findlay, ed. D. Moran (New York: Routledge, 1970) v. 2, p. 211: "*Intention is not expectancy, it is not of its essence to be directed to future appearances. If I see an incomplete pattern, e.g., in this carpet partially covered over by furniture, the piece I see seems clothed with intentions pointing to further completions — we feel as if the lines and colored shapes go on 'in the sense' of what we see — but we expect nothing. It would be possible for us to expect something, if movement promised us further views. But possible expectations, or occasions for possible expectations, are not themselves expectations.*"

intended and which provides the intuitive fulfillment for this intending. "The same object?" What does that mean? How can the object of my not-yet fulfilled intending be the same as the intuited object, if the former is undetermined in many respects from the point of view of its content, while the latter is characterized by its intuitive richness and fullness? Two solutions are excluded from the beginning: that which consists in thinking anticipation as a pre-giving (*pre-donation*), *already intuitive*, of the object (for example, in the mode of an imaginary consciousness which would pre-give the future in the form of phantasms): for this would amount to assigning to consciousness the demiurge's power to be in advance of all possible perception and, literally, to fore-see it; and that which consists in denying that consciousness is nevertheless in advance of itself, always fore-seeing and awaiting. But then what solution do we have? How could we characterize this "emptiness" of our intendings, which corresponds in Husserl to the indetermination of our expectations?

There is no response to these questions within the framework of Husserlian phenomenology. The reason for this lies in the fact that Husserl's analyses short-circuit the linguistic moment inherent in all expecting, taking account of that which would alone allow us to formulate the problem with clarity. What I anticipate, that which I expect, when I perceive a cube, is that which I would be able to *say* about the awaiting. For example, that what I perceive is just a cube. In saying this, I describe the content of my anticipation, and this content is rigorously defined by the use of the term "cube" in this sentence; in saying that I perceive a cube, I say nothing yet about the color of its hidden sides. Likewise, if I say that I expect that the solid earth will not give out from under my steps when I walk upon it, I express quite precisely the degree of indetermination *and* determination that my expectation possesses: I expect that the ground will bear my weight, but I don't expect that the texture of this ground or its chemical composition will be such and such. The degree of determination *and* indetermination of my expectations is rigorously that of what I can say using meaningful sentences; it is not that of an "object" in the sense that Husserl understood it, which must be simultaneously entirely determined, since it is susceptible to being given intuitively, and in part undetermined, since it is intended only "emptily." Put in another way, the metaphor of emptiness and fulfillment, which underpins the entire Husserlian analysis of "expecting ..." as consciousness of the object, does not allow us to conceive to what extent my awaiting is determined and to what extent it remains vague: *this frontier can be traced only by language.* Our expectations on the level of perception are those of what we can say about our actual perception when we undertake to describe it; their object is not a potential given that must be determined in each of its aspects, nor is it an integral emptiness which would prohibit us from conceiving the intention as an expectation of whatsoever.

These considerations apply just as well to the second modality of awaiting which will be examined below, that of an attitude which I can adopt toward a future fact. When I set up a rendezvous with someone at an agreed-upon time and place, many facts may correspond to my awaiting: "I'm waiting for Emily at the café Flore around 6pm," is satisfied by the arrival of Emily, sprightly or gloomy, wearing a dress or a raincoat, showing up at 5:59 or 6:02. The degree of determination of my awaiting is rigorously defined by the degree of determination of the sentence which expresses it, and not by the "degree of vacuity" (supposing that this expression makes any sense) of silent acts of consciousness which would emptily intend an intuitive content potentially given.

Thus, in thinking appresentation and protention (and even awaiting in general) as acts of consciousness, and this consciousness as an object-consciousness, Husserl succumbs to the difficulty according to which our acts of intending or pre-intending should be after all *in part* determined, since they should be able either to be fulfilled in the way they are intended, or to be contradicted by experience. But Husserl does not tell us in what consist both this determination and indetermination. And he *is not able to tell us* this in virtue of the principles underpinning his description. For, to speak here of determination and of indetermination makes sense only in relation to possible expressions of this awaiting. There are no expectations for a mute consciousness, but only for a human being for whom being-in-the-world is essentially determined by speech. As Wittgenstein said, "It is in language that an expectation and its fulfillment make contact."[2] Does this amount to saying that the object of our awaiting is by nature intrinsically linguistic? We must avoid this conclusion. What I await and what I expect is Emily's arrival and not the expression of Emily's arrival in the sentence which corresponds to it. It is a possible state of affairs, and not a proposition which corresponds to it in language. More precisely, it is a fact of the world or a state of affairs *inasmuch as* these can be circumscribed and determined only by their expression. This remark allows us to extend the notion of anticipation beyond beings equipped with speech (a predator can lie in wait for its prey, expect that it will move in such and such direction, anticipate its movement), as long as we specify that the description of animal mobility in terms of prevision and anticipation, on the basis of its peculiar aspects (immobility, preparation for the pursuit) remains a "figure of speech." But above all, these considerations lead to two conclusions on the most general order. First, if the object of awaiting can be determined only by means of language, it does not follow from this that awaiting is a linguistic or "propositional" attitude; I can expect something without, for that matter, having formulated what I'm expecting and without needing to do so. I expect the ground not to give out from under my feet, I expect that my experience goes on without a hiatus, and nevertheless, I've never thought about it (if I do, it is uniquely as a philosopher). Awaiting — in the sense of the anticipation or of expecting something — is thus in no way reducible to determined linguistic behaviors, even if it is not thinkable independently from the possibility of *any* linguistic behavior. It is not of a linguistic order; it is an aptitude underpinning many behaviors (what shows that that which I'm expecting is not only what I say, but just as much what I do: for example, to walk without fear upon firm ground), and,

---

[2]   L. Wittgenstein, *Philosophical Investigations*, §445, third edition, trans. by G.E.M. Anscombe (Oxford: Blackwell, 2001), p. 111.

consequently, a modality of our relation to the world. Its analysis cannot simply depend upon the resources of a philosophy of language; it is indeed a matter for a phenomenology, but a phenomenology attentive to the linguistic dimension of our presence to things and to beings. Second, since the object of our expectations cannot be determined except by linguistic determinations, the "subject" of awaiting can only be a subject engaged practically in the world and possessing aptitudes and capacities (among which the capacity of speech) which necessarily possess a corporeal basis. This subject is never a representative consciousness, which presents objects to itself, nor is it a linguistic consciousness (supposing that something like this were thinkable). We can do nothing else, in order to think foresight and anticipation, than to take as our starting point an existent who is related practically to the world and to himself. Thus we can do nothing else than adopt the inflection which Heidegger subjected Husserlian phenomenology to, in the sense of a hermeneutic phenomenology.

This inflection appears all the more unavoidable if we ask about the relationship between awaiting and memory. What allows me, in effect, to anticipate the hidden aspects of an object, its internal and external horizons, and, more generally, the determinants of a world such as the solidity of the ground I walk upon, the relative stability of things, the permanence of persons, etc.? The answer can be nothing other than: "memory." But which memory? How are we to think memory in order to account for these anticipations, simultaneously elementary and architectonic, which confer upon experience — perceptive experience, for example — its style and continuity? Here, the insufficiency of the Husserlian characterization of our anticipations has as its correlate the insufficiency in his characterization of memory. What is profound, in effect, in Husserl's approach is more the problem, which he is the first to formulate in all its clarity, than the solution he gives to it. This problem is that of a form of permanent anticipation which belongs to the style of experience as such, and which confers upon it its coherence and unity — a style in virtue of which what catches us unawares, what disappoints our particular expectations, does not break apart the unity of experience, nor introduce in it any absolute hiatus, but appears precisely as unexpected on the basis of a more fundamental expectation. But how exactly are we to think these perceptive anticipations, this expectation, which is by no means a particular expectation of this or that, but rather a general and indeterminate expectation according to which experience would continue to unfold following the same "constitutive style"? It is evident that the notions of protention and of appresentation cannot solve the problem raised: not only because they involve us in inextricable difficulties (i.e., how many protentions are there? How to enumerate them? Is there a corresponding protention for each and every aspect of the real of which I can eventually say that I'm expecting it? And if so, then how are these almost-infinite intentions organized with respect to one another?); but more fundamentally, because such anticipation is not a datum for consciousness, it is of an essentially practical nature. Not only do I have no consciousness of anticipating this or that aspect of my experience to come, but I would indeed be incapable of saying all that I anticipate, of establishing a list of assertions regarding it. I anticipate experience by a prolepsis which is indissociably gestural and perceptive, which haunts the very potentialities of my body. In other words, the memory which is here appealed to, which inhabits the powers of my body and confers upon me this general take on the world, is a practical memory which does not allow any explicit and exhaustive account-taking. The beliefs and certainties, which haunt my perception and my very manner of moving-about in the world, are neither conscious intentions of which I might become integrally aware, nor linguistic "givens," the content of which I could formulate exhaustively. They are aptitudes which belong to incarnate memory, in accordance with which my past is present at each instant, in the very dispositions of my body, without being at my disposal in an explicit manner. To think such a memory, we are obliged to think memory otherwise than Husserl did: not at all, in the first place, as retention and re-membering, an intentional relation to past objects and episodes, but as incarnate capacity under the form of aptitudes and habitudes. Such a memory has no need of a thematic consciousness of the past; it does not rest upon it. Anterior to every form of conscious recall, it does not reproduce the past in one form or another, even linguistic; it is a modality of attention and openness toward the present. My recognition of faces and of things, my capacity to orient myself in space, belong to a blind familiarity which is the acumen of a hidden yet lucid memory, of an active forgetting which summarizes and condenses our entire experience under a concealed and subterranean form; it consists in this active memory which lives off unconsciousness and forgetting. We anticipate the future because we are in some way our past, because it is lodged in the arcana of our living and vibrant bodies, or rather because at each instant it makes us what we are, a body perched upon the stilts of time, to use an image by Proust.

The Unexpected

Perhaps we are now able to respond to one of the main difficulties for a phenomenology of awaiting and of surprise. How to think simultaneously the permanent anticipation underpinning even the least of our perceptions, along with the possibility of surprise? How to reconcile the ordered character of our experience, the "pre-indicated" character of our perceptual horizons, with the cropping up of unforeseeable phenomena?

An initial answer is given to us by the thesis according to which the "object" of awaiting is something that I must be able to express, which puts into play my linguistic capacities, and is not an "object" conceived as a potential datum for consciousness. This is neither an object determined in advance, nor an object that is undetermined (for what would "undetermined object" signify if the object is defined as that which is able to be given to a consciousness?); this is by no means an *object* in the sense of a content for consciousness, which it would be necessary for me to foresee in order to then be able to see it. Wittgenstein was right to highlight that the visual metaphor which generally underpins conceptions of awaiting — and which is quite typical of the Husserlian conception of intentionality — is a source of confusion: "I mean: 'If someone could see the process of awaiting, he should see what is awaited' — but that's indeed how it is: the one who sees the expression of awaiting sees what is awaited. And how could he see it in another fashion, in another sense?"[3] If that which I expect did not have the determination and the indetermination which is given to it by language, it would be possible neither for my anticipation to be satisfied (for the sides of the cube which are actually hidden from me would always be other, more brilliant or dull, more clear or murky, than all that I had anticipated), nor for it to be contradicted (for it would *always* be contradicted, and hence, it would *never* be so). The countryside extending below a promontory — is it hilly, as I expect, or is it flat? If expecting were a kind of "seeing," if it must "fore-see" or "pre-give" to itself its object in some way or another, it is clear that no particular hilliness could correspond to my expectation, for it would always be different from what I had anticipated. But if nothing can satisfy my expectation, then nothing could any longer contradict it: there would be neither surprise, nor confirmation. If, to the contrary, it is only by means of language that expecting and its fulfillment meet up, it becomes simultaneously possible to say that my expectation is confirmed (for it turns out that the countryside is hilly) and that the surprise of the discovering is total: this particular countryside is as new and astounding as those which might have been painted by Ruysdael or Courbet. The possibility of the fulfillment of my expectations, as well as that of their non-fulfillment, are thus inextricably bound together: it is necessary to be able to think together the fact that my experience unfolds in a coherent manner in the continuous fulfillment of my perceptive horizons, and that it never ceases to make room for the irreducibly new. Or rather, the sense of the new, *the novum*, is double: there is a novelty which is, in some sense, by right and which belongs to the phenomenality of the phenomenon, even if it does not provoke any sense of surprise, does not thwart any expectation; there is a novelty which is that of surprise when our expectations, as undetermined as they are, enter into conflict with an unusual experience. How can we account for this latter phenomenon?

What is an expectation contradicted? How to think the unexpected? We understand now at least how it cannot be thought. The difficulty in which most conceptions of expecting get mired is, in effect, the following: if it is indeed the future reality which is expected, how can it be expected if it is always new, if it catches us unawares? But this difficulty rests upon a misunderstanding. That which constitutes the object of our expectations, as I have underlined, is not the future reality taken in itself, which, indeed, cannot be anticipated, but rather it is this reality *inasmuch as it is determined by what we might say of our expectation.* Thus, it becomes possible to maintain simultaneously that what is expected is the future (and not, for example, a mental representation which would present it to us in advance), even though this is not the future as it will happen in fact, of which it is true that we know nothing. It is the future and it is not the future: it is the

---

[3]   L. Wittgenstein, *Philosophical Grammar*, §86.

future as an object of thought, that is to say, inasmuch as it is circumscribed by its linguistic expression. In other terms, the object of expectation is not the same object as the perceptible object that will come to fulfill it, neither is it a different object. Here we are dealing with two senses of the word "object." The future such as it will happen is of a different order than the object of my expecting, with the future-as-expected, because the first is a phenomenon always new and the second is an "object of thought," that is to say something which can be "given" only through a description which expresses it. One can thus say with an equal right for *every* phenomenon that it is "unexpected," if one means by this that it is impossible to foresee it in detail, in its richness and in its unforeseeable concreteness, and that it can be expected — and often is, in fact — if one considers it this time in its relation to possible *formulations* of expecting. Unless we make this distinction, we would have to say either that all is always in principle unexpected, or that nothing is so, since the object of expectation is the future itself — and then, one winds up unmistakably at the disastrous conclusion of Husserl, denying all specificity to the future, according to which the protention of consciousness is nothing other than an inverse retention.[4]

How can the present conform itself to our anticipations and appear nonetheless new, and thus unforeseen? The answer is that it is not anticipated and surprising *in the same respect*. One can thus maintain without contradiction, with Bergson, that phenomenality is always new and unforeseen — this novelty defining the present; and that the present very often conforms to our expectations when its novelty arouses no surprise. It is important to highlight that anticipation does not have to be *formulated* in order to be an "effective" anticipation; it is necessary and it suffices that it *could* be so. Certainly, we could have said that the cube had six sides, that the countryside beyond the headland was going to be hilly, like that which we had already traversed on our way up to the panoramic point. But it is generally after the fact, when surprise has torn through the fabric of our expectations, that we realize that we could have said it, that we could have expressed those expectations which, in the meantime, have turned out to be false, even if we did not feel any need to do so. It is the surprise that reveals to us the dispositions which precede it, and that it renders as mistaken. For whereas we feel the need to express our surprise, our expectations themselves remain tacit. The world mends itself on its own, incessantly, in our indifference, behind the minute shocks that destabilized it for an instant.

There is thus the novelty of every present perception — be it expected — and there is the novelty of that which contradicts our expectations: these are not situated on the same plane. But even this last novelty — does it *entirely* take us by surprise? Indeed, no. Let's suppose that, to our surprise, the countryside which stretches beyond the headland is neither flat nor hilly: it is actually a seascape. We had not known that the sea was so close; nothing had prepared us for it, neither

---

[4] E. Husserl, *The Phenomenology of Internal Time-consciousness*, trans. by J.S. Churchill, Bloomington: Indiana University Press, 1964, §26.

this salty odor that we presently recognize very well, nor this strong wind off the sea which we had wrongly taken for an ordinary breeze. And yet. The sea, the vast sea which is spread out at our feet is integrated immediately into our experience, it becomes an integral part of it, it threatens neither its continuity, nor its integrity. Even the surprise which it gives us remains bound to our expectations, not certainly to this particular expectation which was ours (to come out onto new hills, on a similar landscape), but to a more vast and more undetermined expectation, that of the *type* of landscape, which, in general, could come after hills in a region by the sea, a kind of expectation which results from the totality of our past experiences and prolongs them in the present.

We are thus dealing here with a weak sense of surprise, a weak sense of the unexpected. The unexpected, that which thwarts our expectations, remains still a modality of the expected. It thwarts a partial expectation; it is integrated to a general expectation. It does not call it into question. Is this always the case? Is there not a strong sense of the unexpected, such that the unexpected calls into question not only a partial expectation, but our global expectations, our habits, and even our aptitudes (for example, that of saying what it's all about) — tearing experience, destroying its unity, introducing a hole impossible to fill? Such could be traumatic experiences, marked by the imprint of a staggering shock: the palpable encounter with an omnipresent death on the field of battle, for example — unbearable experience, impossible to recount, breaking our ties of familiarity with the world, rendering it unrealizable to the point that it confers upon it an almost dream-like atmosphere. The staggering shock is not only a more intense surprise: it destroys the possibility of the surprise by excess of the surprising; it renders impossible all appropriation of the traumatizing event, and attacks the ground of our presence in the world. In the staggering shock the world gives way under our feet. That which is revealed to us with the weight of the unbearable, in an overwhelming face-to-face encounter, that which reaches us and defeats us, with a reality so real that it tends toward irreality — this, for example is the death of others in its horrifying materiality. And thus also our own death. Staggering shock often goes hand in hand with terror, in which we are struck powerless, incapable of the least response in the face of that which petrifies us. This experience at the limits of all possible experience cannot for this very reason be assimilated into anterior experience: it suspends it and breaks it — by excess.

But this does not apply only to traumatic experiences. Uncanny experiences can make the ground upon which our lives are built waver with an comparable intensity. The birth of an artistic vocation, for example. Alberto Giacometti recounts the following memory: around the age of nineteen, he took a trip in Italy where he discovered the painting of the great masters, Tintoretto in Venice and Giotto in Padua; upon exiting a church, still under the shock of that which he had come to see, he could no longer manage to perceive the people passing in the street under their usual aspect: "The same evening, all of these contradictory sensations were thrown into chaos by the vision of two or three young women who were walking ahead of me. They seemed to me immense, beyond all measure, and all of their being and all of their movements were charged with a horrific violence. I looked at them like a lunatic, overcome by a sensation of terror. It was like a tear in reality. All the meaning, all the relations among things were changed."[5] Terror, hallucination — these deal with the unexpected in its strong sense, close to staggering shock. Human bodies become meteorites in galactic space stripped of all orientation. They are no longer fastened to anything in known space; they float, disproportionate — now immense, now minute. The staggering shock is no longer a negative expectation, a surprise that a new continuity could blur: it is a rupture, a hole in the cohesion and the unity of the meaning of experience. For the sculptor, space is not given once and for all before the sculpture, it is this sphinx which he does not stop interrogating, and which offers no response but the reiteration of its enigma. At the birth of a sculptor's vocation, it is not surprising that there would be this repeated perception of a space without measurable depth, literally im-mense, and frightening in its absence of proportions. A little later, a second analogous experience:

> The true revelation, the true shock which made my entire conception of space topple over and which definitely put me on the path that I am now on, I received during the same period, in 1945, in a cinema. I was watching the news. Suddenly, instead of seeing figures, men who were moving in three-dimensional space, I saw spots on a flat cloth. I no longer believed it. I looked at my neighbor. It was fantastic. By contrast, he took on an enormous depth. All of a sudden I was conscious of the depth into which we are all plunged, and upon which we do not remark because we are so used to it. I went outside. I discovered an unknown Boulevard Montparnasse, dreamlike. Everything was different. The depth transformed people, trees, objects.[6]

This metamorphic regard cast upon the environing world no longer reveals anything that can be assimilated into common experience. The world reveals itself there out of reach and outside of expectation. Here, it is not a particular expectation which appears broken off or suspended, but a more vast, general, and immemorial expecting, which is that of our incarnate practical memory, that renders our world habitual and habitable. Not only would we be unable to foresee what irrupts under the figure of the elusive — we are in the impossibility of saying, even after the fact, what we were expecting — but we remain speechless and incapacitated: certain fundamental capacities of ours are suddenly unavailable, along with the totality of possibilities which depend on them. And since our grounding in the world is precisely that which our aptitudes and our habits give rise to, it is the stability of the world which here is threatened — the base of our possibilities, the very texture

---

5   This remark is reported by Charles Juliet, *Giacometti* (Paris: Hazan, 1985), p. 9. Cf. also Giacometti, *Écrits* (Paris: Hermann, 1990, 1997), p. 247.

6   The remark is related by Jean Clay, in "Alberto Giacometti ...", *Réalités* no 215, December 1963, p. 143.

of our relation to things. An uninhabitable world, absolutely enigmatic, survives this general shipwreck.

If the staggering is the figure of the unexpected which is assumed by the form of a certain number of events, it would, however, be inadequate to maintain that every event is announced to us under this guise. There are events which do not at all surprise us at first sight — or so little. There is nothing exceptional about them: they seem to integrate themselves without difficulty into our existence. An encounter that will eventually be capital can seem insignificant at first: an incurable sickness could take the form of a benign condition at the beginning; a decision the consequences of which appear limited can modify, from top to bottom, the course of our existence. And yet, is there anything in common between these virtually silent events and the striking experiences just mentioned? Certainly. In the one case as in the other, what is changed is not this or that possible, it is the possible in its totality. More precisely, it is not only the possible such as we expect it and anticipate it; it is also and at first the possible such as we project it, and such as we project ourselves onto it, the possible which structures our existence itself as the permanent project of itself, which now appears struck with impossibility, presenting itself to us in a new light. This metamorphosis of the possible (and of the world such as it articulates the possible) is not effectuated all at once; it seems even impossible that it would happen like this. It is only after the fact that an event becomes the event that it was. An event *is* not; it *will have been* an event. Its time is the future anterior. Contrary to appearances, this remark applies as well to the most striking experiences. Whether it happens at the beginning as striking or insignificant, it is not its intensity or its novelty as perceived or recognized at the moment which confers upon a fact its event character. The event appears as such only retrospectively, in proportion to the reversals in projects to which it gives rise — and this, no matter the intensity with which it manifested itself to begin with. Thus, returning to our example, it is the entire reshaping of space such that the sculpture of Giacometti puts to work, which allows us to understand the event that he relates, and not the inverse. It is what is full, in the event, of unaccomplished possibilities which *a posteriori* illuminates it and confers upon it its inaugural, and thus fateful, character. The excess of an experience with respect to our expectations and our projects is not an excess of manifestation that we could welcome immediately, but rather a lacuna, a suspension, an absence. What is eminently a phenomenon, what harbors in itself, as eminent, the mark of novelty in its anarchic and unforeseeable rising-forth, is precisely what appears only in recess and deferred with respect to its proper phenomenalization. The newer an experience is, the more it disturbs the expected, the more it reverses our projects and our possibilities, and the more it refuses itself to experience, the excess reverting into a lack, into disappearance. As Levinas writes, "the 'great' experiences of our life were never, properly speaking, lived through."[7] This is

---

[7]   E. Levinas, "Énigme et phénomène" in *En découvrant l'existence avec Husserl et Heidegger*, 3rd edition (Paris: Vrin, 1982), p. 211.

why the temporality of the event is that of a novelty which is always already past when it announces itself, of a memory which, when it returns to itself, is always already exceeded by what refuses itself to remembering, of an experience which, at the moment when it begins to gather the meaning of what traversed and defeated it, can no longer be its contemporary: irreducibly dia-chronic, the event is that which troubles all synchrony of consciousness, all its infallible presence to that to which it is present; it will have been present but after the fact, by the very metamorphosis of the present and of the presence to the whole world to which it gives rise. Deferred presence of the present taking leave of itself and presenting itself for the first time in the after-the-fact of its retrospection. And yet, even this deferred presence, as opposed to that which Levinas at times affirms, is still a matter of a phenomenology, for only a naïve conception of the phenomenon can equate it with the presently present.

Throughout these analyses, a new sense of the unexpected comes out. An event is surprising *otherwise* than an unexpected fact. As its having-occurred, the surprise which accompanies it is itself retrospective as well; consequently, it endures always. The great events of our life never lose their surprising character, this perennial surprise being their inalienable mark. Even once the astonishment "has passed," they overtake us. Indeed more so, it happens that they do not even astonish us at the beginning. Such a paradox is consistent with the fact that the surprise they provoke is no longer that of a disappointed expectation. It is rather a critical reversal of the possible in its totality — not only of our expectation, but first and foremost of our projects articulated and coordinated, one to the other. It is a rupture of meaning in the cohesion of our history. This surprise, which does not cease once our expectations are re-established, is accompanied by the immemorial evidence of that which is always already there.

Waiting for Something — Awaiting Nothing

We can, at present, return to the analysis of the second modality of awaiting. Until now, we have privileged awaiting understood as a permanent disposition (expecting), which is coextensive with our presence to the world as such. To exist is to constantly expect, thus to be exposed, in essence, to the unexpected. But the unexpected has assumed three main forms: the irreducible to a determined expectation (although partially undetermined, and determinable only by means of language); the irreducible to a general and global expectation which is one with our aptitudes in general, with the very manner by which we inhabit the world, thus the unexpected in the strong sense, the staggering, the impossible with regard, not only to this or that possible, but to our powers in their totality, and which often, in horror, strikes us with powerlessness; finally, what calls into question our existence in project as such, thus our manner of relating ourselves to ourselves and of comprehending ourselves in the light of our possibilities: the unexpected in the sense of the *indefinitely surprising*, the event — whether it is conspicuous and striking, or, on the contrary, "it arrives on the fluttering wings of a dove" (Nietzsche).

Expecting, in the sense that we have examined, is a permanent prolepsis of our existence; it is not an attitude that we might or might not take, adopt or reject: it guides our gestures and our perceptions, it is inherent in all our conduct. It is different from awaiting in its more common sense, in which we can or cannot place ourselves, which is a manner of being or an attitude.

I wait for something. I await, for example, the arrival of a train at 11:15. This awaiting thus understood rests upon a pre-vision, an expectation: only he who expects something can also, and by virtue of this, wait for it. No one can await something without at least expecting that it will come to pass. At least, this is the way it seems at first. One can wish for the impossible, desire the impossible, one cannot await the impossible. Holding something for impossible excludes the awaiting of this something. Awaiting is always only for the possible, and even for the probable.

However, waiting for something is no way the same as foreseeing that something will happen. My foresights (as my beliefs) do not have to be formulated: I live in them; they are fused with my being. But awaiting is an attitude that I take in given circumstances. It is up to me to await or not to await. Does it thus follow from this that awaiting envisaged in this sense is an activity, a kind of behavior? Awaiting is not a behavior. If behaviors characteristic of awaiting exist, none of them, by itself, defines awaiting nor is one with it. I can pretend to wait, pose as waiting. Inversely, I might feign not waiting, while continuing to await. Awaiting is not even a state or an affective disposition in which is placed the one who awaits. One can await joyously or weighed down with boredom; boredom and joy can suddenly disappear, but the awaiting disappears only if I cease to await. Let us not confuse awaiting with the painful agitation which sometimes accompanies it. Awaiting is an attitude in which I am placed. Certainly, it happens that I cannot prevent myself from awaiting, that I await against my will. Strategies for turning me away from waiting, diversions fail. But, even in this last case, the simple fact that some diversions exist manifests, nevertheless, that awaiting is something which I am able to do, something to which I give way even when I balk at doing so. This attitude is turned and held toward the future, toward a fact or an action to come that absorbs me. Awaiting, where I wait for something, is a tension of my being which leaves me no respite; whence its permanent risk of changing itself into boredom or insensibility to the present.

Of course, all awaiting is not menaced by boredom. There are joyous awaitings that are accompanied, rather, by enthusiasm or by impatience. And yet, above all when it tends to be prolonged beyond a certain point, awaiting is intimately exposed to this risk. Boredom besieges it: therein are revealed, indirectly, certain phenomenological traits of awaiting. Boredom places us in step with time in its languor, in its slowness: "longueur du temps" without patience, impatience and elongation of time, which are a stasis, a stagnation of existence. In boredom, we find time long, boredom is always "long," it is the length of time itself, its paralyzing stagnation. Not only is it that no occupation seems any longer able to fill in the punctured vessel of the present, but no thing, no task, no person captures us. No longer have we a taste for anything. Boredom suspends our ordinary curiosities and plunges us into a dismal stupor. It is a "dismal incuriosity [morne incuriosité]" according to the expression of Baudelaire,[8] dismal or morose, for, as Aristotle has already underlined with respect to melancholy in which anxiety grows, it strikes us with the *môrôsis*, with numbness.[9] It leaves us with nothing more than an empty and deserted present, and a consciousness cut loose and unhinged from the occupations and the interests of the moment. It is because nothing can fill in this void that we flee bored into diversions which, in truth, merely render us more sensitive to boredom and more weighed down by it. These diversions, these pastimes, which serve to "kill the boredom" are nothing other than its palpable expression: for we are not bored only by boring things but, when boredom grows and takes over our existence entirely, we are bored just as much by the amusing, the agreeable, the diverting. Passions, affairs, projects redouble the void of boredom instead of lightening our burden by it; they fill in the present only to better evade the bottomless pit. They don't while away the boredom; they intensify it, for this more profound boredom does not have to do with this or that occupation from which it is possible to distract oneself, or as the French say, "*de se désennuyer*" ("to get un-bored"); our lack of interest engulfs everything and leaves nothing outside of it. What 'un-bores' us is always, at base, the boring, what prolongs and deepens the boredom, that which dissipates it only in appearance and, in fact, perpetuates it. In boredom (*inodium*), everything is detestable for me (*est mihi in odio*), including and at first the pastime which turns me away from it. The mortal languor of boredom covers existence in a persistent fog through which no lamp can shine. Its void is an oppressive void that makes of distended and suspended time a parody of eternity.

The risk of boredom finds its way into all waiting, even the least painful. In waiting, we are no longer held in place. Everything glides along and nothing fills up the present, nothing holds our interest, we no longer have the heart for anything, with the exception of that which would come to fill the waiting, or to bring it to an end. Held entirely toward that which it expects, awaiting renders every other attitude difficult, almost impossible: it reduces it to insignificance. It occupies us to the point that nothing more can any longer occupy us, but this very occupation itself is a dis-occupation. Awaiting tends thus to desert the present in favor of dwelling upon a future momentarily unavailable. It is a tautness of our entire being, a tropism where time is deported in the direction of the future, or rather of that which, in it, retains us and obsesses us. Waiting lives only in the day after. But these days-after are apprehended only as the site of a *relative* novelty: all that which does not satisfy the requisites of awaiting generally becomes indifferent;

---

[8] Baudelaire, *Les Fleurs du mal*, Spleen LXXXVI, *Oeuvres completes*, vol. I (Paris: Gallimard, *Bibliothèque de la pléaide*, 1975), p. 73.

[9] Aristotle, *Problemata*, XXX, 953 b5–6.

the novelty of the future is reduced to a single possibility. We understand why Heidegger could say of this awaiting that it tends to realize the future in advance, and by that, to "de-possibilize" it. Awaiting envisages the possible in general only across an expected possible; it is an obsession, a blockage of existence.

But there is another kind of awaiting. Is it possible, in effect, to terminate all waiting for something, even waiting for something entirely vague and undetermined, and to await *purely and simply?* No longer to wait for something, but just to await, to be immersed in an empty, neutral, vast, unfathomable awaiting — incessant and without beginning? To await, only wait, to be entirely in awaiting, but to wait for nothing, to wait without specification, to accept that waiting itself stretches forth and stretches forth toward — nothing. To place oneself in empty awaiting, without any object, which is only the rehearsing [*ressassement*] of awaiting, as the wave is the repeated churning [*ressassement*] of the sea, an anticipation tensed toward nothing, a slackening of all of our awaitings? "The awaiting begins when there is nothing more to await,"[10] writes Blanchot, "not even the end of waiting. Awaiting ignores and destroys all that it awaits. Awaiting awaits nothing." But such a modality of awaiting, is it possible? And if so, what does it teach us about awaiting and about its relationship to the possible, to the future?

Such an awaiting is most certainly possible. It invites us to reconsider the idea that there is only an awaiting of that which one can expect. On the contrary, that toward which this awaiting is held is not a future occurrence, as undetermined as it could be; it is rather the un-awaitable in its strong sense, that which could overturn the entirety of our projects, reconfiguring the possible in totality, that is to say the world. Such an awaiting that awaits nothing frees and alleviates us from our awaitings, understood as awaitings of something; it opens us to the unawaitable that dismantles our awaitings, to the impossible which transfixes our possibilities and which is the purest name for possibility. It disposes us, not only to that which we cannot await, but to that which it is impossible to await; it prepares us not only for that for which we find ourselves unprepared, but also for that which nothing can prepare us for. This awaiting which is tensed toward nothing looks more like a slackening; because it anticipates nothing, it is open to everything; because it excludes nothing, it is susceptible to all welcoming. We can call it "*availability.*" While awaiting something takes place continually in the vicinity of boredom, since in deserting the present it renders it indifferent, turns away from it, availability is a renewed presence to the present, an attention to it in its novelty which cannot be anticipated, a *vigilance*. While the patience of awaiting something takes place always on the border of impatience, this awaiting which awaits nothing drives us to the edge of a vacancy and of a vigilance which are on the opposite side from restlessness, which are rather of the order of peace. This awaiting which is absorbed and absorbs us in itself, in its self-sufficient void, is therefore that which alleviates boredom. That which I await here is nothing; yet, this new figure of the void has a sense opposed to the previous one. There is a void that oppresses us, and

---

[10]   M. Blanchot, *L'attente, l'oubli* (Paris: Gallimard, 1962), "L'imaginaire", p. 39.

another that gives us peace. This is no longer the mortal repose of the stagnation of time, rather it is the profound repose which turns expectation away from itself, allowing it to forget itself, the turn of awaiting against itself in the direction of the unexpected. Here, the unexpected is no longer that which contradicts expectation — that is to say, continues to stand up against it — but it is that which is out of proportion in relation to it. Such availability is without guarantee, lacking certitude. It is not an attitude that one adopts, rather it is the attitude of renouncing any attitude that one would be able to take, or decide to take. It is by lodging us in its center that we can for example begin to think: "To be able to question signifies to be able to wait, even an entire lifetime,"[11] writes Hölderlin. Is not artistic creation also at this price? "The poet finds expression not in searching for his words," says Claudel, "rather on the contrary by getting into a state of silence and having nature pass over him."[12] This awaiting which awaits nothing — is it not the background of prayer itself? Is not true prayer that in which we ask for nothing, expect nothing, but relinquish to God our requests and expectations?

Philosophy does not say much about hope. Without a doubt this is because of the scent of theology that surrounds this term. Hope is omnipresent in all of human life: it is difficult to relate to the future other than through hope. But hoping [*l'espoir*], which must be distinguished from religious hope [*l'espérance*] — can it give to our existences their stance and their orientation? If I leave it up to hope, do I not also leave it up to this paradoxical hope that dwells in the greatest distress and which drives toward renunciation? For hope tricked and deceived can even come to extreme point of hoping for no more hoping. If nothing is stronger than hope, as it is sometimes said, nothing is stronger than despair. But, is it not possible to return, for short moments at least, to this side of hope and of despair, in a this-side of pure neutrality, which is that of intransitive awaiting, or better, of availability? That which, in the midst of the worst trials, can confer a glimmer to our lives is not so much hope as it is availability, this antenna of our fragile — and finished — freedom. This awaiting, having renounced hope, and just *because* it renounced it, can remain open to the unhoped for [*l'inespéré*] in the midst of the worst trials. For it is when one does not hope for the unhoped for, to reverse the formula of Heraclitus, that one can again await it, without expecting it.

Is not this availability the true name of religious hope (*l'espérance*)? Is not religious hope closer to availability than to hope? These questions exceed those to which philosophy can answer. It is not a task for philosophy to attempt an answer — not even, without a doubt, to pose them. But if religious hope is always hope of this or hope of that, if it is not deprived of its residue of waiting-to-see, if it has not reached the appeasement and the lightness, absorbed in an awaiting that is not awaiting anything, does it not risk always being reversed into its opposite? With this question (which is no longer exactly a question), we have returned to the problem with which we began, that which has for its title "phenomenology and

---

[11] Letter of January 1799 to his mother.

[12] Paul Claudel, "Préface à Rimbaud," in *Choix de poèmes* (Paris: Gallimard, 1960).

eschatology" and to which you are, without a doubt, right to expect that I offer a solution.

This expectation, I must profess, will go unmet.

Translated by Ryan Coyne

PART II
Phenomenological Eschatology

Chapter 3

Sacramental Imagination and Eschatology

Richard Kearney

"Only through singularities can we find the divine."

Spinoza

Contemporary philosophical discourse on the religious can generally fall into three categories: protest, prophecy and sacrament. In the present essay, I would like to focus on the third step, beyond the indispensable labor of iconoclasm, apophasis and mourning, namely, the sacramental return to the holiness of the everyday.

Sacraments differ from signs and symbols insofar as they embody the transcendent in the immanent, the extraordinary in the ordinary, the not-yet in the now. I am using "sacramental" here in a more general sense than that of ecclesial "sacraments" (though it can include these) to cover those re-awakenings of the divine within the singular events of quotidian existence. In doing so, the logic of the sacramental obeys that of an inaugurated eschatology. Teresa of Avila argued that true mystical experience testifies to this sacramental movement from mystical meditation back to the ordinary universe. After the forgetfulness of self and detachment from possessions in silent meditation, she speaks of returning to a life of service to others in the world, reminding us of the "sacred humanity" of Christ. The ultimate step in mystical abandonment and eschatological hope is a sanctification of our mundane existence: "Know that the Lord walks among the pots and pans helping you both interiorly and exteriorly."[1] "The Creator," she always insisted, "must be sought through creatures."[2] This sacramental return to the everyday signals a *via affirmativa* after the *via negativa* of detachment and disenchantment. Beyond the dark caesuras of existence — the sunderings of history or of individual souls — the eschatology of the present promises a second consecration of the life-world. It embodies, in Ricoeur's phrase, "*la joie du oui dans la tristesse du fini.*"[3]

---

[1] Teresa of Avila, *Collected Works*, vol. 3, 5.8. I am grateful to Anthony Steinbock whose work, *Phenomenology and Mysticism: The Verticality of Religious Experience* (Bloomington and Indianapolis: Indiana University Press, 2007), examines this question in detail; see especially pp. 64–5.

[2] Teresa of Avila, *Collected Works*, vol. 1, 22, 7–8; cited in Steinbock, *Phenomenology and Mysticism*, 62.

[3] Paul Ricoeur, *L'Homme Faillible* (Paris : Aubier-Montaigne, 1960), 156.

The sacramental invokes the power of "yes" in the wake of "no." This is a powerless power that is ultimately more gracious and effective than the most powerful of powers. It is the possibility of a God after God (*ana-theos*) which signals the return to God after the setting aside (*ana-thema*) of God. Here anathema takes on the double sense of not only heretical condemnation — its colloquial connotation — but also of a radical consecration or setting apart as holy. Condemnation as precondition of consecration. Separation as prelude to sanctity. Withdrawal as precursor to consent. We thus recover the original sense of "anathema" as a thing devoted to the divine.

In the light of this *anathema-anatheos* paradox, I will suggest in this essay that the sacramental return presupposes a certain "negative capability" which keeps us vigilant towards strange signs of the divine beyond the dichotomy between theism and atheism. In other words, the sacramental move, as I understand it, signals the possibility of a second God set apart from a first God of metaphysical dogmatism. It marks an opening towards a God whose descent into flesh depends on our response to the sacred solicitation of the moment. This calls for a special attentiveness to infinity embodying itself in daily acts of eucharistic love and sharing. An endless crossing over and back between the infinite and infinitesimal. Here the highest deity becomes, kenotically, the "very least of these." The Word becomes everyday flesh. On-going and interminable gift. Transubstantiation.

This sacramental paradigm not only characterizes the final movement of what I call "anatheism" (i.e., the passing from protest to prophesy and from prophesy to the retrieval of the sacred in the everyday), it also comprises what I have elsewhere termed a "micro-eschatology."[4] In other words, the consecration of the mundane which, I will suggest, characterizes Merleau-Ponty's phenomenology of the flesh allows us to re-conceive eschatology. No longer forced to choose between the triumphal macro-eschatologies of an omnipotent God and the anonymous causality of atheistic scientism, the retrieval of the eschatological in the everyday allows us to rethink eschatology as occurring somewhere between these alternatives.

A Phenomenology of the Flesh

What, if anything, can contemporary philosophy tell us about the anatheist option of sacramental incarnation? What light might it cast on the everyday marvel of Word becoming living flesh?

The theme of "flesh" was largely ignored by Western metaphysics since Plato. This may seem strange given the fact that almost fifteen hundred years of the history of metaphysics comprised what Etienne Gilson called the "Christian synthesis" of Greek and Biblical thought. But metaphysics (with some notable

---

4   Cf., my contributions in John Panteleimon Manoussakis (ed.), *After God: Richard Kearney and the Religious Turn in Continental Philosophy* (New York: Fordham University Press, 2006).

exceptions like Duns Scotus before scholasticism or Thomas before Thomism) managed to take the flesh and blood out of Christian incarnation leaving us with abstract conceptual and categorical equivalents. There were the mystics of course, whose lives and confessions testified to the mystery of transcendent immanence; but these were invariably sidelined (Eckhart and the Beguines, John of the Cross, Teresa of Avilla, Margaret Porete). The Citadel of Metaphysics was not breached by their heart-felt "heresies," or, if it was, remained deeply suspect. It resisted all such infiltrations of the flesh-smitten spirit from without and from within. Even poor Aquinas, as noted, had the mystical harm taken out of him, his initial nerve and brio reduced to a caricature of itself. The edifice of Onto-Theology admitted of no gaps, no risks, no wagers. Immune to the daring of quotidian incarnation — the constant daily coming into flesh of the divine (*ensarkosis*, as Scotus called it) — Metaphysics stood firm, indubitable, *intactus*.

In terms of mainstream Western philosophy, it would, I will argue, take Husserl and the modern phenomenological revolution to bring Western philosophy back to the experience of "sacramental flesh," that is, the possibility of acknowledging Spirit in our most basic pre-reflective lived experience. Edmund Husserl blazed a path towards a phenomenology of the flesh when he broached the crucial theme of the living body (*Leib*).[5] In order to open up a space where neglected notions of embodiment might be re-visited in a fresh experiential light, Husserl considered it essential to operate his famous *epoche*. This involved the bracketing of all previous presuppositions — in this instance, everything we thought we knew about the flesh. This suspension of received wisdoms ran all the way down, from the heights of metaphysics to the most basic prejudices of common sense: a whole gamut of assumptions which Husserl lumped together under the label of the "natural attitude." In other words, the natural attitude which Husserl's phenomenological method sought to put out of play covered a wide variety of taken-for-granted views about what the "flesh" actually is: accredited opinions informed by inherited speculative systems (realist or idealist), positive sciences like biology, physics and chemistry, or any number of cultural, social and ideological attitudes. And it also, needless to say, included religious doctrines and dogmas about the body, sex,

---

[5] Husserl, *Ideas II*, *Cartesian Meditations* and the *Crisis*. See the excellent commentary by Didier Franck, *Chair et Corps: Sur la Phénoménologie de Husserl* (ed. De Minuit, Paris, 1981) as well as by French phenomenologists like Jean-Luc Marion (*Being Given, In Excess*, and *The Erotic Phenomenon*) and Jean-Louis Chretien (*Hand to Hand*, Fordham University Press, 1993). William Desmond also has interesting philosophical points to make about the sacredness of the flesh in his recent essays on "consecration." See also the work of Catherine Keller, *Face of The Deep: A theology of Becoming* (London and New York: Routledge, 2003) and John Manoussakis, *God after Metaphysics: A Theological Aesthetics* (Bloomington and Indianapolis: Indiana University Press, 2007). Nor should we omit reference here to Gabriel Marcel's intriguing philosophical reflections on incarnation and embodiment, which exerted a considerable influence on the "religious" phenomenological writings of Ricoeur and Levinas.

desire and sin. Once all such inherited attitudes were suspended, Husserl wagered that the phenomena themselves would be allowed to speak for themselves in their simple, ordinary everydayness. The hypothesis was that *after* the *epoche* of received opinion, the things of experience would be invited, without censure, to show themselves forth from themselves as they are in themselves, that is, in all their multilayered — sensible, affective, intelligible, spiritual — *thereness*. In this manner, experiences of the flesh, all too often neglected by Western metaphysics, would be re-described in a new and unprejudiced light.[6]

Husserl himself, however, only pointed in this direction. He blazed the trail and took some steps along the path, but he did not enter or occupy the terrain. His own work, however pioneering, remained a matter of promissory notes, missionary manifestos, half finished charts, logs and maps. For all his talk of returning us to the "things themselves," Husserl remained caught in the nets of transcendental idealism and never quite escaped the limits of theoretical cognition. It would be for his followers to drop anchor and bring the expeditionary flotilla to shore. Heidegger, one might argue, advanced the project of a phenomenology of flesh with his existential analytic of "moods" and "facticity," but the fact remains that Heideggerian *Dasein* has no real sense of a living body: Dasein does not eat or sleep or have sex. It too remains, despite all the talk of "being-in-the-world," captive to the transcendental lure. Other disciples of Husserl went further, but while Scheler and Stein made sorties into a phenomenology of feeling and Sartre offered fine insights into shame and desire, it is really only with Merleau-Ponty that we witness a fully-fledged phenomenology of flesh. Here at last, the body is no longer treated as a mere project, cipher or icon, but as *flesh itself* in all its ontological depth. The ghost of metaphysical idealism is finally laid to rest. We return to the body in all its unfathomable *thisness*.

It is telling, I think, that Merleau-Ponty chose to describe his phenomenology of the sensible body in sacramental language. This terminological option amounts to nothing less, I submit, than a eucharistics of profane perception. Let me take some examples. In the *Phenomenology of Perception* (1944), we read:

> Just as the sacrament not only symbolizes, in sensible species, an operation of
> Grace, but *is* also the real presence of God, which it causes to occupy a fragment
> of space and communicates to those who eat of the consecrated bread, provided
> that they are inwardly prepared, in the same way the sensible has not only a
> motor and vital significance, but is nothing other than a certain way of being in
> the world suggested to us from some point in space, and seized and acted upon

---

[6] See James Morley, "Embodied Consciousness in Tantric Yoga and the Phenomenology of Merleau-Ponty" in "The Interreligious Imagination" issue of the *Religion and the Arts*, ed. R. Kearney (Brill, 2008), pp. 144f. See also Edmund Husserl's statements on God, transcendence and the absolute cited in my "Hermeneutics of the Possible God" in *Givenness and God*, ed. Ian Leask and Eoin Cassidy (New York: Fordham University Press, 2005), pp. 220f.

by our body, provided that it is capable of doing so, so that sensation is literally a form of communion.[7]

This is a bold analogy for an existentialist writing in France in the 1940s, a time when close colleagues like Sartre, de Beauvoir and Camus considered militant atheism *de rigueur*. Merleau-Ponty goes on to delineate this eucharistic power of the sensible as follows:

> I am brought into relation with an external being, whether it be in order to open myself to it or to shut myself off from it. If the qualities radiate around them a certain mode of existence, if they have the power to cast a spell and what we called just now a sacramental value, this is because the sentient subject does not posit them as objects, but enters into a sympathetic relation with them, makes them his own and finds in them his momentary law.[8]

It is a curious paradox that when Merleau-Ponty traces the "phenomenological return" all the way down to the lowest rung of experience (in the old metaphysical ladder, the *sensible*), he discovers there the most sacramental act of communion. This is intimately related to his notion of chiasmic crossing of ostensible contraries: the most in the least, the first in the last, the invisible in the visible. Here we have a reversal of Platonism and Idealism, and a return to flesh as our most intimate "element," namely, that which enfolds and envelopes us in the systole and diastole of being, the seeing and being seen of vision. Phenomenology thus marks the surpassing of traditional dualisms such as body/mind, real/ideal, inner/outer, subject/object. This is how Merleau-Ponty describes the enigma of flesh as mutual crossing-over in his posthumously published work, *The Visible and the Invisible* (1964): "The seer is caught up in what he sees ... the vision he exercises, he also undergoes from the things, such that, as many painters have said, I feel myself looked at by the things, my activity." So much so that "the seer and the visible reciprocate one another and we no longer know which sees and which is seen. It is this Visibility, this anonymity innate to Myself that we have called flesh, and one knows there is no name in traditional philosophy to designate it."[9] It is here, I suggest, that Merleau-Ponty gets to the heart of this nameless matter and descends — in a final return, a last reduction that suspends all previous reductions — to the incarnate region of the "element":

---

[7] Maurice Merleau-Ponty, *Phenomenology of Perception* (London: Routledge, 2002), 246. I am grateful to John Panteleimon Manoussakis for this reference. See an extended discussion of this theme in chapter seven of his *God after Metaphysics*.

[8] Merleau-Ponty, *Phenomenology of Perception*, 248.

[9] Merleau-Ponty, *The Visible and the Invisible* (Evanston: Northwestern University Press, 1968); cited in my *Modern Movements in European Philosophy* (Manchester University Press, 1986), 88–9.

The flesh is not matter, in the sense of corpuscles of Being which would add up
or continue on one another to form beings. Nor is the visible (the thing as well as
my body) some "psychic" material that would be — God knows how — brought
into being by the things factually existing and acting on my factual body. In
general, it is not a fact or a sum of facts "material" or "spiritual."

No, insists Merleau-Ponty:

the flesh is not matter, is not mind, is not substance. To designate it, we would
need the ancient term "element," in the sense it was used to speak of water,
air, earth, and fire, that is, in the sense of a *general thing* midway between the
spatio-temporal individual and the idea, a sort of incarnate principle that brings
a style of Being wherever there is a fragment of Being. The flesh is in this sense
an "element" of Being.[10]

Returning to examples of painting — Cézanne and Klee — in *Eye and Mind*
(1964), Merleau-Ponty expounds on this chiasmic model of the flesh as a mutual
transubstantiation of the seer and the seen in a "miracle" of flesh:

There really is inspiration and expiration of Being, action and passion so slightly
discernible that it becomes impossible to distinguish between what sees and what
is seen, what paints and what is painted ... There is no break at all in this circuit;
it is impossible to say that nature ends here and that man or expression starts
here. It is mute Being which itself comes to show forth its own meaning.[11]

In *Signs* (1960), a collection of essays devoted to questions of language and art,
Merleau-Ponty repeats his claim that the flesh of art is invariably indebted to the
bread of life. There is nothing so insignificant in the life of the artist, he claims,
that is not eligible for "consecration" in the painting or poem. But the "style"
which the artist creates converts his corporeal situation into a sacramental witness
at a higher level of "repetition" and "recreation." The art work still refers to the
life-world from which it springs, but opens up a second order reference of creative
possibility and freedom. Speaking specifically of Leonardo da Vinci, he writes:

If we take the painter's point of view in order to be present at that decisive
moment when what has been given to him to live as corporeal destiny, personal
adventures or historical events, crystallizes into "the motive" (i.e., the style), we
will recognize that his work, which is never an effect, is always a response to
these data and that the body, the life, the landscapes, the schools, the mistresses,
the creditors, the police and the revolutions which might suffocate painting are

---

[10]   Ibid., 89.

[11]   Merleau-Ponty, *Eye and Mind in Continental Aesthetics*, ed. R. Kearney and D.
Rasmussen (Blackwell, 2001), 288f.

also *the bread his work consecrates.* To live in painting is still to breathe the air of this world.[12]

In short, the bread of the world is the very stuff consecrated in the body of the work.

Merleau-Ponty is no theologian and certainly no Christian apologist, but he has an intriguing interpretation of Christian embodiment as a restoration of the divine within the flesh, a kenotic emptying out of transcendence into the heart of the world's body, becoming a God *beneath* us rather than a God *beyond* us:

> The Christian God wants nothing to do with a vertical relation of subordination. He is not simply a principle of which we are the consequence, a will whose instruments we are, or even a model of which human values are the only reflection. There is a sort of impotence of God without us, and Christ attests that God would not be fully God without becoming fully man. Claudel goes so far as to say that God is not above but beneath us — meaning that we do not find Him as a suprasensible idea, but as another ourself which dwells in and authenticates our darkness. Transcendence no longer hangs over man; he becomes, strangely, its privileged bearer.[13]

When it comes to expressing love for another human being, Merleau-Ponty sees the presence of this "transcendence" in the promise we make to another beyond what we can know or realize in the present moment. The absolute which the lover looks for beyond our experience is implied in it. Just as I grasp time by being present, I perceive others through my individual life, "in the tension of an experience which transcends itself." There is thus, Merleau-Ponty suggests, "no destruction of the absolute ... only of the absolute separated from existence. To tell the truth, Christianity consists in replacing the separated absolute by the absolute in men. Nietzsche's idea that God is dead is already contained in the Christian idea of the death of God. God ceases to be an external object in order to mingle in human life, and this life is not simply a return to a non-temporal conclusion. God needs human history. As Malebranche said, 'the world is unfinished'." Merleau-Ponty realizes that official Christianity might not concur with this, but he suggests that "some Christians might agree that the other side of things must already be visible in the environment in which we live."[14]

Finally, in his Lectures on "Nature," delivered at the Collège de France between 1956 and 1960, Merleau-Ponty adumbrates what I would consider to be some basic anatheist insights. Arguing the need to think God in relation to Nature, Merleau-

---

[12] Merleau-Ponty, *Signs* (Evanston: Northwestern University Press, 1964); cited in *Modern Movements*, p. 85.

[13] Ibid., pp. 83–4.

[14] Maurice Merleau-Ponty, "Inaugural Lecture to the 'Société Française'" in *The Primacy of Perception*, ed. James Eddie (Evanston, Il: Northwestern UP, 1964), pp. 27f.

Ponty objects to any theism which takes God out of the world. This he associates with a certain Christian "acosmism" — or anti-worldliness — epitomized in the equation of true and total being with a God beyond the world. Such a removal of divinity from the natural and human world threatens to plunge this world into a state of non-being or nothingness. Merleau-Ponty links this to a special "malaise of Judeo-Christian ontology" which he defines thus: "Such a monotheism carries along with it in all rigor the consequence that the world is not. 'From the moment when we say that God is Being, it is clear that in a certain sense God alone is.' Judeo-Christian thinking is haunted by the threat of acosmism."[15] But this a-cosmic expression of Judeo-Christian belief is of course historically specific; it is a particular metaphysical account of the divine, and its relationship to nature, which became dominant in western philosophy and theology. Like Nietzsche before him, Merleau-Ponty identifies this orthodox account with a disguised nihilism: to equate God with a timeless, otherworldly Being, which is the sovereign cause of itself and has no desire for nature or humanity — as Descartes and the rationalists did — is to reject the sanctity of the flesh. "To posit God as Being is to bring about a negation of the world."[16] And it is also, Merleau-Ponty hastens to add, a betrayal of the original message of Incarnation — the Logos becoming Flesh and entering into the heart of suffering and acting humanity.

In reaction to this version of metaphysical theism, Merleau-Ponty calls for the recognition of a genuinely a-theistic moment in the Christian story of incarnation and crucifixion where Christ experiences a radical abandonment before the father: "My God My God why have you forsaken me?" Merleau-Ponty concludes by contrasting acosmic theism with a genuine Judeo-Christian alternative that he identifies with the sacramental engagement with the world, epitomized by the Worker-Priest movement in France in the fifties which also found expression in liberation theology and in the attention to what he calls "minorities," namely, the marginalized and rejected ones. This is his critical diagnosis of acosmic theism: "God is beyond all Creation. Theism comes from this position, and moves towards that of no longer distinguishing the critique of false Gods ... And as Kierkegaard said, no one can be called Christian; faith must become unfaith. There is an atheism in Christianity, religion of God made man, where Christ dies, abandoned by God."[17] But Merleau-Ponty does not end there. He appends the following summary prognosis: "It may be, says a hymn, that the passion of Christ is not in vain ... See the adventure of the priest-workers, as awareness that we cannot place God apart from humanity suffering in history; hence, so that God may be realized,

---

[15]   Merleau-Ponty, *Nature: Course Notes from the Collège de France*. Compiled by Dominique Seglard (Evanston: Northwestern University Press, 1995), p. 133.

[16]   Ibid., p. 137.

[17]   Ibid., pp. 137–8.

(we need) the sorting out of humans who are the furthest from God … because minorities are the salt of the Earth!"[18]

In short, Merleau-Ponty believes that we need a new, non-dogmatic relation to Nature and thus to God that opens onto the minor, the different, the incarnate. Recognizing the radical consequences of incarnation for our understanding of both God and Nature is, for Merleau-Ponty, an ana-theist alternative to the endless doctrinal disputes between theism and atheism. In this sense, I suspect that Merleau-Ponty might have agreed with the proposal by post-secular thinkers like Bonhoeffer and Ricoeur that we move beyond those "religions" disfigured by otherworldly metaphysics to a faith in the divine potential inherent in the everyday secular life of action and suffering, of attention and service to others. But where Merleau-Ponty seems to differ somewhat from Bonhoeffer and Ricoeur is in supplementing their "prophetic" voice of protest (informed by their war experience of imprisonment) with a "sacramental" acoustic of existence. In this he might be said to add a more "Catholic" style to the "Protestant" iconoclasm of Bonhoeffer and Ricoeur, though in both cases we are speaking of a post-religious expression of these confessional cultures. By relocating the moment of sacred transcendence in the immanence of nature, Merleau-Ponty is restoring Logos to the flesh of the world. And, by extension, he is replacing the idea of a triumphal eschatology with a micro-eschatology of the incarnate now.

Phenomenological Method and the Sacramentality of the Sensible

This insight of "immanent transcendence" is not of course unique to Merleau-Ponty. Many Christian mystics — from John of the Cross to Hildegarde of Bingen and Meister Eckhart — said similar things, as did Jewish sages like Rabbi Luria and Rosenzweig, or Sufi masters like Rumi and Ibn'Arabi. Indeed I am also reminded here of the bold claim by Teilhard de Chardin that God does not direct the universe from above but underlies it and "prolongs himself" into it. Or indeed of the suggestion by Max Scheler that Francis of Assisi's sacramental vision of the natural world represented a profound "heresy of the heart" which broke from previous metaphysical doctrines of Christianity as acosmic denial of the flesh. Scheler is of special relevance here, given his close links with phenomenology. Arguing that the sacrament of the Eucharist shows how Christian love may "acquire a footing in the living and organic, through its 'magical' identification with the body and blood of our Lord under the forms of bread and wine,"[19] Scheler suggests that these came to be virtually the *only* natural substances, in a very ritualized setting of Holy Communion, which permitted a union with the cosmos

---

[18]   Ibid., p. 138. My thanks to Kascha Semon for bringing many of these passages to my attention.

[19]   Max Scheler, "The Sense of Unity with the Cosmos" in *The Nature of Sympathy* (Routledge and Kegan Paul, 1954), p. 87.

— until, that is, mystics like Francis and Claire of Assisi came to embody this communion in their everyday lives, restoring sacramentality to the living universe of nature, animals and humans. Francis's bold "heresy," in Scheler's view, was to have challenged the enormous *gulf* between humans and nature, introduced by "traditional Christian doctrine," addressing as Francis did both fire and water, sun and moon, animals and plants, as "brothers and sisters." Against the a-cosmic tendencies of mainstream Christianity, Francis's bold achievement was to combine love of God with the sense of "union with the life and being of Nature."[20] His greatness was to have expanded the specifically Christian emotion of love for God the Father to embrace "all the lower orders of nature," while at the same time uplifting Nature into the glory of the divine.[21] Most of Francis' contemporaries thought him "strange and unconventional," some heretical and mad. Here was a mystic who dared conjoin transcendence and immanence, the sacred and the secular, by calling all creatures his brothers, and by looking with "the heart's keen insight into the inmost being of every creature, just as though he had already entered into the freedom of glory of the children of God."[22] This view that God is in all beings was condemned as atheistic blasphemy by many orthodox Christians before and after Francis. But for Francis, as Scheler recognizes, it was a way of restoring God to the world, of rediscovering a living God amidst the ashes of a dead one.[23]

Merleau-Ponty would, I think, be in agreement with many of these expressions of sacred immanence, found in different mystics of the great Wisdom traditions. But Merleau-Ponty is a philosopher, not an apologist nor an historian of religions. What he provides is a specific philosophical method — namely, a phenomenology of radical embodiment — to articulate this phenomenon of sacramental flesh. And it is to be noted that a number of recent phenomenologists have followed Merleau-Ponty's lead when seeking to inventory the sacred dimensions of the flesh. I am thinking here especially of Jean-Luc Marion's writings on the "flesh" as a saturated phenomenon in *On Excess* or Jean-Louis Chrétien's hermeneutical commentary on the *Song of Songs*. But Merleau-Ponty has the advantage, in my view, of not only being the first phenomenologist to explicitly explore the sacramental valence of the sensible but also to observe a certain methodological agnosticism with regard to the theistic/atheistic implications of this phenomenon, an agnosticism which opens up the anatheist option.

Merleau-Ponty is no crypto-evangelist. On the contrary, he consistently sustains the methodic suspension of confessional truth-claims recommended by

---

[20]   Ibid., p. 87.

[21]   Ibid., p. 87.

[22]   Ibid., p. 88.

[23]   Scheler's work was informed by Husserl's phenomenological investigations but lacked the rigor of the phenomenological method, opting instead for a more romantic, eclectic and holistic view of the subject in his writings on feeling and sympathy, cf. *On Feeling, Knowing and Valuing* (Chicago: University of Chicago Press, 1992).

Husserl. And this chimes well, it seems to me, with the poetic license enjoyed by artists and writers when it comes to the marvel of transubstantiation in word, sound or image. For poetic license entails a corollary confessional license from which no one is excluded. In this respect, we could say that the phenomenological method — which brackets beliefs — is analogous to the literary suspending of belief and dis-belief for the sake of inclusive entry to the "kingdom of as-if." This suspension allows for a specific "negative capability" (Keats) regarding questions of doubt, proof, dogma or doctrine, so as to better appreciate the "thing itself," the holy *thisness* and *thereness* of our flesh and blood existence. The attitude of pure attention that follows from such exposure to a "free variation of imagination" (the term is Husserl's) is not far removed, I believe, from what certain mystics have recognized to be a crucial preparatory moment for sacramental vision, calling it by such different names as "the cloud of unknowing," the *docta ignorantia* or, in Eastern mysticism, the *neti/net* — neither this nor that — a moment which paves the way for the deepest wisdom of reality. True belief traverses non-belief. In the free variation of imagination, indispensable to the phenomenological method, everything is permissible. Nothing is excluded except exclusion. All is possible. By allowing us to attend to the sacramental marvel of the everyday without the constraints of particular confessions, Merleau-Ponty offers fresh insights into the eucharistic character of the sensible.

Messianic Time

Another aspect of micro-eschatology is what Walter Benjamin calls "weak messianism." This seeks to honor the forgotten voices of history by retrieving their "impeded possibilities," thereby emancipating the past into a future.[24] This eschatological giving of a future to the past is witnessed for example in Gen 3.15 when Yahweh tells Moses that he is not just the God of ancestral memory but the promise that "will be" with his people in their struggle for emancipation. "I am who will be with you." I am the God who may be, can be, shall be, if you listen to my summons and choose liberty over slavery, life over death, *eros* over *thanatos*. And this same eschatological paradox of past-as-future is at work in the Palestinian formula of the Passover which instructs us to remember the feast of the Passover "until he comes." It is reprised in the Christian invocation of "anticipatory memory" at the Last Supper (I Corinthians 11:25–6: "for as often

---

[24] See also Paul Ricoeur, *Memory, History and Forgetting*, trans. Kathleen Blamey and David Pellauer (Chicago: The Chicago University Press, 2004) and also our discussion of giving a future to the "unfulfilled possibilities" of the past in "Capable Man" in *Paul Ricoeur: the New Hermeneutics*, ed. Brian Treanor and Henry Venema (forthcoming). For a fuller treatment of this theme of messianism in relation to Derrida, Levinas and Ricoeur in Chapter 3 of my *Anatheism: Returning to God after God* (New York: Columbia University Press, 2009).

as you eat this bread and drink the cup, you proclaim the death of the Lord until he comes"); and it finds additional echoes in John the Baptist's famous avowal of Jesus "The one who is coming after me ranks ahead of me because he existed before me" (John 1:15).

The Messianic exists before us ("before Abraham was I am") as the possibility which lies ahead of us. It heralds the one who comes *after* every "god" we presume to possess, the sacred stranger who is always in front of us, always to come. Which is surely why Jesus refuses the allure of self-possessed power, priority and privilege, insisting that he be baptized by John rather than the contrary. "I need to be baptized by you," says John bemusedly, "and yet you are coming to me?" (Matthew 3.15). The washing of the apostles' feet (John 13) and subsequent enduring of death for others rather than the assumption of imperial power, signals the eschatological conversion of sovereignty into hospitality. It epitomizes the anatheist option for self-emptying service to strangers.

The eschatological reversal of Sovereign Being is echoed in the overturning of Sovereign Knowledge. Jesus does not *tell* his disciples who he is; he *asks* them who he is! "Who do they say that I am" (Mark 8:27). And just as the voice in the burning bush refuses to impart some sacred name of magical power, replying instead with a riddling pun: "I am who I shall be" — so too Jesus resists all attempts to apprehend him in any definite or categorical way. In fact it is only the demons who claim to *know* Jesus, as in the exchange with the unclean spirit at Capernaum who called out "I *know* who you are — the Holy One of God!" To which Jesus responds: "Be quiet! Come out of him" (Matthew 1.24). Even when Peter announces "You are the Christ," Jesus warns him to tell no one and actually denounces him as "Satan" for trying to dissuade him from going to his death (not a thing an omnipotent God should do!) (Mark 8:30–33). Is it not significant, moreover, that whenever Jesus is pressed to reveal himself "as he is," he constantly refers to the Father, or the Pentecost or the "least of these"? Is it not highly telling that he defers to *others* in a process of kenotic self-emptying? So that if he indeed admits he is the "Way the truth and the life," it is always a way that leads to others, a way that opens onto other ways. "You cannot reach the Father *except* through me," he boldly announces, calling for the radical exclusion of exclusion itself. For who cannot be counted among the "least of these"? Or among the "strangers" who hunger and thirst? The messianic way leads from Sovereign Self to excluded stranger, breaching the highest in the name of the lowest, the first in the name of the last. Which is why, as I argue elsewhere, I keep repeating that interconfessional hospitality towards other faiths and cultures is not just an option for Christians but an imperative. Christian *caritas*, as a refusal of exclusivist power, is a summons to endless *kenosis*.[25]

---

[25]   See R. Kearney, *Anatheism: Returning to God after God* and also *Exploring Kenotic Christology: The Self-Emptying of God*, edited by C Stephen Evans (Oxford: Oxford University Press, 2006), and Sarah Coakley's illuminating chapter on "Kenosis and Subversion: On the Repression of 'Vulnerability' in Christian Feminist Writing" in her

It is in a similar spirit, I suggest, that we may choose to read the frequent injunctions against idols and graven images in both Judaism and Islam. Namely, as a refusal to possess the sacredness of the wholly Other in anthropomorphic projections and illusions. In all three Abrahamic traditions we find evidence of a *via negativa* which safeguards the "strangeness" of the divine. This is why it is so important to constantly recall the anatheist moment of *not-knowing* at the very heart of spiritual experience: not as a threat to faith but as an integral part of the journey towards the Other. The anatheist wager is not some postmodern gloss on Descartes's doubt but a movement of decision recognized as essential to genuine spiritual quest, as Steinbock points out in his analysis of the testimonies of great mystics of the Abrahamic tradition: Ruzbiahn Baqli in Islam, Rabbi Dov Baer in Judaism, and Teresa of Avila in Christianity.[26] And one finds powerful instances of this wager in numerous other mystical texts from Gregory of Nyssa's notion of an unbridgeable gap (*diastema*) between human understanding and the irreducible strangeness of God to Bonaventure's famous definition of faith as a never-ending "pilgrim's progress" of many winding paths (*itinerarium mentis in Deum*). These all testify to an anatheist gesture of detachment from assumed faith which prizes open space for a possible return to second faith. That is why Teresa of Calcutta's diary confession of loss of her original belief should not, I suggest, have provoked world-wide scandal but been seen as a salutary part of her spiritual maturation to a deeper belief.

Perhaps there can be no anatheist wager without this moment of atheism? And if this be so I am tempted to compare such a cycle of faith to the ancient Patristic figure of "circumcession" (*perichoresis*) where different persons move endlessly around an empty centre (*chora*), always deferring one to the other, the familiar to the foreign, the resident to the alien, the self to the stranger. Without the *gap* in the middle there could be no leap, no love, no faith.

Anatheism cherishes the Siamese twins of theism and atheism and celebrates the fertile tension between them. The bracing oscillation between doubt and faith, withdrawal and consent, is the aperture which precedes and follows each wager. It is the guarantee of human freedom before the summons of the other. The choice to believe or not believe is indispensable to the anatheist wager. And it is a choice made over and over again.

---

volume, *Powers and Submissions: Spirituality, Philosophy and Gender* (Oxford: Blackwell, 2002), pp. 3–39.

[26] For a very illuminating discussion of comparative mystical experience in Jewish, Christian and Islamic traditions see Anthony Steinbock, *Phenomenology and Mysticism*.

Chapter 4

The Promise of the New and the Tyranny of the Same

John Panteleimon Manoussakis

Nothing oppresses us more than the weight of an irrevocable past. In front of the past we are powerless: the things we have done and the things done to us assume an undeniable authority as *facts*, as the things-themselves that, furthermore, give shape to who we are. Nothing undermines our freedom more than a predetermined and given nature, our fixed facticity. Most of us understand ourselves as who we have been — our identity is like a record in which every action, deed and thought is written down indelibly. Think here of police records, credit records, academic transcripts, professional résumés and medical files. In all these cases — and for each institution that they represent, the police, the academy, the market, and the medical establishment — we simply *are* our past. This archival orientation is best illustrated by the example of the *shadow* — the past, like a shadow, follows us and grows on us and it is impossible to get rid of it. It is only in the Church, as I would like to argue in this essay, that we are not who we have been but who we *will* be. Against this archeological logic the Church retorted with a new logic — the logic of the new, the *novum*, the doctrine of *de novissimis*. In Revelation (21:5) the "new things" coincide with the last things and together they form what is known as eschatology. Against the things-themselves stand the things-to-come.[1]

The reason for our society's obsession with the past is the fact that our epistemology is entirely *protological* (in giving ontological priority to what comes

---

[1]   The references here are, of course, to phenomenology and eschatology. "Back to the things themselves" was the battle cry of the father of the phenomenological movement, Edmund Husserl, at the beginning of last century. By that he meant the return to the reality that Kant had refused to things as a result of the bifurcation of the World into phenomena and noumena. The bridge that Husserl had discovered between phenomena and noumena was consciousness itself, and specifically the intending character of consciousness, what became known in phenomenological parlance as intentionality. What could be, if any, the relation between eschatology and phenomenology, between the things-to-come and the things-themselves? At first it seems that any possible relation is exhausted in their antithesis: the two have nothing to do with each other — not only because presumably they come from two different worlds, that of faith and reason, but because of the fundamental difference in their orientation: the things-themselves are precisely *not* the things-to-come. In spite of this opposition, I would like to suggest that reconciliation is possible in the retrieval of the things-to-come *in* the things-themselves.

first). In other words, our knowledge is based by necessity on experience (one needs only to refer to the opening lines of Kant's Introduction to the *Critique of Pure Reason*), and experience is always experience of what has been and has come to pass, what, in other words, can be measured, observed and written down in files and records like those mentioned earlier. In everyday life we reason according to such protological paradigms — the origin holds the truth of the thing or the person in question. A careful examination of the violence directed toward the Other (in the many forms of racism, sexism, xenophobia, homophobia, etc.) would reveal that in the root of such violence lies the simple prejudice that gives priority to what has been, either in terms of a biological beginning (nature, essence) or in terms of one's own history. It is the beginning, after all, that determines the end and not the other way around. And how could it be differently? The beginning functions as the *cause* of what has thereby its beginning — and does not the cause come always before its effects? Not for theology. The chronological and ontological primacy of the cause is challenged by a series of events, such as the Creation, the Incarnation, the Crucifixion, and the Resurrection. These events do not fit in the protological paradigm of causality that we described above. What would be, for example, the "cause" of the crucifixion? Does the cross make any sense at all if seen by itself, that is, as the effect of what has preceded in the life of Jesus? We would argue that the cross becomes the cross only once it is seen from the future, that is, from the point of view of the resurrection that follows it. Theologically, then, it is the resurrection that is the "cause" of the crucifixion. And the resurrection itself — would it make any sense to say that the resurrection is the "result" or the "effect" of Christ's passion? "In Paul's mind," John Zizioulas writes, "even the historical event of our Lord's resurrection would make no sense if there was not to be a final resurrection of all human beings *in the end*: 'if there is no resurrection of the dead, then not even Christ was risen' (1 Cor. 15:13)."[2] And Jean-Yves Lacoste concurs when he writes that the Hegelian understanding of History as progress and progression towards the future "could only be right, finally, if the resurrection of the Crucified did not have to be interpreted as a promise, and was nothing but the meaning of the last fact — of the reconciling Cross."[3] Theologically speaking then, the cause of the things that happen and have happened lies *not* in their beginning but "in the end" — for they come *from* the kingdom of God, for it is the kingdom that is, properly speaking, their origin. "It is not at the beginning (in the morning of consciousness and at the dawn of history) that man is truly himself."[4] For, as Heidegger would say, the beginning determines man and history only insofar as

---

[2]   Metropolitan of Pergamon John D. Zizioulas, "Towards an Eschatological Ontology," unpublished paper delivered at King's College in 1999.

[3]   Jean-Yves Lacoste, *Experience and the Absolute: Disputed Questions on the Humanity of Man*, trans. Mark Raftery-Skehan (New York: Fordham University Press, 2004), p. 138.

[4]   Ibid., p. 137.

it "remains an advent."[5] "Meaning" Lacoste writes, "comes at the end."[6] In this respect, eschatology is *anarchic* through and through, for it alone can effect such a radical subversion of the *arche*: of principles and beginnings.

Eschatology, as we shall see, reverses the naturalistic, essentialist and historistic models by making the seemingly improbable claim that I am not who I am, or even less, who I was and have been, but rather, like the theophanic Name of *Exodus* (3:14), I am who I *will* be. Eschatological theology is deep down a liberation theology. The protological example of the shadow (*skia*) is properly reversed as in the *Letter to the Hebrews* (8:5 and 10:1) and in the *Colossians* (2:16–17): the shadow now does not follow but rather precedes reality, so that, in Christian typology, the present condition as the things-themselves is merely an adumbration of the things-to-come.[7] This implies, at the very least, that the validity of the things-themselves depends upon the things-to-come and, therefore, the former have no intrinsic value of their own.[8]

Christian Eschatology

Most religions share some form of an eschatological vision: more commonly it is a vision that anticipates the end of the physical world, the coming of a better world. Such apocalyptic events are usually structured around the coming of a Messianic figure. None of these elements of eschatology, however, is particularly or properly Christian. In order to find what is proper to Christian eschatology we need to look away from the narrations of cataclysms and catastrophes.[9] The particularity of

---

5   "Der Anfang bleibt als Ankunft." Martin Heidegger, *Elucidations of Hölderlin's Poetry*, trans. Keith Hoeller (New York: Humanity Books, 2000), p. 195.

6   Lacoste, *Experience and the Absolute*, p. 137.

7   Zizioulas, "Towards an Eschatological Ontology."

8   What is implied here is the Lutheran doctrine of the "orders of creation" (*Schöpfungsordung*) that regarded such worldly institutions like nations and states and civil conventions like marriage as belonging intrinsically to the creation and thus "good." This doctrine gave rise to a *Theologie der Ordungen* that did not hesitate to support Nazi ideology (since the Third Reich could be seen as part of God's creation). Dietrich Bonhoeffer criticized such theories by changing the terminology from "orders of creation" (that would imply a permanent validity) to "orders of preservation," making them, thus, part of the transient scheme of this world that has its justification only in relation to the eschaton; cf. *Creation and Fall*, trans. Douglas Stephen Bax (Minneapolis: Fortress Press, 1997), p. 140. The same notion is expressed by Bonhoeffer's eschatological concept of the "penultimate"; cf. *Ethics*, trans. Reinhard Krauss, Charles C. West, and Douglas W. Stott (Minneapolis: Fortress Press, 2005), p. 160ff.

9   Moltmann, after going through a list of similar apocalyptic visions and prophesies, concludes: "All these ideas and fantasies are certainly soundly apocalyptic, but they are not Christian. The Christian expectation for the future has nothing at all to do with final solutions of this kind, for its focus is not the end of life, or history, or the world. It is rather

Christian eschatology, I believe, is best summarized by three statements (although, it is in no way exhausted in them):

a. The eschaton is *not* the End of History,
b. The eschaton *is* the Incarnation, and
c. The eschaton is the Incarnation as unfolded in History through the celebration of the Eucharist (we will treat this last statement in the third part of this essay).

What these three statements have in common is the desire to refuse a rather dominant tendency in Christian theology of assigning eschatology to a semi-utopian time at the End of History, that might, one day, come but most likely not during our lifetime. This tendency is reflected by the arrangement of the articles in the Nicene Creed — the phrase "I expect the resurrection of the dead and the life to come" is, fittingly it would seem, the last one. Similarly then, the talk about the last things comes always *last*: eschatology has traditionally been the last chapter of any systematic exposition of theology. And it is against this tendency that I would like to argue today: by relegating eschatology to a realm beyond experience, we have come up with the perfect alibi for our getting all too comfortable with the world in its current state. We have found the ideal justification for our forgetting that this is not our home, our goal, our destination; that the categories of this world are not and should not be the paradigms and the concepts of our thought. By exiling eschatology to a time beyond time we have precluded ourselves from the wonderfully subversive effects of the future, of the reversals that the new might bring. Without an eschatological awareness in our interaction with the everyday we cannot but become immune to surprise and, therefore, to the kingdom of God which has surprise as its very mode of manifestation (Matt. 24:27, 50, Mark 13:36, Luke 12:40, 17:24).

The Eschaton is not the End of History

A common mistake that one finds even today in manuals and handbooks of Systematic Theology is the identification of the Eschaton with an End (the end of the World[10] or of History), that is, the confusion of the *eschaton* with the *telos*.

---

the beginning ..." See, "Is the World Coming to an End or Has Its Future already Begun?" in *The Future as God's Gift: Explorations in Christian Eschatology*, eds David Fergusson and Marcel Sarot (Edinburgh: T&T Clark, 2000), p. 130 and also his Preface to *The Coming of God: Christian Eschatology*, trans. Margaret Kohl (Minneapolis: Fortress Press, 1996), p. xi.

[10]　It is highly problematic, I think, to speak of the "end of the world" from a Christian perspective. *The Revelation*, in all its apocalyptic imagery, presents us with the transformation of the world and its renewal ("Behold, I make all things new," 21:5) but not

Eschatology, however, is not a teleology. Such a *teleological* eschatology has no place in theology but only in cosmology. The eschaton can be found on either side of the End of History, or on both sides, before it and after it, but it should never be identified with that End itself. Hence the impossibility of telling *when* the kingdom will come. This impossibility is not based on the unknown but rather on the unknowablility of the kingdom's coming. It is not so much that we do not know when the kingdom will come, but rather that we *cannot* know, because its coming is necessarily situated outside time and history, where the question of "when" has no meaning. The kingdom of God does not coincide with the culmination of History, that is, with a *totality*, but it signals a breach in the body of history, a rupture occasioned by the encounter with the Other. By placing the coming of the kingdom either *after* history or *within* history, we avoid identifying it with History — as in the (ontotheological) eschatologies of Hegel and Marx.[11] By doing so, we guarantee history its own freedom. History is then allowed to unfold in its own ways — without being constrained by a predetermined route, leading to a predestined outcome. History has no program, and even less a program already known and given before the ages. That idea would condemn God to boredom and humanity to a fatalistic passivity. To presume such a right for either God or for humanity is to turn the eschatological dream into the nightmare of either a theocratic or a secular totalitarianism.[12]

The Eschaton is the Incarnation

This statement distinguishes Christian eschatology from its monotheistic counterparts in the Abrahamic tradition. Whereas Judaism and Islam have *one* eschatological center, fixed in the future, Christian eschatology unfolds as this tension between *two* eschatological nodal points: between the *already* of the Incarnation and the *not yet* of the Parousia. This tension finds expression in the formula of the Fourth Gospel "the hour is coming and is now here" (John 4:23,

---

with its annihilation or destruction. It is questionable if the world as God's creation can be destroyed, especially after the event of the Incarnation, given that God has united the world with Godhead in the human nature of Christ as the doctrine of the Ascension would imply.

[11]   Wolfhart Pannenberg regards these eschatologies as fundamentally anti-Christian and thus as structures of the anti-Christ; see, *Systematic Theology*, vol. III (Grand Rapids: Eerdmans, 1998), p. 636. As their common characteristic, Pannenberg identifies the tendency to place value on the general, or the abstract, over and against the particular and the individual.

[12]   To remember Levinas: "eschatology institutes a relation with being *beyond the totality* or beyond history … It is a relationship with *a surplus always exterior to the totality*" of history; see *Totality and Infinity: An Essay on Exteriority*, trans. Alphonso Lingis (Pittsburgh: Duquesne Press, 1969), p. 22. And as he writes later, "When man truly approaches the Other he is uprooted from history" (ibid., p. 52).

5:25). John's eschatology is *realized*[13] in the revelation of Christ, or, better yet, *inaugurated*[14] by the Word's coming to the World (the judgment takes place "now" [John 12:31] or "already" [John 3:18]; the resurrection of the dead is also taking place in the "now"[John 5:25]). Thus, for Maximus the Confessor, "the end has come upon us"[15] insofar as the "humanization" of God has already been accomplished while what is still pending is its corollary, i.e., the deification of Man. And even that has already begun with baptism and is being perfected little by little by the Eucharist. In that, Lacoste is right, I think, to speak of a "splitting" of the end or of the *eschaton* into two: the eschaton of the present (at the end of times) and the present of the eschaton (in the everyday).[16] Inaugurated eschatology seems to be also the principle through which the author of the *Letter to the Hebrews* understands his own times (1:2, 9:26), while it is not unknown to Paul either (1 Cor. 10:11). Von Balthasar summarizes it in the following words:

> The Biblical experience of God in both the Old and the New Testaments is characterized as a whole by the fact that the essentially "invisible" and "unapproachable" God enters the sphere of creaturely visibleness, not by means of intermediary beings, but in himself. (...) This structure of Biblical revelation should neither be sold short nor overplayed. (...) It could be overplayed by the view that all that God has instituted for our salvation, culminating in his Incarnation, is in the end only something preliminary which must finally be transcended by either a mystical or an eschatologico-celestial immediacy that would surpass and make superfluous the form of salvation, or, put concretely, *the humanity* of Jesus Christ. This last danger is not so far removed from the Platonising currents of Christian spirituality as one would hope or want to believe: *the impulsive search for an immediate vision of God* that would no longer be mediated by the Son of Man, that is, by the whole of God's form in the world

---

[13]   See, Raymond E. Brown, *The Gospel of John and Epistles of John: A Concise Commentary* (Collegeville: The Liturgical Press, 1988), p. 19.

[14]   See, Georges Florovsky, "Bible, Church, Tradition," volume I of the *Collected Works* (Vaduz: Belmont, 1987), pp. 35–6.

[15]   St. Maximus the Confessor, *Ad Thalassium* 22, trans. Paul M. Blowers and Robert Louis Wilken in *On the Cosmic Mystery of Jesus Christ* (Crestwood: SVSP, 2003), p. 117.

[16]   Lacoste, *Experience and the Absolute*, p. 138. "Reconciled existence" Lacoste writes in the next page "takes place therefore in an interim between the eschatological blessings already granted and the eschatological blessings that still remain within an economy of promise" (emphasis in the original). It is this bifurcation of the eschatological that enables what Richard Kearney has described as a micro-eschatology; see Richard Kearney, "Epiphanies of the Everyday: Toward a Micro-Eschatology" in *After God*, John Panteleimon Manoussakis (ed.), (New York: Fordham University Press, 2006), pp. 3–20 as well as Kearney's contribution in this volume.

is the conscious or unconscious basis for many eschatological speculations. (...) *The Incarnation is the eschaton and, as such, is unsurpassable.*[17]

For if it was otherwise, if incarnation was *not* the unsurpassable eschaton, one would have been justified in anticipating a time where I could have a more direct, full, unmediated understanding of the Other.[18] In anticipation of such a time, however, I begin cheapening (relativizing) my encounter with *this* Other, my neighbor, as it is given in the here and now of everydayness. Such an *eschaton* beyond incarnation would offer me the metaphysical alibi to overlook the Other in front of me, to ignore, neglect or underestimate him/her in expectation of a more authentic encounter with another Other (perhaps, the wholly Other, *tout autre*) at the end of History, conceived as some metaphysical totality *à la* Hegel.

Eschatology and the Forgetfulness of the Spirit

Eschatology's reduction to the time of the Parousia, and to the apocalypse associated with it, might have been the result of disassociating eschatology from Pneumatology. Luther complained once that most of his contemporaries made "fine Easter preachers but very poor Pentecost preachers" because they preached "solely about the redemption of Jesus Christ but not about the sanctification of the Holy Spirit," or, as he put it in another occasion, they had "devoured the Holy Spirit, feathers and all!"[19] One could say perhaps that, from Origen to Barth, theology has become almost exclusively Christocentric, and at times even Christomonistic. There is, of course, a good reason for that: almost all doctrinal controversies in Church History, from Arianism to iconoclasm, have been Christological. And it is through such controversies that doctrine and dogma is clarified, defined and promulgated. Indeed, the creedal definition of Nicea-Constantinople gives only one line to the Holy Spirit, and an incomplete one at that, as it focuses exclusively on the language of the Old Testament ("And in the Holy Spirit ... who spoke though the prophets") with no reference, as one might have expected, to the role of the Spirit in the New Testament and in the life of the Church.

---

[17]   Hans Urs von Balthasar, *The Glory of the Lord: A Theological Aesthetics, vol. I: Seeing the Form*, trans. Erasmo Leiva-Merikakis (San Francisco: Ignatius Press, 1998, pp. 301–2).

[18]   Paul's phrase about seeing now "through a glass, darkly" while then "face to face" (1 Cor. 13:12) concerns only the mode of the manifestation but not its content. What I see now, *sub specie tempore*, i.e., the Other in the person, will also be the eschatological manifestation of the personal Other *sub specie aeternitate* (cf. Acts, 1:11).

[19]   Martin Luther, "On the Councils and the Church," *LW* 41–114 and "Against the Heavenly Prophets," *LW* 40:83, both passages as quoted by Jaroslav Pelican in *Bach Among the Theologians* (Philadelphia: Fortress Press, 1986), pp. 7–8.

This forgetfulness of the Spirit by theology and her domination by Christology (becoming thus a mere *logology*[20]) has had a number of theological repercussions on ecclesiology and soteriology. As far as liturgy is concerned, however, the emphasis of our worship on Jesus Christ (a historical person) and, subsequently, on a series of (historical) events related with his life on earth (crucifixion, resurrection, ascension) bound our worship to history and oriented it permanently towards the past. The original experience of doxology gave its place to the kerygma, our reading of Scripture became evidential and didactic, even the Eucharist itself became strictly or overwhelmingly a memorial — and a memorial of the past, instead of, as the Eucharistic prayers suggest, the future. What was lost in all this was the opening up of the Christian community to what lies beyond history, to the *eschata*.

After all, pneumatology and eschatology are intimately interconnected. It is the Spirit that announces the *erchomena*, the things-to-come (John 16:13). In a manuscript variation of Luke's account of the Lord's prayer, the phrase "your kingdom come" is replaced by the phrase "your Holy Spirit come."[21] The "kingdom of God" is theologically synonymous to "the Spirit of God." And when Paul speaks of "the spiritual body" (1 Cor. 15:44) he is not using an oxymoron but simply refers to the eschatological reality of our bodies after the common resurrection.

One could look for examples of eschatology's interrelation with pneumatology in other fields beyond scripture — in Mahler's 8th Symphony, for example. There the creative imagination of the composer combines two texts that might seem *prima facie* unrelated: the Latin hymn *Veni Creator Spiritus*, and the last act from Goethe's *Faust*. He combines them not only in the sense that he brings them together by setting them in music within one single composition, but even more interestingly by exposing their inner relatedness. For at the very end of the Symphony, as the *chorus mysticus* sings in rapture the accomplishment of an eschatological vision[22]

---

[20] Sergius Bulgakov uses the term rather contemptuously; see, *The Comforter*, trans. Boris Jakim (Grand Rapids: Eerdmans, 2004). In a different sense, it is used by Dietrich Bonhoeffer in his lectures on Christology; see, *Christ the Center*, trans. E.H. Robertson (San Franscisco: Harper, 1978).

[21] In particular, uncial codex 162 and 700, also attested by Marcion and Gregory of Nyssa (*PG* 44, 1157).

[22] It is of interest, I think, to read how Mahler himself understands those closing lines of Goethe's *Faust*, in helping us to understand the eschatological character that permeates them. As Mahler writes to his wife (in June 1909): "All that is transitory (everything that I have presented to you here on these two evenings) is nothing but images, inadequate, of course, in their earthly manifestations; but there, liberated from earthly inadequacy, they will become reality, and then we shall need no paraphrase, no figures, no images. What we seek to describe here in vain — for it is indescribable — is accomplished there. And what is that? Again, I can only speak in images and say: the Eternal Feminine has drawn us on — we have arrived — we are at rest — we possess what we could only strive and struggle for on earth" (quoted in Michael Steinberg's program notes for the performance of Mahler's 8th Symphony by the Boston Symphony Orchestra on October 23, 2004).

("Das Unzulängliche hier wird's Ereignis, das Unbeschreibliche hier ist's getan"), the orchestra repeats *tutti* the theme of the Symphony's opening line: *Veni Creator Spiritus*.

Eucharistic Eschatology

In the Eucharist, however, this link between eschatology and Pneumatology is preserved — most importantly perhaps in the *epiclesis*. That makes the Eucharist the most genuinely eschatological event and eschatology the most authentic interpreter of the Eucharist. It is needless, of course, to emphasize here the importance of the Eucharist — for it is in the fellowship of breaking the bread and sharing the common cup that the Church, in her catholicity, takes place. Here we should focus only on what the Eucharist has to teach us about the Church's eschatological orientation. The question of the Eucharist's eschatological character raises inevitably the question about the nature of the Eucharist. The predominant interpretation of the Eucharist — already attested by the Marcian and Pauline tradition — places at its heart the *anamnesis*, i.e., the remembering of Christ's sacrifice: "every time that you eat this bread and drink from the cup, you offer witness to the death of the Lord, until He comes" (1 Cor. 11:26). Besides the fact that the early Christian communities did celebrate the Eucharist *prior* to the development of this *theologia crucis*, and thus the interpretation of the latter cannot limit the understanding of the former, the Q Sayings, among other sources, testify to a different tradition, more eschatological in its orientation, and quite innocent of the passion narrative.[23] Things become even more clear when we turn to the Eucharistic tradition as recorded in the *Didache*, where there is no mention of the passion but, in its place, one finds an acute eschatological awareness ("… just as this broken bread was scattered upon the mountains and then was gathered together and became one, so may your church be gathered together from the ends of the earth into your *kingdom* …" and again "remember you church, Lord … and gather it, from the four winds into your *kingdom* which you have prepared for it …"). These prayers testify to a yearning for the coming of God's kingdom that culminates with the eschatological as well as Eucharistic exclamation "Maranatha!"[24]

At the end of the day, it is the Eucharist itself that should instruct us as to its meaning and interpretation — and the Eucharistic text, once the layers of superimposed interpretation are removed, leaves no doubt about its eschatological character. At the Eucharistic gathering the faithful assemble in order to re-enact

---

[23] There might even be a connection between the Q document (as "reconstructed" by modern scholarship) and the structure of the Eucharist itself. For this argument see, Petros Vasileiadis, *Lex Orandi* (Athens, Indiktos, 2005).

[24] *The Apostolic Fathers* trans. J.B. Lightfoot and K.J.R. Harmer (Grand Rapids: Baker Books, 1989), pp. 154–5.

the coming of God's kingdom — their orientation, therefore, is always towards the future and never towards the past. There is no text that speaks more eloquently of the eschatological character of the Eucharist than the prayers of the two ancient liturgies that have been handed down to us under the names of St. Basil the Great and St. John the Chrysostom (still in use today by the Orthodox Church). Both liturgies begin with a telling doxology "Blessed is the *kingdom* of the Father and the Son and the Holy Spirit" (as opposed to "blessed is our God ..." that commonly opens the services of the divine office, or the "in the name of the Father ..." formula that we find in the Roman Missal and the rites that are influenced by it). At the very beginning of the liturgy, then, the kingdom is proclaimed as a reality and not as an expectation. It is this bold experience of the kingdom that enables the celebrant to say during the *anaphora*, that is, the consecration prayer: "Remembering ... all those things which came to pass for us: the cross, the grave, the resurrection on the third day, the ascension into heaven, the sitting down at the right hand, the second and glorious coming ..." (PG 63, 916). Here logic is violated and history is left behind. How could it be that we remember the "second, glorious coming"?[25]

The Eucharist is thus more of a *prolepsis* than an *anamnesis*, since the events that we recall lie, from the historical perspective, in the future — a future made present in the Eucharist and by the Eucharist. To remember the future, to have already experienced what is still to come, this is something that goes against our protological categories of thinking. To grasp what is at stake here we need to implement and juxtapose *anamnesis* as recollection (essentially a Platonic concept) with *anamnesis* as repetition (as Kierkegaard understood it).

The Greeks knew of two different phenomena of temporality that have come down to us as *chronos* and *kairos*. Our difficulty in grasping what is essential in the experience of the future in the Eucharist lies precisely in lacking a distinction between these two terms. An understanding of liturgical temporality (and by implication of eschatology) that lacks the category of *kairos* is bound to run into all kinds of impossibilities and, therefore, to revert to a vulgar understanding of both liturgy and temporality (I mention here only the names of Albert Schweitzer and Oscar Cullman[26]). *Chronos* is time seen either as sequence or duration — invariably constituting a chronology: every minute passing by accumulates in those layers of dead time that compile the chronicle of our lives. This time is nothing more than an indefinite series of "nows": the present is the "now" that "is," the future is the

---

[25]   This is only one of the many instances in the Eucharistic prayer that an experience, and not any more an expectation, of the kingdom is indicated: earlier we hear the celebrant saying "Thou didst bring us from nonexistence into being, and when we had fallen away, didst raise us up again, and didst not cease to do all things until thou hadst brought us up to heaven, and hadst bestowed upon us thy kingdom to come" (*PG* 63, 915). Notice the past tense of the verbs.

[26]   For an assessment of their eschatologies see J. Moltmann, *The Coming of God: Christian Eschatology*, trans. Margaret Kohl (Minneapolis: Fortress Press, 1996), pp. 7–13.

"now" that one day will be but is not yet, and the past is the "now" that once was but is no more. But between that which "is not yet" and that which "is no more" there is nothing.[27] Every present "now" thus comes from nothing and rolls back to nothing. Hence the homonymy between *chronos* and *Kronos*: the Greeks saw in this chronological experience of time the mythical figure of Kronos or Saturn, the god who devours his children. Nothing could be farther removed from the eschatological spirit than this view.

Against this concept of time as *chronos* (the passing of time) stands a different understanding of temporality as *kairos*. If chronological time is seen in a horizontal way, that is, as sequence and duration, *kairos* could be represented as vertical and dis-continuous. If *chronos* is measured in minutes, seconds, hours and years, *kairos* cannot be measured at all, since it occurs only in the moment. What we call here "the moment" is nothing else but what has been known as the *Augenblick*[28] or the *Platonic Exaiphnes*. For even if it were possible to put all the kairological moments together that still would not give us any measurable sense of *kairos*, since each moment of *kairos* (contrary to different units of time) is, in a unique way, always the Same, in the sense that it recurs in repetition. This is evident in how the Church presents liturgically events of the past (such as the birth of Christ, his Crucifixion, etc.) as always taking place "today" — a survey of the hymns of the Church will show that the Church knows of no other temporal category than this "today."[29] Kierkegaard was right to see in repetition a new temporal category — that is to be juxtaposed over against Platonic recollection. Recollection, he writes, allows us to "enter the eternal backwards," while repetition is decisively futural, or better yet, adventitious, and in its advent-like character pushes us to

---

[27] See Sartre's remark: "ce qui sépare l'antérieur du postérieur c'est précisément *rien*" (*L'Être et le Néant*, p. 64). Before Sartre, Augustine had said, "But the two times, past and future, how can they *be*, since the past is no more and the future is not yet? On the other hand, if the present were always present and never flowed away into the past, it would not be time at all, but eternity. But if the present is only time, because it flows away into the past, how can we say that it *is*? For it is, only because it will cease to be. Thus we can affirm that time is only in that it tends towards not-being" (*Confessions*, XI, xiv, p. 219). See also, M. Heidegger, *Being and Time*, trans. Joan Stambaugh (New York: State University of New York, 1996), p. 391.

[28] Here are some key references to the concept of the "moment" (*Augenblick*) from *Being and Time*: "The Moment brings existence to the situation and discloses the authentic 'There'" (p. 319). "The present, as the Moment, discloses the today authentically" (p. 362), "... the Moment that lies in resoluteness ..." (p. 353). *Der Augenblick* is Luther's translation of Paul's "twinkling of an eye" (I Cor. 15:51) that undoubtedly belongs to an eschatological context.

[29] "The Virgin *today* gives birth to the one who is beyond being" (from the *kontakion* of the feast of the Nativity); "*today* the nature of the waters is being sanctified" (second *idiomelon* of the feast of the Epiphany; "*today* is lifted on the tree He who suspended the earth among waters" (*antiphonon* of Good Friday's Passion service). The examples, of course, abound.

"enter eternity forwards."[30] It is by means of such temporality that the faithful in celebrating the Eucharist enter God's kingdom. Every time that Christians gather together around the altar, the kingdom of God comes a little bit closer, the *basileia* becomes a little more possible.

In the New Testament the "when" of the *kairos* corresponds to the "how" of the *exaiphnes*:

> ... you do not know *when* the appointed time [*kairos*] will come. It is like a man traveling abroad. He leaves home and places his servants in charge, each with his own task; and he orders the man at the gate to watch with a sharp eye. Look around you! You do not know *when* the master of the house is coming, whether at dusk, at midnight, when the cock crows, or at early dawn. Do not let him come suddenly [*exaiphnes*] and catch you asleep. (Mark 13:33–6)

Allow me to dwell a bit more on the semantics of the term *exaiphnes*, as it is solely on this term that the connection among eschatology, incarnation and liturgy depends. The passage from the *kairos* to the *exaiphnes* marks a passage from temporality to phenomenality: *exaiphnes* is commonly translated as "suddenly" and thus, as a term that denotes a temporal category. Its etymology, however, implies the phenomenality of appearing out of the invisible or the unapparent (*ex* = out of, *aphanes* = the invisible). The term occurs for the first time in Plato's *Parmenides* (156d–e) as a third category that defies all binary oppositions according to which metaphysics operates. We also find it in Plotinus' *Enneads* (e.g., V 3 17 36, VI 7 36 19–20) and in the Neoplatonic successors of Plato in the Academy (e.g., Damascius the Diadochos, in his *Dubitationes et Solutiones De Primis Principiis*). Fascinating as the philosophical development of this term might be, we cannot follow it further here; what interests us instead is the usage of the *exaiphnes* by Christianity as a technical term that punctuates three different "moments": the enfleshment of the Word, the coming of the Kingdom and the celebration of the Eucharist in history (and thus we part ways with the exclusively existential understanding of Bultmann's kairological eschatology[31]). All three events share the same structure, so to speak, of the *exaiphnes* and all three are to some extent referenced in the New Testament (although these connections continue to occur in

---

[30]   *The Concept of Anxiety*, trans. Howard V. Hong and Edna H. Hong (Princeton: Princeton University Press, 1980), p. 90. However, there are times in Kierkegaard's analysis of repetition that his inability to distinguish between repetition as *continuity* and repetition as *recurrence* becomes clear. One could protest that we are splitting hairs by pursuing this kind of distinction; I believe, though, that it is essential not to confuse repetition with a crypto-metaphysical sense of eternity. Repetition is not realized by a *continuous* moment (in the way that eternity is "made up" by the *nunc stans*), but by a *recurring* moment.

[31]   R. Bultmann, *History and Eschatology* (Edinburgh, T&T Clark, 1957).

texts well beyond scripture[32]): the first is Mark 13:36, that we have already quoted, which links the *exaiphnes* with the eschaton; Luke 2:13 relates the *exaiphnes* with the moment of Jesus' birth[33] and in particular with the so-called "celestial liturgy" of the angels; the other two occurrences of the exaiphnes in the New Testament are found in the book of the *Acts* (9:3 and 22:6), both times describing the light that blinded Paul on his way to Damascus:[34]

> As he traveled along and was approaching Damascus, a light from the sky suddenly (*exaiphnes*) flashed about him ... Saul got up from the ground and although his eyes were open he saw *nothing* ... (Acts, 9:3, 8)

That light was the light of Christ, or better yet, Christ Himself — but notice how this moment of epiphany "out of nothing" (i.e., *exaiphnes*) turns the things-themselves (the visible) into nothing — the very nothing that Paul sees. In the moment of the *exaiphnes* the things-themselves have to retreat, and indeed "disappear," in order to allow the unapparent and the unseen (that is, the things-to-come), to show themselves.

The light of the eschaton — of the consummation that has already begun — keeps reaching us at the present; the daybreak of that eighth day, still to dawn, sheds its light on the now, on the momentary and the fleeting, on the ephemeral

---

[32]   Golitzin mentions — besides Dionysius — the *Acts of Judas Thomas*, Athanasius' *Life of Anthony*, and Ephrem the Syrus' *Hymns on Nature* and *Hymns on Paradise*. An examination of these texts allows Golitzin to conclude with the following words "thus, again, we find the term linked with the mystical vision, Christ, light, and the liturgies of both heaven and earth"; see, "'Suddenly, Christ': The Place of Negative Theology in the Mystagogy of Dionysius Aeropagites," in *Mystics: Presence and Aporia*, eds Michael Kessler and Christian Sheppard (Chicago: Chicago University Press, 2003), p. 24. Beyond the milieu of early Christian literature, one finds frequent references to the *exaiphnes* as an indicator of the divine in the work of Philo of Alexandria (especially in *De Somniis, Quod Deus sit immutabulis, De sacrificiis Abelis et Caini* and *De mutatione nominum*). For a recent treatment of the relevant passages, see Jean-Lous Chrétien, *The Unforgettable and the Unhoped for*, trans. Jeffrey Bloechl (New York: Fordham University Press, 2002), pp. 99–118.

[33]   The entire *Third Letter* of Dionysius the Aeropagite attests to the relation of the exaiphnes with the Incarnation. Here is Dionysius' *Third Letter* in its entirety: "'Suddenly' [*exaiphnes*] means that which has come forth unexpectedly and from the hitherto invisible into manifestation. And I think that here theology is suggesting the philanthropy [i.e., the Divine Economy] of Christ. The superessential has proceeded out of hiddenness to become manifest to us by becoming a human being. Yet He is also hidden, both after the manifestation, and, to speak more divinely, even within it. For this is the hidden of Jesus, and neither by rational discourse, nor by intuition can His mystery be explained. But instead even when spoken, it remains ineffable, and when conceived, unknowable."

[34]   For an analysis of the *exaiphnes* in these texts, see Alexander Golitzin, "Suddenly, Christ" (cited above).

and the arbitrary, and makes each and every thing visible — *while itself remaining invisible*.

I speak of light: it is of course an old metaphor but a telling one. As light that illuminates everything renders things visible while it itself remains hidden — or rather it is us who, by seeing only what thus comes to light, remain "blind" to light itself, so our preoccupation with the things-themselves "blinds" us to the things-to-come, although it is in this expectancy that the things-themselves assume their proper shape and character.

How, then, does the Eucharist defy this blindness? By effecting a *reversal*. In order to make visible the invisible, that is, in order to make present the futural, the Eucharist has to let the visible and the present sink into the background in order to allow what lies there, unnoticed, to become manifest. In other words, if the world in its worldliness were a photograph, the Eucharist would be its negative. It is this insight that Wolfhart Pannenberg elaborates in the following passage:

> ... the eschatological truth is already a *present reality* even if in hidden form. Thus judgment as well as life is already present with Jesus Christ in the world (John 12:31, 47–8). Similarly the disarming of the forces of this world is already taking place. The hidden present of the eschaton is the present of salvation only for faith, but the truth of things that will be revealed in the future, their true essence that will come to light at the eschaton, generally defines already their present existence even though in one way or another this may still have a radical change ahead of it. *Only within a general ontology of the present reality of beings as this is constituted by the eschatological future of its nature do the statements of theology about the eschatological present of salvation achieve full plausibility.*[35]

The future is present in the present, hidden like the mustard seed in the soil (Matt. 13:31) and thus, already underway to its surprising transformation. The things-themselves, therefore, can be opened up so as to expose "hidden in them" the things-to-come only by a means of radical *reversal* — what I have called elsewhere, following Levinas and Marion, "an inverted intentionality" analogous to the inverted perspective that characterizes the Byzantine icons.[36] The invention of perspective by Late Medieval thinkers and Renaissance artists gave rise to modernity, subjectivity and the Enlightenment.[37] This is the point made by Karsten

---

[35]   Wolfhart Pannenberg, *Systematic Theology*, vol. III, p. 605, emphasis added.

[36]   See, "The Phenomenon of God: From Husserl to Marion" in the *American Catholic Philosophical Quarterly*, 78:1 (2004), pp. 53–68.

[37]   Karsten Harries, *Infinity and Perspective* (Cambridge: MIT Press, 2001). On the other hand, however, it has been argued that perspective, by introducing the false impression of a third dimension, destroys the painterly character of the painting which is essentially two-dimensional. Thus, it cancels out the liberating effect brought about by painting which, in loosing the spatiality of three-dimensionality (representative of sculpture), freed itself

Harries in his *Infinity and Perspective*. And I would like to say that it is this very notion of perspective that has distorted in a decisive way our understanding of eschatology. A genuine eschatology operates by surprise, in allowing a counter-movement of history, not only *toward* the kingdom but also *from* the kingdom.[38] This structure of counter-movement in the flux of History needs to be paired on the personal level with a counter-movement of perception and understanding. The *from*-the-kingdom movement that runs against the forward current of *pro*-gress, but also propels it by exercising an irresistible attraction towards itself, has as its aim the disarmament of our predictability, that is, our prejudice. The eschaton is like the new wine that cannot be contained in the old wineskins because we all know what happens then. The old wineskins are nothing else but the concepts and categories of this World, the thinking process that we are used to and familiar with — let's call it, our *perspective*. If I am Greek it is the Greek perspective from which I judge the world, and if I were a Jewish it would be the Jewish perspective that becomes the measure of my judgment — there are many such perspectives that have become canonical over others (the white over the black, the male over the female, and so on) so much so as to forget that by coming to occupy this privileged locus that our perspective affords us we take up the place reserved for the kingdom, *we become our own eschata* and thus, in denying the kingdom of God for the sake of the kingdom of Man, we become the anti-Christ.

Thankfully, everyday there are moments in which, in anticipation of God's kingdom, our perspectives are confronted and reversed. When this happens — and it does happen — we speak of a "transformation" (like the one that is undergone by Schönberg's *Verklärte Nacht*) or of a moment of "epiphany" (like the ones described by Joyce). When this happens, when my perspective is countered, inversed, returned to me, I am no longer the privileged subject that establishes and constitutes the objectivity of the world (the thinghood of the things), *but merely a dative*, I become this "to whom" the world, as the world-to-come, is given. For only then can be there a world given, when I make myself available as a receiver, as gifted with the gift of givenness. Without such a change of attitude, without an inverse perspective, without an eschatology, which enables us to receive, there would be no charisma or *charis*, that is, grace received.

The paradigm of inverted perspective, as exemplified by the Eucharist (where in receiving the gifts we also receive ourselves as gifted), the hymn (that instead of being comprehended by us becomes amplified in chanting as to comprehend us) and iconography (where we become the "objects" of the icon's gaze), in all

---

from the constraints of universality. For painting as a the "Christian" paradigm of art, effected by the Incarnation, see, G.W. Hegel, *Aesthetics: Lectures on Fine Art*, vol. II, T.M. Knox (trans.), (Oxford: Oxford University Press, 1975).

[38] This is the groundbreaking insight of the eschatology of the Metropolitan of Pergamon John Zizioulas, see "Towards an Eschatological Ontology" (quoted above) and his "Church and the Eschaton" (in Greek) in *Church and Eschatology*, ed. Pantelis Kalaitzidis (Athens: Kastaniotis Publishers, 2001).

these cases, the structure of the eschaton is outlined as the future that flows into the present, as the moment that cuts an in-cision in the flux of time and therefore, calls for a de-cision. It calls us to decide either to refuse it or to receive it, either to accept things as they are and let them be what they are (the things-themselves) or to desire things otherwise, as the things-to-come.

Eschatology and Phenomenology

The association between eschatology and phenomenology might seem strange to the reader: what does the theology of the things-to-come have in common with the philosophy of the things-themselves? I would like to propose that phenomenology, especially as it has been recently formulated by a new generation of phenomenologists like Jean-Luc Marion, Jean-Yves Lacoste and Richard Kearney,[39] can be a very helpful instrument at the hands of eucharistic eschatology in its effort to rescue eschatology from the twin risks of either immanetizing it or relegating it to an end-of-times utopia. Furthermore, we will suggest that intentionality in general and imagination in particular disclose the eschatological orientation of consciousness.

The relation between the things-themselves and the things-to-come can be taken to be analogous to that of the particular to the universal or of the actual to the possible. The reference of the particular to the universal is manifold and not all of the ways are helpful or even appropriate to serve as an analogy for the correspondence between the things-themselves to the things-to-come. Nevertheless, and in a certain way, the particular belongs to the things-themselves: it is in its realm that we encounter the concreteness of the everyday. On the other hand, the eschaton could be envisioned as the realm from which the manifoldness of the everyday world draws its unity and therefore its intelligibility. This analogy, however, is not applicable to eschatology insofar as it comes from the logical or cognitive schema. In other words, the eschaton cannot be made the "universal" of the things-themselves in the same way that a concept is the universal of a particular object (although this is a position upheld by Dionysius' and Maximus' doctrine of

---

[39]   All of the three authors engage, each to different degrees, a eucharistic eschatology in their phenomenological analysis (although sometimes it is difficult to tell whether it is not actually an eschatology engaging phenomenology that is the case). None of them, however, draws the concrete conclusions that we formulate here. Marion treats the eschatological character of the Eucharist in his *God Without Being* (in particular pp. 169–176) but no ecclesiological or ethical implication is drawn as a result of it. Kearney is aware of the ethical significance of such an eschatology but his understanding of the Eucharist is rather weak and therefore his analysis lacks a firm theological grounding. Lacoste (in his *Experience and the Absolute*) is closer to us here but his preoccupations against Heidegger and Hegel give an altogether different color to his discussion. Needless, of course, to say that their work remains crucial to this study.

the *logoi* of beings). The eschaton can only be an *indeterminable* "universal," to which the thing-themselves refer (otherwise it would not be possible to recognize them as such) but their reference remains open-ended. Indeed, there is such a category where the particular refers to a universal that one cannot determine but needs to somehow provide. Let me offer an example: Galileo's law of acceleration of falling bodies is a particular law of physics which, at the time of its proposition, was lacking its universal — that came about a hundred years later with Newton's law of universal gravitation. This relation, of a particular to an indeterminable universal, is employed by Kant in the analysis of aesthetic judgments. The object of an aesthetic judgment (e.g., this rose) is a particular that refers to a universal that cannot be determined[40] (it is not, for example, the concept of the "rose," or that of a flower and so on, as in the case of understanding). On the other hand, the particular rose in its aesthetic manifestation (i.e., as a *beautiful* rose) needs to be recognized, that is, to be subsumed under a universal. Could the beautiful itself be that concept? Kant's answer might come as a surprise: the beautiful is not a concept and therefore cannot serve as the universal of the particular beautiful rose.[41] Similarly, the things-themselves are particulars that refer to an indeterminable universal, i.e., the things-to-come. The latter cannot be determined or known but they can only be awaited and anticipated. It is not that the things-to-come lack reality, intelligibility, or content. Their indeterminability, their unknowableness as we would say in theological language, is not due to their emptiness nor to their transcendence but to mode of their manifestation, which remains unpredictable.

The digression to Kantian aesthetics is indeed necessary for it will provide us with the main concepts that Husserl employs in defining the phenomenological understanding of imagination and in exploring imagination's teleological character. The universal *a priori* idea of aesthetic judgments is for Kant purposiveness, that is, as we would see, an eschatological orientation of imagination (of course for Kant eschatology is only teleology, that is, an eschatology without recourse beyond the creaturely character of nature within which it exhausts itself).

---

[40] "Judgment in general is the ability to think the particular as contained under the universal. If the universal (the rule, principle, law) is given, then judgment, which subsumes the particular under it, is *determinative* ... But if only the particular is given and judgment has to find the universal for it, then this power is merely *reflective*"; Immanuel Kant, *Critique of Judgment*, trans. Werner S. Pluhar (Indianapolis and Cambridge: Hackett, 1987), pp. 18–19, emphasis in the original. All aesthetic and teleological judgments are reflective.

[41] "*Beautiful* is what, without a concept, is liked universally"; Kant, *Critique of Judgment*, p. 64, emphasis in the original. Furthermore, "... beauty is not a characteristic of the object [as, say, the redness of the rose] when taken in its own right" (p. 221). That means that a thing is never beautiful *in itself*, as if beauty was a quality, but its beauty lies with the feeling aroused in the subject. So, "... apart from a reference to the subject's feeling, beauty is nothing by itself" (p. 63). Of course, this does not imply a subjectivism along the lines of "beauty is on the eye of the beholder." The whole purpose of the third Critique is to establish the universality of aesthetic judgments.

Kant's definition of the beautiful as that which, without a concept is pleasing to all (*das, was ohne Begriff allgemein gefällt*) presents us with a paradox insofar as the beautiful is a pleasure — and thus something that exists only in the subject — but a pleasure that is not "subjective" — varying, as it were, from subject to subject — but rather universal. Therefore, the beautiful is a universal pleasure or what one finds pleasurable universally. The first implication of such an understanding of the beautiful is that it is not a property or a quality of the object, like color or size. Beauty as pleasure makes no sense without a reference to a subject — for if it is pleasing it must be so to *someone*. The second implication is the tension between the characterization of the beautiful as a feeling (*Gefült*) and its claim to universality. One could indeed understand such a claim if the beautiful was mediated by a concept, but a *feeling* — how could it be universal? Here we arrive at the crucial point of Kant's exclusion of the concept (*ohne Begriff*). What does this qualification, so explicitly stated, achieve or what does it avoid? Kant offers us two remarks. The first explains how the beautiful would be mediated by the concept only if it had a practicality. But the beautiful, we are told, cannot be practical insofar as it is devoid of all interest. The second remark says "if we judge objects merely in terms of concepts, then we lose all presentation of beauty (59)." This is a rather strong statement for it asserts that concepts, in fact, prevent beauty, for if beauty was conceptual then it would have to be compulsory ("No one," Kant writes, "can use reasons or principles to talk us into judgment on whether some garments, house of flower is beautiful (59)." Thus, the following characteristics of the beautiful emerge: the beautiful is essentially free, disinterested and unpractical.

However, it is a mistake to assign these characteristics to the thing judged as beautiful for they should rather be attributed to the judgment itself. When Kant explains the necessity that judgments of taste be devoid of interest he writes "the judging person feels completely *free* as regards the liking he accords the object (53–4)." It is not, therefore, the beautiful object that is free or disinterested but the subject who, by not being compelled by any interest (be it the monetary or emotional value of the object he or she admires), can declare it "beautiful." My apprehension, then, of the beautiful is personal (insofar as it is highly subjective) but in such a way that every personal trait is left behind.

It is here that one should locate the universality of that pleasure that is the beautiful. In my finding this or that thing beautiful I carry not personal interests — neither my origin nor my desires, neither my education nor my preferences, in short, nothing in my past, and above all the past itself plays a role. I like it not as a "me" but as man — any and at the same time every man. Hence, as Kant notes, my demand that you too find it also beautiful. It is as if the subject in the moment of aesthetic apprehension became all subjects (or the subject in general — *allgemein*) and yet remained himself. As if, when I say "this is beautiful," I was speaking on behalf of all humanity — liberated from the constraints of the natural. How can beauty afford us such a perspective where I am everywhere, insofar as I am everyone, and yet my own self here and now?

The answer lies in the crucial — although often taken as rather obscure — role played by teleology. What holds together the two, seemingly disparate, parts of the *Critique of Judgment* is beauty's purposiveness. "Beauty is an object's form of purposiveness insofar as it is perceived in the object without the presentation of a purpose (84)." What was earlier expressed under the condition "without a concept" is now formulated in the condition "without a purpose." In judging something as beautiful we do not make an assessment with regard to its purpose. That would have turned aesthetic judgments into judgments of practical reason (i.e., morality) or into judgments of pure reason (i.e., understanding). But the beautiful is neither the good nor the true.

On the other hand, we can grasp objects only teleologically — as if things were organized according to a "will that would have so arranged them in accordance with the presentation of a certain rule (65)." Thus, the beautiful is given through the idea of a purpose without purpose, that is, through the form of purposiveness. Again, we should emphasize that this form of purposiveness is not endemic to things but to the subject's mind. "The very consciousness of a merely formal purposiveness in that play of the subjects cognitive powers ... is that pleasure" [i.e., the beautiful] (68). The play in question is the "free play" between imagination and understanding to which Kant refers in a number of passages. The play is "free" because in aesthetic judgment imagination stands in a different relation to understanding than in cognition. In cognition imagination is constrained by understanding (reproductive imagination) whereas in aesthetic judgment imagination is free and unrestrained (productive imagination). It becomes clear that the entire structure of aesthetic judgment from top to bottom and from the beginning to the end is sustained thanks to imagination which can posit that which without a purpose, without a concept and without interest is liked universally.

Imagination foresees, previews the future and affords us a view that no here and now could furnish, not even at the final state of things. It is not, therefore, that through the dioptra of imagination we can get a glimpse of what lies ahead but rather that teleological imagination "opens" the present by adding along with the incomplete state of the present thing the image of its completion, that is, of its perfection. If, indeed, only the end (in the double sense of *telos* as finality and purposiveness) makes things perfect (*teleia*), then imagination keeps reminding us of such perfection amidst incompletion and imperfection. It is as if the human mind were indeed made in such a way as to understand only the perfect and the complete. For even if this is lacking in the present state of things (and it can only be lacking) then it feels compelled to supply it by itself.

How are we to understand this ability of imagination? It is precisely at this point that we need to turn to a phenomenological inquiry of the eschatological. It would seem that the first (that is, the most fundamental and the most readily available) intuition of eschatology is that of awaiting or expecting.[42] But what would such an intuition have been without the idea of purpose, that is, of fulfillment

---

42   See, for example, Lacoste's and Romano's essays in this volume.

of one's anticipation, even if we were to know not what or whom we are waiting for? More fundamental then than waiting is this waiting-for, that is, the structure of a purpose (purposiveness). Whence can we phenomenologically derive such a structure? First of all, from the very character of intending. Intentionality, even prior to intending this or that, always intends a purpose; in fact, it *is* purposive. In every fulfillment, in every filled intention, one can observe the structure of the eschatological. Kant spoke of pleasure precisely on these terms[43] and we believe that it is the joy of the kingdom to come that is foreshadowed in the feeling of satisfaction that every filled anticipation yields. The very passage from an empty intention to a filled one (that is, the passage from absence to presence) is such an eschatological indication for in all these common structures of anticipation the absolute anticipation, i.e., the anticipation of the absolute, is reflected.

But by speaking of anticipation we are already in the realm of imagination of which anticipation is one of its modes. The association of imagination with the eschatological deserves a more attentive study that exceeds the limitations of the present essay. We could, however, say that such a connection is indeed to be discovered in imagination's ability to posit things otherwise without allowing presence to fully collapse into the present. One should, however, distinguish between *imagination* (as our sole capacity to envision the eschata) and *fantasy* (as what hinders our vision of the eschaton by "binding" us down to the things-themselves). What fantasy does is present things as our only possibility precisely by presenting us with the phantasmagoria of their (infinite as it would seem) possible transformations.

Without imagination (in its broad, existential sense) there can be no freedom. Man is thus engulfed in the inertia of his nature unable to expect or wait for what comes beyond the natural. Eschatology in a very fundamental sense is counter-intuitive — by that we mean to say that that for which the Church waits cannot be given empirically as present-at-hand; if it were, her waiting would have been canceled out. That for which the Church waits cannot be presented to us unless by means of hope and expectation, that is, of imagination. At the same time, one needs to stop imagination before she completes her work, for the risk in that is canceling out surprise as the mode of eschatological manifestation. This can be done by realizing that one's imagination would never succeed in representing the ultimate (lest it becomes an idol) and, therefore, the proliferation of images in which imagination takes comfort is nothing but the very indication of its inability in capturing the singular.

---

[43] "The very consciousness of a merely formal purposiveness in the play of the subject's cognitive powers, accompanying a presentation by which an object is given *is* that pleasure" (*Critique of Judgment*, p. 68, emphasis added). "For the basis of this pleasure is found in the universal, though subjective, condition of reflective judgments, namely, the purposive harmony of an object (whether a product of nature or of art) with the mutual relation of the cognitive powers (imagination and understanding) that are required for every empirical cognition" (p. 31).

If, in other words, we leave ourselves only to perception and cognition we deprive ourselves of the possibility of the eschatological. If, on the other hand, we indulge in our imagination's infinite possibilities we have somehow already given ourselves the eschaton and, therefore, we need no more wait for its coming. Biblical language trod down the middle path between these two extremes by providing prophecy and parable. Imagination is indeed employed (e.g., "the kingdom of heaven is likened unto ...") but also left undone by its very resources, that is, the Biblical imaginary of the kingdom is so imaginative that becomes prohibitory to imagination's own attempt to appropriate it.

Chapter 5

John Zizioulas on Eschatology and Persons

Douglas H. Knight

The Orthodox theologian John Zizioulas is most often associated with the Christian doctrine of the person. The concept of the person holds together the two issues of communion and freedom. Zizioulas argues that if there is one person there must be many persons: the concept is intrinsically plural, relational and yet safeguards our particularity. By making a distinction between person and individual, Zizioulas contrasts the human who is related and integrated, and the human who is disengaged and isolated from all others. According to Christian doctrine, Christ is the person in whom we may all be persons. Christ comes to individuals without relation to anyone else, and brings them into communion so that they become persons, related to all others, indeed related to everything that is not themselves. This catholic being who is simultaneously one and many is coming into being in history, and at the eschaton will turn out to be the truth of all humanity. In Christ, time and history move towards this reconciliation in which all creatures discover their proper unity and difference; this coming together of all things makes itself known in history in the Church and in the event of the eucharist. For Christian theology, the concept of the person relates to time and purpose and so to eschatology. His confidence in the theology of the Greek Fathers enables Zizioulas to lay out the logic of the Christian doctrine of the person with the utmost clarity, and it is this that makes his account of personhood distinctive and rewarding.

Zizioulas' central concern is human freedom. His first insight is that communion and freedom are not opposed, for freedom is enabled, not restricted, by our relationships with other persons. God is intrinsically communion and freedom, and he extends this communion and freedom to us in the body of Christ, the communion of the Church. The persons gathered into this communion will come to participate in the freedom of God, and through them all creation will share this freedom. The freedom promised to humanity has been inaugurated in this body; all particularity is being perfected in it so that in this communion the diversity and very existence of creation will have no limits.

Communion means both oneness and otherness, difference as well as unity. The Father, Son and Holy Spirit are the criterion and guarantor of this otherness. These divine persons are truly other, and the source of all otherness. It is they who establish and confirm us as different from God, and different from one another. The divine persons are the guarantee that there is any distinct thing at all, and that the profusion of beings and creation as a whole are no aberration. As evidence of his intention to promote and sustain this profusion of particularities, God has planted his communion as a community in the world. This community is the Church, the sign and inaugurating event of this plurality in communion.

Persons or Individuals?

Zizioulas' account of human beings is at odds with a great part of the Western intellectual tradition, for which it is a basic prejudice that we cannot both be together and free. This tradition conceives man as an isolated unit, separable from all other beings, and believes that each of us must assert ourselves against all that is not ourselves. The individual struggles against his neighbors and against society as a whole, alternately reaching out to them and withdrawing from them, but he is ultimately unable to establish his own identity. Since no creature is finally able to recognize anything that is not themselves, the otherness and very existence of every creature and thus of the world, is in doubt.

Zizioulas regards the individual as essentially cut off and separate from all that is not himself, so the individual is a tragic, even demonic, concept. A person on the other hand is not an individual, but a plural being who includes and represents the entire world of relationships.[1] The identity of a particular person is not to be found somewhere deep inside him or her: he has no self, center, soul or other form of private existence before coming into relationship with others. The identity of each person is constituted and sustained everywhere and by everyone. Zizioulas is not saying that one person is the function of *many* other persons, for then the question would be *which* persons and *which* community? Rather, each person is the function of *all* persons; all the persons will be constitutive of the being of each and every person in the world.

The logic of this statement is theological and eschatological. Even working in complete harmony the whole world is not sufficient finally to sustain the being of a single creature in it. But this world has no other logic than as the creation of God, and its Creator is free to be present to his creatures in it, so that they exist in one economy with him. The trinitarian persons are constitutive of all other persons of creation and must therefore be included amongst the persons of the world. God calls into being that which is not himself, and he sustains it so that it may answer his call in freedom; our reception of his call and God's reception of us gives us our existence. The triune persons of God, who are fully able to give and return their being to another, are also fully able to give and return our being too, and so are the full and sufficient condition of human persons. Because God *empersons* others, the conditions of personhood for all are met.

---

[1]   John D. Zizioulas, *Being in Communion: Studies in Personhood and the Church* (London: Darton, Longman and Todd, 1985) pp. 27–65. He offers more on this contrast and its relation to the theology of Cappadocian Fathers in *Communion and Otherness: Further Studies in Personhood and the Church* (London and New York: T&T Clark 2006) pp. 171–7.

The Predicament of the Creature

Considered apart from God, the creature is an individual. The individual is tragic.[2] To sustain ourselves we break open animal bodies and consume them, and extend our lease on life through their death. We come into existence through sex, and we are drawn together to another person with them to reproduce ourselves; but we do not thereby reproduce or sustain ourselves, but reproduce only children who, however much they are like us, are not us, and who finally replace us altogether. We are driven by our desire to be with others, but the bounds of our own body deny us this communion.

The Augustinian theological tradition assumed that death came to creation to punish the disobedience of man. Against this tradition Zizioulas insists that, since all created things have beginnings and are demarked by boundaries, they also have ends, and so mortality is intrinsic to the world. Yet each creature is created to move through boundaries on its way to freedom and communion. "Nothing was created perfect from the beginning. Everything, including especially the human being, was meant to grow into perfection."[3] In isolation from the eschaton, each creature remains in immature form, and creation as a whole remains confined within mortality. Since it is not the source of its own life, creation remains liable to dissolve back into nothingness: all created things, left to themselves, tend to divide and drift into isolation and eventual dissolution. Without man to make it free, creation remains disordered so that nothing in it comes to fulfillment. Unlike the Augustinian tradition, Greek patristic theology relates the concept of sin to eschatology, for sin relates to freedom as the end towards which everything is orientated. Sin is not deviation from an original state but from what *will be*.

God intends no less than absolute freedom for man.[4] If man does not succeed in becoming free, creation loses all hope of a long-term future. It is not because he demanded freedom that man fell, but because he has not exercised the mediatory role for creation for which he is made. Despite the fall, it is vital that man aspires to freedom. Man is called to bring freedom into creation and thereby give it a future: this eschatology is central to the Christian doctrine of creation.

Man as Mediator of Creation

If the world is to live, death must be overcome. But only a relationship of love, freely willed on both sides, can overcome the limits of our life. Death is the ultimate limit. Created beings are safe from death as long as they are in communion with the

---

[2]   Zizioulas, *Being in Communion*, p. 51.

[3]   Zizioulas, 'Towards an Eschatological Ontology' (Unpublished paper delivered at King's College, London, 1998) p. 6.

[4]   Zizioulas, "Preserving God's Creation: Three Lectures on Theology and Ecology" (*King's Theological Review* 12, 1989, pp. 1–5, 41–5; 13, 1990, pp. 1–5). Third lecture, p. 3.

life that, being uncreated, is without limits. Man was offered the freedom of God to decide freely, and on behalf of all creation, for participation in the communion and life of God. Because all creation makes up his body, materiality participates in man's decision. "The material creation would in this way be liberated from its own limitations and by being placed in the hands of man, it would itself acquire a personal dimension; it would be humanised."[5]

The future of the world, and the survival of creation as the project of God, depends on man.[6] Zizioulas explains that because it had a beginning, creation is finite and likely to come to an end, and since this is the case, the meaning and the truth of every part of it is in question. Man's reluctance to take his freedom in relationship with God has delayed the arrival of this freedom for creation, so creation continues to be held back by its own mortality. If creation is not going to survive, its very truth is in doubt. Creation therefore awaits the arrival of the being who is determined, not by his beginning, but by his goal — mankind who shares the freedom of God.

Man is made for relationship with God, who always intended to be with man, and intended that man should know this and be glad of it. From the first, God meant to be incarnate for man: had he not fallen, man would have been transformed incrementally into Christ, that is, man-with-God. Now in one instance man — Christ — has acted decisively as this mediator. He has established relationships with all men, brought each into relationship with all others, and through them united all creation to God within his own person. Christ is the truth of man and creation, sustained through all limits by unlimited communion with God.

Although man initially refused to act as priest of creation, in Christ man takes up this task and acts within the freedom of the end rather than the constraint of his origin. He overcomes the mortality inherent in these beginnings and ends, and so liberates creation for life with God. So it is not how things began that is ultimately determinative, but how they reach their goal and are fulfilled. The end re-determines the beginning: "It is the eschaton that gives being to history."[7]

Only God, who is free and who seeks nothing for himself, can disinterestedly and so truly give us recognition and so establish who we are. God is not threatened by the existence of anything, since it is by his will that anything comes into existence. He is free to love and confirm all his creatures without limit, and in love he extends this freedom to us. So it is finally due to its reception and acknowledgment by the Father that anything has the identity and existence that it has. Christ presents us to the Father, regarding us, and all creation, as integral to himself. He raises us continually to God, and he will present us to God finally: because the Father receives us from him, our existence is affirmed. And we can decide in freedom that

---

[5]   Zizioulas, "Preserving God's Creation," Third lecture, p. 4.

[6]   Zizioulas, *Lectures in Christian Dogmatics* (London and New York: T&T Clark, 2008), Chapter 14, "The Doctrine of Creation."

[7]   Zizioulas, "Towards an Eschatological Ontology," p. 10.

we have indeed been properly identified, that our freedom and our existence are finally secured, and thus we can be glad.

The beginning is reckoned from him who is at the end and from whom all beginnings and ends take their orientation. By taking the world into his hands and creatively integrating it and referring it to God, Christ brings man into communion with God. "Man and the world are no longer imprisoned in their past, in sin, decay and death. The past is affirmed in so far as it contributes to the end, to the coming of the kingdom."[8] As man raises creation up to God, it is freed from its own limitations, and becomes personal.

Our formation in the Body of Christ requires an account of time, which is what eschatology is. The beginning, and the present state of affairs, does not have the last word. Creation is made up of many voices issuing, and taking up, many invitations. But only Christ, man with God, can hear and give adequate response to all these many created voices and bring them all into harmony.

Christ is their proper audience, their "end" because he can hear, interpret and so truly and finally make something of all the beginnings that these invitations represent. All take their orientation from Jesus Christ who alone can finally hear and affirm them.

> We have to think of history as a movement consisting of two kinds of directions: one is the direction toward the end for which the world was created; the other is away from this end. Since the end decides finally about the truth of history only those events leading to the end will be shown to possess true being, or being *tout court*. The historical events of revelation, therefore, are true and real only because they lead to the end from which they came into being, not in themselves.[9]

So, following Saint Maximus the Confessor, Zizioulas suggests that what is real is what has reality in the end. Jesus Christ is empowered in the resurrection to be the truly determinative man, the high point and purpose of creation and guarantee of its survival. The future is determined by Christ, man with God; by taking the world into his hands, and referring it back to God, this complete man liberates creation from the failed custody of man without God. He will receive and re-determine all beginnings, and he who is the audience and goal of creation will turn out to be its origin too. Saint Maximus sets out this eschatological ontology in his *Ambiguum* 7:

> The inclination to ascend and see one's proper beginning was implanted in man by nature. Whoever by his choices cultivates the good natural seed shows the end to be the same as the beginning. Indeed the beginning and the end are one. As a result, he is in genuine harmony with God, since the goal of everything is given in its beginning and the end of everything is given in its ultimate goal. As

---

[8]   Ibid., p. 19.

[9]   Ibid., p. 9.

to the beginning, in addition to receiving being itself, one receives the natural good by participation: as to the end, one zealously traverses one's course toward the beginning and source without deviation by means of one's good will and choice. And through this course one becomes God, being made God by God.[10]

According to Saint Maximus, all things orient themselves to the Word and so participate in the conversation that the Logos initiates and sustains. Creatures exist as they find their place in the ordered work and creation of God and move towards him, gaining self-control as they do so. Whatever is denatured does not find this orientation; it falls silent and does not survive.

Son and Spirit

Enabled by the Holy Spirit, it is the proper action of man to say that he is not God. He has no knowledge of God until God gives him that knowledge. God is known within his own communion, so the Father is known by the Son who is known by the Holy Spirit. The Holy Spirit glorifies Christ and is always with him; he cannot be recognized as "Christ" outside the body which the Holy Spirit sanctifies for this purpose. An implication is that we cannot know any human being apart from all other human beings in the communion that enables such free mutual acknowledgment in love.

The Spirit makes Christ who he is. Christ is eternally accompanied, supported and even constituted by the Spirit, so he "exists only pneumatologically."[11] Because he shares in the communion of God, the Son is intrinsically plural, and in the form of the Church he allows the world to participate in this plurality:

> The Person of Christ is automatically linked with the Holy Spirit, which means with a community. This community is the eschatological company of the Saints who surround Christ in this kingdom. This Church is part of the definition of Christ. The body of Christ is not first the body of the individual Christ and then a community of "many", but simultaneously both together.[12]

Jesus Christ shares the communion of God with the people who are his body. We cannot know Jesus Christ (the one) without simultaneously acknowledging his community (the many). The Spirit brings us into this communion so that we may know Christ and through Christ may enter communion with all other creatures.

---

[10] Saint Maximus the Confessor, Ambiguum 7, in *On the Cosmic Mystery of Jesus Christ* (Paul M. Blowers and Robert L. Wilken, eds, Crestwood, New York: St Vladimir's Press, 2003), pp. 58–9.

[11] Zizioulas, *Being as Communion*, p. 111.

[12] Zizioulas, "The ecclesiological presuppositions of the holy Eucharist," p. 342.

Failure to acknowledge the indivisible unity of Son and Spirit has an unfortunate consequence for the unity of the world. When the Son and Spirit are seen in isolation from one another, the temporal world divides into ostensibly opposite movements of "past" and "future." The past is what Christology, without pneumatology, describes: the incarnation of Christ took place back there in the past; Christ is confined to an increasingly distant moment, and time appears to carry him ever further beyond our reach. Then the same appears to be so for all the rest of us: time bears us away from all earlier generations. Without pneumatology, christology represents the givens of history, but each particular given is borne away and subject to endless division and dissolution.

The other movement relates to the Spirit who, when considered apart from Christ, is equated with freedom and spontaneity. For a pneumatology without Christology, the universal and the particular are opposites: the result is the passing of time represents a flight, away from all particularities, into disembodied universality. When past and future are regarded as antagonists, time, conceived as necessity, pushes up between them. Without Christology, pneumatology becomes a totalizing principle that erases every particular person: without the specific persons of Christ and the Holy Spirit, either freedom destroys communion or communion destroys freedom.

Zizioulas insists that only a properly pneumatological Christology holds time together, redeeming all time past, and giving all our separate times a common future, and so revealing all time to be the good work of God for man. When we concede that the unity and distinction of these persons are fundamental we gain the specific communion of the body of Christ. The Spirit makes Christ the fundamental and finally indivisible *particular*, the person, than whom there is no more fundamental particle. In Christ we may also become particulars, whom nothing in creation will ever be able to break up. In the person of Christ, the Spirit holds us together and so is responsible for our unity; within Christ each of us may be a unique and irreplaceable particular, so that we are irreducibly many persons.

It is the communion of God, known to us as the Church, that holds together all time as the good time of God for man: man and communion will not finally be divided, dissolved and carried away by time; rather, time will be held together, rescued from death, redeemed and brought into a single unity, the eternity of man with God. Time will not dissolve the communion of God for man, rather God will sustain man in time without limit and forever. The communion of God, opened to us in the form of the Church, is more fundamental than time. Time does not divide the Church: the Church unites time.

Catholicity

God has put his communion in the world, and so revealed all other communities to be merely partial, not yet the whole truth. All other communities and cultures ultimately fail to sustain the real otherness of their members; because they represent less than the whole truth, they will not last.

> The Church, as sign and image of the eschatological community, continues to portray in history the genuine ethos of otherness ... the Church is the place where ... the fear of the Other is replaced in the Eucharist ... by the acceptance of the Other *qua* Other.[13]

The Church points towards the whole because it is that whole in miniature, arriving from the future. It gathers together the fragments of which the world is so far comprised. If the Church did not make its offering from every part of the world, the diversity and even the existence of the world would remain in doubt. The Church points towards the reconciliation of all things: its very existence demonstrates that a barrier has been broken, and that the world is no longer propelled by the forces of division and dissolution. Now the parts are no longer mutually antagonistic, but assembling around Christ and renewed from him, each is an instantiation of the whole. The Christian people is a vast assembly that includes those who for us are in the past and the future. This assembly makes itself present in each locality in which the Church is found, in each eucharist.

We are being brought into relationship with those who are presently living and with those who are, to us, dead. Though they are dead to us and to each other, they are not so to Christ; he does not allow death's individualizing to prevail over them. They are alive because he does not end the relationship he has with them; as long as he does not let go, they are sustained and cannot die. Though we are presently hidden from one another in different pockets of time, in his communion Christ sustains all in life and sends each into encounter with all others.

The resurrection means that you will be raised to me and I will be raised to you: the relationship we once had will be restored, and the relationship that we never had will now begin. Though we may run away from people, in the event of the resurrection each of us is turned around so that we run into all those whom we have been fleeing. Our sudden encounter and consequent transformation into catholic beings — persons — is what the resurrection is. You will give me my life and I will give you your life as we both receive life from Christ: he will receive us back from one another again, authenticating our reception of one another. Then each human being will be garlanded or anointed with all other persons, "Christ-ed" as it were, with Christ's whole people.

The eschaton, in which all are raised to all, slowly spells itself out to us in time. It gives us only as much of itself as we are ready to take. Like Jacob sending his flocks ahead to Esau, Christ sends us many people ahead of him. We have to receive him by receiving all of these; we may not refuse any, nor define ourselves by any smaller or more exclusive group. Through discipleship, each of us is purified of our fear and consequent aggression, and turned outwards toward others; so we are

---

[13]   Zizioulas, *Communion and Otherness*, p. 88.

transformed from one degree of Christ-likeness to another, from partial to whole and perfect, to become catholic persons in unconfined relationship.

Freedom and Time

If God were a universally manifest and inescapable fact, freedom would be impossible. So God withholds his glory, so that it is a mystery, revealed and known only in freedom, by faith. If our own identities were simply given to us complete at birth, freedom would be equally impossible. So it is not enough that Christ gives us our identity: we must also take it up in freedom. Our identity becomes truly ours as we receive all his creatures as our own. We must love them as he does: this love will be free, because it will be our own response to, and participation in, the love that we have received.

Our life and work, enabled by the Holy Spirit, consists in recognizing and acknowledging the otherness of other persons and so of attributing absolute particularity to each of them.[14] Christ calls us into reconciliation, in his body, so that none of us remains at war with any other. Christ does not regard himself as complete without us. He listens for us and regardless of how long it takes, he waits for each particular person to hear and answer in freedom. However deep we are buried, he hears us, and can uncover and restore us. He is able to wrest us out of one another's grasp, tell us apart from all others and confirm who we are. As Christ waits, his whole sanctified communion waits, and we must also wait for each other.

God intends that we be free. If the future were fixed or necessary, it would not be future, but simply more of the present. No future can be foisted on us. We can only be said to be beings with a future if we become, and remain, free: we must be willing contributors to it, for our identity will not be decided without our collaboration. His invitation to the freedom of a life shared with him and with all his people is what the future is.

Our lives are therefore part of a history, enabled by the Holy Spirit which, because we must all participate in it, unfolds through time. Time exists because we are waiting for other people to join us. In this faith we look for the resurrection that will make the body of Christ complete. In the prayers of the eucharist we ask God to give us all whom we are waiting for, and we mourn for those who are not yet present, for their absence means that we are not yet present as we want to be. The identity of other people is not to be established without our participation and consent, but we ourselves may affirm it gladly. Through the patience of the Holy Spirit we may learn how to return acknowledgment to one another, and this education in love unfolds through time. Each call from God is a new invitation and summons that frees us to act, and to do so by receiving one another in love. The whole Christ, and our own very being, is waiting for them.

---

[14]   Ibid., pp. 13–98.

The proper drawing together of all things produces the fellowship which we call the body of Christ. In it all persons, and within them all creation, come into mutual encounter, and finally into mutual recognition and love. The eucharist is the whole, making itself felt among the parts, interrupting their claim to be self-sufficient or complete and inviting them to their much larger future. It brings a taster of the fellowship of the Holy Spirit and so is the drawing together of all things towards integration and order. Left to itself, all creation is splitting and disintegrating. The gulf between each thing and every other is widening, we become confined within ever more constrictive units, and drift towards eventual dissolution. The resurrection is the reversal of this drift apart and the eucharist is the diffident and interrogative presence of the resurrection into our time.

From the concept of person that emerges within the theology of the Greek Fathers, Zizioulas argues that freedom and communion are equally fundamental. Christ is the whole of humankind, and the Church is this whole, offering itself to us in time. Christ sends us installments of this whole so that, in the eucharist, its outline is always set before us, to be received or refused. When each of us is able to receive all others and affirm their identity in love, this whole will have arrived: each human being will become anointed with the whole plurality of man in Christ. This theological eschatology, which is based in this pneumatological Christology, gives us this account of the absolute particularity of each human person, and so a very high account of humanity.

God is the first audience of man. He calls each of us into being and presents each of us to every other so that we can affirm one another in freedom: when each of us is ready to acknowledge that we are known and loved, and is glad of it, man's life will be underway at last. Though presently concealed to us, in the communion and body of Christ, the future of creation is coming into being and all identity and difference is being established.

PART III
Eschatological Phenomenology

Chapter 6

The Eschatology of the Self and the Birth of the Being-with; Or, on Tragedy

Ilias Papagiannopoulos

Experience and/or Identity

The present investigation sets out from the question about the relation between, on the one hand, the field of experience and therefore the field of human existence as well, and the self or human identity, on the other. For the most part, within the framework of contemporary philosophy, this appears to be a highly problematic, if not impossible, relation. More precisely: it seems to be the negative relation of a mutual exclusion: either identity or experience. After Heidegger, phenomenology has often come to define the unfolding of experience as a departure from every sort of "identity," as an irreversible deliverance to its negation, to non-identity as the free work (or the responsibility) of a negative transcendence, which would amount to the paradoxical truth of singular existence. Does this philosophical decline of the notion of identity occur necessarily due to the inner logic and the orientation of the phenomenological method itself, marking its definite character? Does it exhaust the full range of its innovative perspectives? Or could it also be that the detachment of the notion of experience from all positive reference to a notion of identity remains indirectly subordinate to fundamental presuppositions of Western metaphysics, though, or precisely because, it reverses them?

Crucially, such a gesture of reversing metaphysics points back to the roots of metaphysics and discloses the reality of which metaphysics developed as negation. In other words, this deconstructing negation of negation is a return to — and an affirmation of — the *initial event* against which metaphysics reacted. Or, even more accurately: it is the *primary* activation of that event, since it could not have been activated without the mediation of its imaginary other — only this mediation reveals the undetermined character of the initial event as such, its freedom beyond any given necessity. This event defines the common place of metaphysics (when appearing in its negated form) and simultaneously of its phenomenological critique (when appearing in its affirmed form). Metaphysics is thus revealed in its hidden and renounced truth; but this truth, in turn, is itself defined in relation to the metaphysical renunciation. The question, therefore, would be: can we perceive the renounced truth not in relation to metaphysics, i.e., not (at least, not *ultimately*) in relation to the imaginary structure that we tried to impose upon it? Can we perceive this *phenomenologically*? Which amounts to the question: is there or is there not a site of experience, and therefore of existence, *beyond* the one characterized by the dialectic between the imaginary Ego and its endless estrangement?

It is clear that the possibility of a positive notion of identity depends on an affirmative answer to this question. Only if the deconstruction of an imaginary will does not end in an estrangement can 'identity' escape its coincidence with constructed closure. In other words, only then can we think of the possibility of linking openness to identity and not to its opposite. It is also obvious that such a perspective implies a major ontological differentiation as well, or, more precisely, a differentiation between definitions of ontology — a differentiation that concerns the understanding of Being. And here we touch upon an important issue at stake: is phenomenology bound to a certain ontology, to a certain understanding of what ontology is, independently of whether it affirms or rejects this understanding, or could it also introduce a different ontology, i.e., *a process of alteration of our ontological coordinates*? Could a certain unfolding of the phenomenological method perhaps lead to a different understanding of the identity of singular existence, insofar as it gradually leads beyond the ontological coordinates of Western metaphysics and beyond their preservation in their reversed and renounced form? Could phenomenology liberate itself even further from metaphysics by claiming to move *forward* (and, of course, not to detour) the process of reversal beyond the reversed — by claiming, in other words, that there is a site of experience not only beyond the closure of an immortal essence, but also beyond the various forms of openness-towards-death as its reversed form? In such a case, existence would be more than a broken closure, more than trauma and mourning. And Being would be more than the coming to itself of a restless negativity. What we have here in mind is phenomenology *as this very alteration* of anthropological and ontological levels, a transformation which would amount to the truth of the subject and, at the same time, to the truth of Being itself.

Being and the Eschatology of Nothingness

Heidegger was the one who clearly demonstrated to us that the reasons for the dissociation of experience and identity lie in the field of ontology. Ever since ancient Greek thought set the principles of Western ontology, the notion of identity has always been bound to a notion of Being, and specifically to an essentialist understanding of Being. According to this understanding, Being is identified as an order of autarky, as an ontological perfection-in-itself, i.e., as an absolute closure. In these terms, openness cannot acquire primary ontological significance. It suggests rather the opposite of Being, since the relationality that openness as such indicates is a rupture of every imaginary autarky. In an essentialist context, openness exists ontologically only as an internal region of closure, as an elucidation of its inner structure — which amounts to an ontological neutralization of openness. Thus, openness and nothingness seem to form a tautology.

But if openness belongs to the site of nothingness, then the same has also to be true of experience — at least if experience is understood as an ec-static movement, as a step outside of every substantial order. Doesn't authentic experience consist in the departure from presupposed reality and, consequently, from an *a priori* subjectivity too, from the very idea of a positive agent of experience — is it not the very process of coming to existence by receiving alterity *ex nihilo*, by being surprised at the unknown and the unfamiliar, the uncanny? Being such an initial opening towards radical otherness, experience cannot but indicate a hovering of Being, a self-deliverance to the site of nothingness, to an endless negativity. This is a reversed transcendence leading downwards to the ungrounded. It is an estrangement, a *dépaysement*, that occurs at the very center of experience, facing the *unheimlich* (speaking with Freud) and the *ungeheuer* (speaking with Heidegger) nature of a natal and, within the very heart of that nativity, also deadly exteriority. The initial step beyond closure leads to a coincidence between presence and absence of the existent. But it also leads to an analogous ontological ambivalence of otherness as well: the other is present only as a phantasmatic trace. Here, being-with takes the paradoxical form of an encounter within nothingness. And, consequently, death seems to be the site not only of personal existence, but of community as well.

At this point, we may be standing before two different perspectives. According to the first one, this event of rupture, this breakage of substantial totality, already marks the end of any existential and any phenomenological process. In that case, we remain attached to Being conceived of as a totality, though that totality is an impossible one. It is precisely this impossibility that designates the ultimately negative character of the event of experience as openness towards an infinitely distant exteriority. An exteriority whose presence *is* this very distance, a disturbance and an irruption of the unknown into the order of the known. I am here particularly thinking of two important figures that influenced contemporary phenomenology, Lévinas and Derrida, who, in a characteristic gesture, defined Being as totality, giving the primacy thus to non-totality, to lack, in terms of an encounter of a present-absent otherness. Here they paradoxically met with certain aspects of German idealism (and, still further, of a certain tradition of western mysticism) and its philosophical idea of God, according to which not only human transcendence but also God Himself is linked to lack rather than to plenitude. Whether this can itself be thought of ontologically or not (which means then: ethically), is perhaps less important than the fact that the primacy of openness is linked to a primacy of a painful lack. But precisely this seems to remain indebted to a "protological" structure of thought, since what defines Being and non-being, plenitude and lack, actually remains, throughout the phenomenological process, *the same*. In other words, the primacy of the absence of any imaginary closure, or, equally, in different phenomenological variations, its constant escape in the ambiguity of the future, do not alter the presuppositions of essentialism, since the ontological pole of punctuality[1] remains intact.

---

[1]   The terms "punctuality" and "punctual" are used here in the sense of a selfhood disengaged from intentional experience (cf. Charles Taylor, *Sources of the Self: The Making*

A different perspective could, perhaps, consist in conceiving this event of estrangement not as ultimate, not as the definite coincidence of birth and death, of presence and absence, but, on the contrary, as a *beginning*. Which means to think of the alteration of ontological coordinates as the very nature of the event itself; to think, therefore, of the alteration of the notions of Being and of identity as the very meaning of experience and, consequently, of the unfolding of the phenomenological analysis as well. The lack of Being is here solely in reference to the first ontological pole and to the initial reality: to nothingness as the primary ontological site of human existence. Because, at the same time, this very nothingness cannot and does not appear alone, in itself and absolutely, as a static given. On the contrary, its nature is dynamic: nothingness emerges as an arrow pointing somewhere else — it *is* this very pointing beyond itself, introducing a radical ontological bipolarity.

In this analysis, nothingness emerges only within an event of a call, in the most radical form that a call can take: the call to be. It emerges as the *first truth* of the called-in-himself, that is, as his ontological origin. Nothingness is the site where a call-to-be can be heard, it is the site that a received call-to-be indicates. Within the event of the call, existence is shown to have no ontological foundation in itself; i.e., within nothingness, existence is shown as called-to-be. Nothingness is thus not absolute, it is only the site of "to-be," the site of a paradoxical entity hovering between its original inexistence and its potential existence which always lies ahead of it, initiating an incessant movement towards it. In other words, strictly speaking the called entity is not, but simultaneously, this very negativity emerges only in the light of an Existence which, from a site that is not yet realized for the called, attracts non-existence beyond itself — which, in other words, *donates Being*.

This paradoxical knowledge of the self, a knowledge that precedes its own agent, is the *reception* of the call that otherness as such is. It is only by receiving the calling presence of alterity that the primary self-knowledge (knowledge of nothingness moving towards Being) can be attained. But the truth of the call itself, of the primordial event of the call, lies only in the possibility of *answering* the call. And that means: of transcending the initial ontological status of the called entity, or of transcending nothingness. The call is received within nothingness, but it is answered within Being. If its reception marks a beginning, then only an answer marks its end. In that sense, in Being nothingness would find its own eschatological truth, since nothingness is but the called that has not yet responded. In responding, nothingness becomes what it is: self-transcendent Being.

Thus, the ontological origin of beings is *not* their truth; their truth is the potentiality to alter their own ontological status, by way of what could be called an existential tuning, an imitation, in Christian terminology, of otherness's calling gesture, i.e., of the transcendence that defines otherness's being. Tuning and imitation, which cannot but be dialogical. The response, as coming to one's own truth, is being in the mode of saying, of a primordial referring to otherness. Being

of Modern Identity, Cambridge: Harvard University Press, 1989, pp. 159–76).

and referring here constitute a tautology. Consequently, the eschaton does not have the meaning of a "last word." Such an understanding of eschatology, not unusual within contemporary phenomenology, is, as I have already claimed, merely a reversed protology, remaining still under the influence of an essentialist context. Instead of identifying Being with the autarky of silence, such an understanding of eschatology identifies Being with pure relationality, with pure reference to otherness. Whereas nothingness is the field of silence, the eschaton is an event of dialogue, of a living encounter. Which, conversely, means that *openness does not indicate a lack of Being, but the very plenitude of Being*. Being emerges here not as a static and closed substance, but as the very gesture of opening: of calling otherness to be, of appearing before the other and seeking or exposing oneself to a profound relation to him. Appearance and relation, without which nothing exists, neither God, nor any human person (not even nothingness can appear here — we may thus be dealing with the primary truth of appearance in general).

We find here an access to a certain theological tradition according to which God is primarily the Father and not a substance. The Father is a Person who exists in His absolutely free, creative mode — a creation which, at the same time, is radical relationality: calling otherness to be. Thus, creativity is love and vice versa. Ontology and ethics meet in a single event, within which, at the level of human existence, truth takes place. It is where I become myself by calling you to be, transcending nothingness as my initial ontological status by *deepening* that very nothingness as a response, as a creativity which would not differ from responsibility. I am (my self-transcendent truth is) by perpetuating the metaphysical fertility that creates Being as Being-in-common out of isolation's nothingness.

A mode of personal existence and a mode of personal identity constitute the very unfolding of the world as Creation. The world in the sense of Creation is not what it already is: this is only its beginning, a potentiality. But the truth of the world, its ontological reality, according to such an approach, phenomenological and theological *in nuce*, is the response of the world towards the exteriority lying at its roots. Such a response would not transubstantiate its createdness to something different, it would not negate death; on the contrary, it would understand createdness as the passion of creativity, it would understand death as the very movement towards life. Passivity and creativity would then coincide.

Let us summarize our steps. In *moving from hearing to answering the call*, the called entity, absolutely creative and absolutely passive at the same time, would simultaneously alter, personally (since it is in the mode of a radical relationality that it makes it be), its ontological status. Nothingness, as claimed, appeared only in the form of the "to-be," as a missing absolute, as a called nothingness. And this also means: it appeared only in view of an absolute otherness, whose modality is radical relationality as such: "Let there be." Thus, the truth of nothingness is not itself, not its origin in itself — it is not its protological status. It is rather that which lies beyond it, which transcends it, but which, at the same time, exists as what causes its movement towards its own being. My being thus emerges as an answering being, as a radically relational being, *ad imaginem* of the relational

Otherness. "Cause" is here a paradoxical inversion of our usual understanding of cause, it is rather an inverted cause: it ontologically locates beings not by designating them necessarily, nor by binding them under a law of dependence, but by liberating them from every ontological necessity, by giving them freedom — by giving them giving as such. "Ontologically located" thus means, not fixed in given identities, but on the contrary, being called to self-transcendent openness. Openness is not a lack of Being, but its own modality, the mode of its fullness and its perfection.

Nothingness is thus the site where the potentiality to be is given: it is where Being is donated, or, where truth as the donation of Being is manifested. The truth of the donation does not indicate a singular ontological pole; on the contrary, it indicates the very difference between two distinctive ontological poles, between Nothingness and Being. And the other way around: this polarity emerges not as an internal determination of some still broader totality, a process which one single ontological term has to undergo in order to realize itself. But it emerges only as a gift, the gift to be, only as the surprise of self-transcendence and, therefore, of a transcendence of nothingness. What we are facing here is the potentiality of a change of ontological sites — and this is exactly what we identify as "eschatology": an understanding of beings according to neither their own essence (their origin in itself), nor an abyssal otherness, but according to an initial donation, which always remains to be responded to.

This might be a possible phenomenological transcription of the Christian doctrine of creation *ex nihilo*. Or, the other way around: what a certain phenomenology would allow is an understanding of the tension between two different ontological sites, Nothingness and Being, at the heart of Christian theology. The very distinction between Being and Nothingness arises only if we ascribe to alterity ontological importance. In terms of an ontological monism, there is no place for nothingness as an absolute category. But if Being is in itself already a relational movement, if God is primarily not a substance but a loving Father, then he exists as relation to his exteriority, i.e., as creativity. Thus nothingness is a first name for the reality of ontological otherness — but a reality and an otherness which can be true not by itself, but by tuning to the mode of relationality. To the one ontological pole (to Being) this relationality means Creation, to the other (to Nothingness) it means self-transcendence, i.e., it means the potentiality of an alteration of ontological sites, of existentially perceiving a radical donation.

The notion of such an alteration is often missing from contemporary phenomenology. Within its framework, nothingness is but the inner rhythm of Being itself. Whence, e.g., the idea of a becoming or an imperfect God, a God united ontologically to the fate of the world, to temporality and thus, inevitably, to death, an idea which since Schelling has influenced many attempts to articulate an alternative religious modality next to metaphysics. But such an alternative reproduces the ontological fundament of metaphysics, i.e., the coincidence of fullness and closure, and, consequently, of openness and lack. Eschatology here risks remaining a mere inversion of protology, a doubling of the same, since punctuality survives as the main reference point, even if it escapes from presence towards absence. An alternative would, in my opinion, consist less in inverting the Aristotelian scheme of *dynamis* and *energeia* by ascribing primacy to potentiality. It would rather consist in seeing in the motility of *dynamis* the birth into the ontological perspective of Being, the *reception* of a call to be, the movement towards openness — nothingness as the site of the relative self-knowledge of temporal and created beings, as relative openness; nothingness as their *first truth* (or, as the protological aspect of truth): the truth of their otherness in relation to Being. And it would also consist in seeing in *energeia* the *response* to that call, the ever-moving arrival (*aeikinitos stasis*, in the words of Maximus Confessor) at the site of absolute openness — at Being-in-relation as absolute self-knowledge or as the *last truth* (the eschatological aspect of truth).

The arrival at absence would be the first event of truth, the arrival at presence the last one; none of them exists in itself, they indicate each other. But the ontological importance that movement attains here rests on the very difference between two distinctive ontological polarities, each of them moving, though in a different sense, because of their ontological difference (*diaphora*, according to Maximus Confessor) — and because that very difference is not a manifestation of a division (*diairesis*, again according to Maximus Confessor), but of a relation. A relation defined, otherwise than by Lévinas, as the very transcendence of every systemic, non-personal interdependence. Proximity would thus be the very poetic cause of distance, its eschatological truth the cause, depth, and unfolding of its protological truth. Here we depart not only from the Hegelian understanding of movement, but also from the Heideggerian one. Finitude in itself can illuminate movement as inadequately as infinity in itself. An important challenge for contemporary phenomenology might consist in transcending those ontological presuppositions that identify Being with closure, and thus permitting one to see experience and existence not as constant withdrawal from Being, but as the very movement towards it — as the call to *incarnate* it by tuning into the mode of responding to a radically exterior call.

The thoughts which I will try to sketch now, constituting an attempt to follow such a scheme at the anthropological level, will remain in an indirect though constant dialogue with certain contemporary thinkers, including Jean-Luc Marion, Jean-Luc Nancy and Richard Kearney. At the same time, the structure of such a phenomenological inquiry, unfolding as it does in a process of changing and becoming, expresses itself very well in the narrative mode. For that purpose I am going to turn now to a great literary example that will help me illustrate, in narrative, some aspects of such a phenomenology; I am going to read and interpret some aspects of the double Sophoclean drama of the myth of King Oedipus, *Oedipus Rex*, and, especially, *Oedipus in Colonus*. I also wish to suggest a different genealogy of the person: we might find here a kind of dramatic ontology, departing not only from the substantialist presuppositions of ancient Greek ontology, but also from the need to reject ontology in order to rediscover the primacy of the encounter with the other — a dramatic ontology which, from a path different from but relative to the Jewish one, announces Christianity.

Otherness as the Natal Call to Absence

Let us briefly recall some of the major elements of the myth and of Sophocles' elaboration of it. Everything begins with the oracle of Delphi telling Laius, king of Thebes and Oedipus' father-to-be, that he must not have any son, because this son will one day kill him: the son is the death of the father. Laius, nevertheless, ignores the warning of the oracle, and Jocasta, Laius' wife, gives birth to a child. But then they get afraid, and Jocasta turns the little child over to a shepherd with the order that he should kill it.

From the very beginning, the problem is located at a traumatic emergence of alterity. Laius denies that the son will "kill" him, i.e., that the future, which culminates in the son, may put into question the closure that defines the father's primary identity. Laius denies the future as that which he cannot control, as that which exposes him as dead, which exposes his closed individuality as a non-existing entity.

The initial point of the myth is this emergence of an ontologically threatening otherness, which opens me to the temporality of the future as that which comes to me from outside, as the unknown — an opening which is always already a death. Laius does not want to die, cannot die, thus he cannot allot anything of his own self to otherness, cannot be generous; in a word, he cannot be a father. And such a denial of the traumatic otherness which is the son as the future cannot but end in a murder, in the violent negation of an annihilating exteriority.

We have to understand all this in the first place not in terms of morals, but in terms of a phenomenology of human existence. Laius cannot sacrifice his closure, not because he is an exceptionally or unusually immoral man, but only because he supports a certain idea of existence, which is in fact our common idea of existence, whether we are aware of it or not, whether it takes civilized forms or not. Laius characterizes "normality," or the first stage of subjectivity, illuminated at an ontological level and not a psychological or moral one.

However, the shepherd takes pity on the little boy and abandons him at the mountain of Cithaeron. There he is found by another shepherd, coming this time from Corinth, who takes the boy with him and brings it to Polybius and Merope, royal pair of Corinth, who adopt the child because they did not have any children of their own. At the time when the boy is coming of age, during an evening of wining and dining, someone tells him that he is not truly a child of his parents: the natal rupture emerges anew. His parents of course deny those words, but Oedipus is alarmed enough to ask the oracle of Delphi about it, the same oracle who had spoken to his equally alarmed father. Instead of answering that question, the oracle gives the well known answer that Oedipus will kill his father and marry his mother. After that, Oedipus leaves behind what he thinks to be his homeland, in order to avoid the verification of the oracle's divination. But as his fate unfolds, he comes to a crossroads where he meets some strangers, one of which is his own father, whom of course he does not recognize. None steps aside to allow the other to pass, it comes to a conflict, and Oedipus kills his father. As Oedipus is afterwards about to reach Thebes, he comes across the Sphinx, a mythological monster, which poses the famous riddle about the identity of the being that walks with four legs, then with two and finally with three. Oedipus manages to solve the riddle, the Sphinx dies, and Oedipus becomes king of Thebes and husband of Laius' widow.

Oedipus manages to solve the riddle of identity and temporality, which means that he succeeds in turning the *mysterium* of what exceeds him into an interior territory, he manages to represent exteriority in the order of his mind. This actually bears witness to the strength of his will. Moreover, the encounter with the foreigner at the crossroads is indicative: Oedipus will not diverge from his own path for any reason or for the sake of anyone.

The most important thing about Oedipus is this self-referential will. Independently of all psychoanalytical assumptions about whether he wanted to kill his father or not, Oedipus is clearly driven by his strong will. Even his refusal to accept the oracle has to be understood in terms of his will: Oedipus wills not-to-kill his father. But why? Does an affirmation of the other render the essence of the individual will? For Kant and for the whole metaphysical tradition the answer is affirmative. For Sophocles, however, it is not. For Sophocles, the will not to harm is already harmful, because it originates from the fiction of a self which exists before the threatening contact with otherness and, thus, which is moral without being in relation to otherness — it is rather moral in order to avoid its rupturing presence.

Remember the prophecy: Oedipus will kill his father and marry his mother. Is this not a double form of the same statement: you will deny the rupture that gives birth to you? Is the father not the one who, in a sense, repeats the birth by activating, in a higher level, the separation from the mother and, at the same time, the separation from non-existence? Is the father not the primary face of temporality and, thus, of singular existence itself? By denying those statements, Oedipus denies, not evil, but the word of exteriority that exposes him to his existential birth as the content of his future, the future of a human being. The oracle tells him that human life is a denial of an initial separation, of an initial birth — and doing so, it indirectly tells him of this initial, singularizing event itself. It is this event that Oedipus denies by denying the oracle. It is an escape from his own birth in the face of exteriority that his moral will is trying to establish — an attempt covered under the mantle of collective usefulness, i.e., to be as successful as possible.

The beginning of the Sophoclean drama finds Oedipus at his throne, regarded by his people as a king that has served public safety — precisely against the Sphinx as the memory of death and, therefore, as the memory of the aforementioned rupture. But this is being said at a peculiar juncture: a delegation of the city has come to talk to Oedipus about a plague from which the city is suffering. The plague is due to an old and forgotten murder that had never been resolved, and it will not end if that past evil is not revealed. However, in that very dialogue between the city itself and Oedipus, we already have the key to what the plague is all about. The city acknowledges in Oedipus a man who rescued it from the threat of nothingness; in other words, a man who established a certain being-with without its mediation through a reference to otherness's first form. Oedipus does indeed stand for all that, and at the same time realizes his role as a protective ruler, and one gets the impression that we stand before a scene of mutual mirroring, where every part (the city and its king) stands for the idol of the other's will, i.e., of the other's fictitious self. In that sense, we stand before a *false dialogue*, a dialogue which does not serve the naked appearance before each other, the real presence of the persons, but on the contrary, it serves the very hiding behind a mask — a mask which again serves a fictitious security, a detachment from the traumatic presence of the other, from his natal and deadly call to appear before him, in relation to him. It is detachment from nothingness as the very center of singular existence, a loss in an interior non-existence, which would prove at the same time to be an imaginary absolute existence. The sickness of the city, explicitly defined as the impossibility of birth among humans and the rest of the physical world, can be read as the outburst, at the level of phenomenality, of precisely this masquerade, of this ontological distortion, of the abandonment of the world by enclosing oneself within a well-organized society of detached minds, and of the deeper nothingness that this masquerade sought to hide: "sickness lies on all our company, and thought can find no weapon to repel it" (*Oedipus Rex*, 169–71). The reality of the persons appears first of all in the form of falling masks, in a major disturbance of representations, which is but a birth to death.

This outburst is exemplified once again in a dialogue, but this time a dialogue opposite to the previous one. This time no mirroring can take place. It is the dialogue with Teiresias, the blind prophet, whose blind eyes do not return to Oedipus a wishful image of his own, but the very absence of such an image. Teiresias' sight is like a dark or empty mirror: therein Oedipus finds himself as a missing, absent identity. Teiresias bears Oedipus to the question of his origin, of his birth and of his identity, he bears him into the burden of his singular existence: "Do you know from what stock you come? ... you are unaware of being an enemy to your own beneath and above the earth ... now you have sight, then you shall look on darkness ...," and finally the most crucial point: "this day shall be your parent and your destroyer" (413–38).

The self-inflicted blinding of Oedipus must be read rather as an inner darkness of man that is illuminated as such. It is not that he could see before, and that he subsequently loses his sight; on the contrary, now for the first time he acknowledges that he had imposed a mantle of darkness, i.e., of absence, above everything: now he can see for the first time, he can see this very absence of the others as the first form of their very appearance. Otherness appears primarily as a negated otherness, a negation which is the essence of violence — and that is why the event which tragedy consists in includes a fundamentally moral aspect. In fact, we are talking about the birth of the moral consciousness — but this consciousness does not appear any more within the will of a subjectivity which is *a priori* good, but within a tragic subjectivity, which emerges as the transcendence of the indirectly nihilistic subjectivity of the autonomous self. It is in the breakdown of the organization of the individualities that the first form of being-with and of singular existence emerges. But, especially in view of Levinas and other contemporary thinkers, we should not overlook the fact that this event does not yet take place between me and the other, as we both really are, but between the two forms of our absence. The event of true relation belongs to a later stage, to which we will turn our attention presently.

In the same sense, it should also not escape our attention that Oedipus becomes, within his self-inflicted blinding, similar to Teiresias, the blind prophet, a creature of the underworld and the heavens simultaneously, and imitates his higher access to the world. The event of blinding is seen negatively only within a psychological view, or within a view that insists in ascribing ontological significance to an unbroken, punctual totality — namely, in opposition to nothingness as primary openness. It is clear that Oedipus now knows for the first time: he knows that he did not know till now, because he could not see any real others, as Teiresias tells him; and for the first time he commits himself to a free act. As Laius negated the future in order to avoid death, Oedipus negated his past in order to avoid his birth: two aspects of the same structure. The self-inflicted blinding is a metaphor of a birth into the world, of a verification of the otherness which has been negated until now, a verification which is the first act that Oedipus does, not as someone else, not as a false imitation of the father's first form (Laius), but as himself, truly imitating the father's last form (Teiresias). The self-inflicted exile of Oedipus to Cithaeron that follows and completes the drama may thus be read as the first form of being-with and being-himself, both defined by their revealed negativity: Oedipus has arrived at the site of *nihilum*.

How distant is the situation of Oedipus from our own intellectual situation? As I have already argued, a great part of contemporary philosophy sees the alternative to the essentialist subjectivity, self-referential and closed, in a definitely lacking self. Is it not true that once we have rejected the violently autonomous and holistic subject, we tend to reject all plenitude as false plenitude, every notion of entity as the construction of a violent idealism? Does not Hegel's and Heidegger's legacy consist in a self which is but the melody or the rhythm of an absolute Being in being the singular site of an emptiness, of a nothingness desiring its *ab initio* lost self-sufficiency? When Freud declares the Thing as *a priori* lost, and when Lacan and his contemporary descendants speak about the desire, do they not remind us of Kant's *Ding an sich* and of the Hegelian idea of an impossible closure, of an opening due to an eternally unfulfilled desire of autarky? Is it not true that contemporary thought about otherness is still largely taking place within a framework where openness is derived from the impossibility of a fullness, which is exclusively understood as a totality? That is, are our ontological terms not still those of totality, even if they have reversed its value? Does the idea of the open subject as an ontologically suspended entity not indirectly perpetuate the old metaphysical presuppositions in their inversed form? Here the theological implications arise anew: we need only consider God primarily as a self-referential essence, and its romantic analogue, a God who opens himself creatively to otherness exactly because He does not yet exist in plenitude, who creates out of a desire for such a self-referential closure.

Is an eschatology understood in terms of a constantly escaping fullness, an eschatology which risks underestimating the Incarnation, whose interpretation of Resurrection is rather exhausted in the event of the empty grave of Jesus — is such an eschatology free of the old metaphysical terms? Is our phenomenology already liberated from such terms and presuppositions?

Otherness as the Resurrecting Call to Presence

I, for my part, think that the theological origin of such presuppositions indicates that any alternative must also begin with fundamentally theological insights. I shall, by the end of my essay, come back to the idea of a creating God, who is primarily defined neither as a self-referential essence (an idea which entails that God's relation to the world and men's relation to each other and to God remains highly problematic), nor as an imperfect God, open due to his lacking fullness, but, on the contrary, a God who creates *because* he exists in fullness, who is radically open because he exists in a state of relation. This is God as Father, a primarily relational entity.

But at this point I would like to raise the question about the direct phenomenological and anthropological access to such ideas. I wonder about the possibility of their emergence within the horizon of a human being ultimately shaped by the experience of a natal nothingness, by the site of the tragic, similar to the one I analyzed through the fate of an "ontological hero" (as Hermann Melville calls Ishmael and Ahab, his humans *par excellence* in *Moby-Dick*) such as Oedipus. But for Sophocles the self-inflicted blinding, the deliverance of man to otherness in terms of an existential hovering, is not the last phenomenological word. On the contrary, it is the first one. The fate of man, as described in *Oedipus Rex*, marks the beginning of the truth, or, in theological terms, the activation of Creation. But Creation was not completed by its mere emergence in materiality; it only began at that point. The beginning is not the end: the beginning is only a *relative truth* through its reference to the *absolute truth*, which is the end, or, in the terminology again of the Church Fathers, the *Logos* of the beings. A relative protology of nothingness exists only through an absolute eschatology of being — as an arrow that appears by the very act of pointing to the purpose that sustains its meaning.

Turning back to the anthropological level of our drama: if Oedipus is born into the very question of who he is, if otherness there marks a deliverance to an existential motion, where is the end of this movement located, the final horizon that permits the appearance and the existence and the meaning of all this?

Twenty five years after writing *Oedipus Rex*, Sophocles returns to this myth in order to complete its perspectives. He writes his most extended drama, *Oedipus in Colonus*. The drama begins with Oedipus, supported by his daughter Antigone, again reaching the territory of a city. What has intervened was nothing less than a period of exile, a wandering in a wasteland. Oedipus now reaches Colonus, a northwestern part of ancient Athens. The city he enters is not the city he left; it is a city with which no physical bonds would connect him: here he is only a stranger.

The whole previous history of Oedipus and the fact that he now exists as a stranger is translated geographically as the place in which Oedipus comes in touch with the new form of collectivity. The point of encounter between the exile and the city, a bridge or a passage (*peschach* in Jewish, *pascha* in Greek, "passage" is the name for the Holy Week), is the sacred grove of the Eumenides, goddesses which in mythology have an impact very much like the one that Medusa has: they bring a terror resulting from the mirroring of the one who sees them. Eumenides like Medusa follow the structure of otherness-as-an-empty-mirror, of a mirror that shows the absence or the blindness of the one that achieves primary self-knowledge.

"Child of a blind old man, Antigone, to what regions, or to what men's city have we come? Who on this day will receive Oedipus the wanderer with scanty gifts?" (*Oedipus at Colonus,* 1–4). Echoing Odysseus and the meaning of his wandering, as it is to be heard in the first three verses of the *Odyssey*, Oedipus does not know where he has arrived at and whom he will meet. The distance from his previous mode, where the encounter with the other was under the imperative of an all-encompassing knowledge and control, could hardly be greater. Oedipus is delivered to the unknown, towards which he appears now as a non-being: "take pity on this miserable ghost of the man Oedipus" (109). This has something of an achieved innocence, and that is the reason why Oedipus may walk in a sacred and forbidden territory without being endangered: the Eumeniden already delimit the territory of his life, they are already the history of his subjectivity.

In this marginal region, in this nocturnal threshold, a question is asked from the chorus. It is as if this region *is* this very question: who is he? (118). And Oedipus answers exactly the same way as Abraham answered when God called him by his name: "I who am here am he" (cf. *Gen.* 22:1), and complements: "for I see with my voice, as they say" (138). Within nothingness, identity emerges not as an "I", but as a "Me", as receptivity, or as a response — an appearing before the eyes of him who calls me to appear, before an otherness that defines the site of the real as such. I am, then, as appearance, or as response, as dialogical speech. I myself cannot see such otherness, I cannot make it my object, I recognize it only by hearing it and responding to it. Being already beyond myself, I attune myself to it through dialogue. Not seeing, but being-seen is now what defines identity, a coming to the open space of "here," or, to *the spatiality of presence as openness*. "Here" is a place of a new absoluteness, it marks a second fundamental event, after the "where?" and the "who?," the hovering and the loss themselves, that marked the first event. This now is the event of true subjectivity.

"Here" is the site of an event of absoluteness, of sociality as the event of truth. Openness and presence form a tautology: I am present only as openness, since I exist only as a response to the inaugural call, which exteriority as such is. There is not any otherness prior to this call, and similarly I do not exist prior to this call. The call does not come after being, it is not a gesture from a being, which is previously constituted as such and then calls, i.e., communicates. On the contrary, according to a paradoxical logic, I am, everything is, in the very social event, in an event of absolute, natal relationality. And this ultimately means that relationality does not restrict being; on the contrary, it is the very site of being as being, an image of absolute personal freedom.

If Oedipus started becoming a subject through the rupture of the totality of a false form of collectivity, which formed a deeper denial of existence, a rupture indicated finally in the exile from the city and in the wandering in an empty space, then the final form of this very abandonment itself is but a new entry in the field of being-with, a sociality which is marked by appearing and listening.

The truth of the subject would thus be seen within a double-sided event, by which the ontological hero, as I called him, would finally come to his eschatological self. The first of those sides is hospitality: Oedipus, who appears now as a naked existence, is received and verified from otherness. Hospitality is not a moral category, but an ontological one, which is the exact opposite: within hospitality, the wanderer is called from exile to relation, from non-being to being. But he is, thus, also calling the host to an encounter, i.e., he invites the host to an opening. In these terms, the one who offers himself as a powerless being, who falls back on the *real presence* of the other, is not simply passive, but he is actually free and creative: he creates life as common life, he creates truth. We would speak of a *creative passivity*, or of a *receptive freedom*. It is in precisely that sense that the event by which the double drama of Oedipus is completed is the very elevation of him to the throne — an elevation of a stranger to the center of the common life, i.e., to the creation of true subjectivity as sociality. Let us now turn briefly to this last part.

The scene of the dialogue with the Athenian chorus, with the collectivity itself, is completed by the arrival of Theseus, king of Athens (551–85). Theseus tells Oedipus that he too has experience of exile and that he is thus ready to offer Oedipus hospitality, to receive this worst among the criminals on earth within the limits of his city. Because, as he says, "I know that I am a man, and that I have no greater share in tomorrow than you have" (566–8). The dialogue with Theseus is the continuation and the completion of the dialogue with Teiresias. It is an absolute speaking, a speaking where the faces are present — and they are present because they encounter each other within the site of an abandonment. While speaking, they are both located (actually: locating each other) in the middle of the exile, and thus, in the middle of the city. Teiresias was blind, Theseus has known exile, which is the same thing: both are metaphors for nothingness as the first site of existence or the beginning to be. Both talked crucially to Oedipus, the first calling him to see his darkness, the second calling him to see his light.

Teiresias called him to his past, but now Theseus calls him to his future. And this future is a common future, or *the common as future*. It is the "share in tomorrow" of which Theseus speaks. But this tomorrow is very different from the controlled one that Oedipus had in mind when he denied the oracle, the controlled and invented future that Laius had in mind, a future without death, a future without temporality, according to a past without birth, a being without existing. This was the existential program of Oedipus, until he was *found by time*, as the chorus says in a crucial verse in *Oedipus Rex*, describing what the disclosure of truth consisted in. (Oedipus was not only found by time, he was also found by his own criminality, as is repeatedly stated in the second drama (cf. 266–7; 539–40; 987).)

But now his being-found, his essential receptivity, attains a different character. It is a sharing of tomorrow, which proves to be radically creative. What Oedipus creates is a new site of being, being-in-common. In the last part of the drama, Oedipus is heading for a certain place where he is going to die, albeit not in a physical way. Being called there alone by a god, he disappears in a blinding light; only Theseus may stay near him till the end, and may learn the secret of the bond between the human and the divine.

Oedipus, a stranger, becomes king anew, initiates anew a mode of being-with. But this time being-with is initiated not through power, but through powerlessness. Being absolutely receptive, Oedipus in the end proves to be absolutely creative: he creates a novelty out of the given, he creates common-life as an absolute life.

Oedipus set out as someone who tried to invent an identity in order to remain autonomous. The first phenomenological site is one wherein the protological insistence on a fictitious individuality is ruptured by the violent irruption of a terrible otherness, which mirrors the non-existence of the subject. At this point, at the point of the annihilation of his substance, the subject begins to move toward his truth. His truth is not his substance, his truth is *the very transcendence of his substance*, since such a transcendence is pointed at *within his substance*. In other words, the substance is nothing but the arrow that shows us its very transcendence as its truth and purpose.

The substance is a nothingness that is called to be. It is the final absolutely- and truly-being that permits the appearance of nothingness as an arrow towards it, as the beginning of a motion to it. Emptiness exists only as being-called-to-plenitude. And this plenitude *is* the very answer to the call of the other. If lack is the reception of the question "Who am I?," plenitude is the reception of my name, the reception of my identity. But this reception and the response are already an attunement with the creative call itself, the engagement in a dialogue that makes things be, where I hear my name only by calling otherness to be, in other words, by donating life as relation. The call "children" opens and closes the first drama on Oedipus, and it functions as the secret motif of the second one as well. It is not accidental: if Oedipus at first reproduces a constructed paternity as power, at the end he becomes a real father, he identifies his being with generosity as a metaphysical fertility beyond any biological bond.

We meet here a notion of plenitude that is known to us from the Greek Fathers of the Church, and especially from Maximus the Confessor. Plenitude is here not a substantial closure, and openness is not lack: openness is the very modality of plenitude. And this can happen only in terms of an eschatology, which at the same time is nothing other than the gradual reception of alterity as the very meaning of experience and of being-created. Delivered to its very "beyond," the experiencing subject is opened to its being as donation from outside, as a call-to-being received *ex nihilo*. Within the decomposition of the negative, imaginarily closed self, within the event of this inaugural loss, the offer (the self as offered) reveals itself as such.

This means that the participation in the world takes place already within the framework of freedom. But "within freedom" does not mean that we are already and necessarily free, it means that the site of our truth is not creation as an end in itself, as a binding fact, but it is rather, paradoxically, *the liberation from any factuality through creation*, as a work of our freedom. According to this paradoxical logic, our birth is paradoxically "caused" by our resurrection, the given is "caused" (i.e., ontologically located or specified) by the liberated, precisely in the perspective of its final, liberated truth. Located, and not determined, since we are dealing here with a notion of cause as the very liberation of the caused. Liberation from non-existence, liberation to otherness, liberation as relation, which is the exact opposite of liberation as *causa sui*.

This means that the event of emptiness *does not yet* designate the field of sociality, but rather indicates it as the end of the movement, *the movement that the emptiness as such is*. The end, the plenitude of being, a profoundly social reality, is the eschatological meaning of nature and being-created. I cite Maximus the Confessor:

> Everything that has been created endures movement as passion [*paschei to kineisthai*] because it does not constitute self-movement [*autokinesis*] or self-enforcing [*autodynamis*]. Therefore, if the logical beings [i.e., human beings] are born ones, then they are anyhow in motion. Because, as is natural [*kata physin*], due to the fact that they exist, they move voluntary from a beginning to an end, with a view to achieving well-being [*eu einai*]. Because the end of the motion of everything that moves is, precisely, to be always in well-being [*en to aei eu einai estin*], whereas the beginning of the motion is being itself [*auto to einai*]. And this is God, the giver [*doter*] of being and donator [*charistikos*] of well-being, because God is the beginning and the end. (Maximus the Confessor, *Ambigua*, PG 1073 B–C).

By seeing in nothingness the very passion of a movement towards God, a reception of a call to be, the beginning of truth, and by seeing in the response to that call the creative imitation of God, the fullness of being, Maximus forwards the anthropology of the ancient drama and permits us to think of a phenomenology and an anthropology liberated not only from metaphysical essentialism, but also from its contemporary counterpart, an anti-essentialism which identifies openness with a mere lack of identity. For Maximus, and perhaps also for a phenomenology such as the one that I have briefly tried to explore here, this is still a protology — which can be deepened (and not negated) by an eschatological phenomenology of creative receptivity, of a self in plenitude as pure relationality.

Chapter 7

Being and the Promise

Jeffrey Bloechl

The Eschatology of Being

If it has been an early tendency of phenomenology to emphasize our intimacy with the world in which we find ourselves, it has nonetheless turned only slowly toward a complementary emphasis on our estrangement from it — that is, on the fact that we are not entirely *of* that world even while we are indeed *in* it. The earlier tendency is present already in Husserl's philosophy, and most noticeably in his second, genetic works, which trace the modes and structures of intentionality back toward the original proximity of what is not yet subject and what is not yet object. Simple question: what accounts for the emergence of subject and object? Simple conclusion: in order for a thing to stand as object over against me as subject, it must first exercise a greater claim on my attention than do the other things also there before me; and I for my part must focus attentively on that one thing and not the others. Phenomenality, it seems, presupposes an original tension that is resolved in the discharge of focus. But since all of this occurs within the lived time of a subject who, moreover, has a past that influences its present, it likewise presupposes a world: the drama of givenness always occurs within a shared setting imbued with the style of my own being, and this setting is neither a thing itself nor the totality of things but the horizon within which they are always found.[1]

If we summarize, for Husserl then, the world is that in which I live and within which I encounter the things that give themselves to be seen; it is that by which the meaning of each thing is constituted according to my perspective. This means that the world, at least for Husserl, is thus the condition for the impossibility of the absolutely foreign or unique. What is new in the world is already intelligible precisely as a modification or alteration of what is familiar. And that intelligibility is thus insured insofar as it submits to laws already in place in the world that it enters. This much begs a question as simple as it is old: is there not an intelligibility that neither is dependent on submitting to the laws of this world nor however opposes the intelligibility of the world as such? Against the primacy of the world and the rule of its laws, one might call for the transcendent category of mystery. Mystery, it is necessary to insist, exceeds what is merely novel because what is mysterious

---

[1]   For indications in support of this Husserlian account of historicity, see e.g. E. Husserl, *Analysen zur Passiven Synthesis. Aus Vorlesungs- und Forschungmanuskripten 1918–1926*, published as *Husserliana* XI (Den Haag: Martinus Nijhoff, 1966), pp. 35f.

remains by definition beyond the reach of the laws that prevail where it reveals itself. What is mysterious arrives with an intelligibility that has its own laws.

There is no need to associate this preliminary definition of mystery with what the monotheisms call "God" in order to anticipate that it will play a unique role within the phenomenology that discovers a place for it, and in any case phenomenology has come to that effort in the later philosophy of Heidegger. Would that later philosophy have appeared under greater pressure from any other theme? Indeed, with the advantage of hindsight we might now suppose that all of the capital achievements of his earlier works are directed to an encounter with this very theme: it is, from the beginning, a matter of our being-in-the-world, or rather of what Heidegger contends is the proper way that we, as Daseins, discover it: not according to the rational faculties by which we secure an environment but in and through the particular mood of anxiety. A condensed account of the experience will do: in anxiety, "all things and we ourselves sink into [the] indifference" in which neither any objects nor our own existence finds support in any of the usual acts that sustain us.[2] Fastening on the fact that this does not occur by our own initiative but precisely suspends all possible initiative, Heidegger concludes that we do not negate all that falls away but instead find ourselves exposed and vulnerable to the nothing that *itself* nihilates — exposed, as it were, to the initiative of the nothing that has been there all along, concealed by every movement of our being-in-the-world, until approaching in anxiety. What anxiety thus teaches phenomenology — what it lays bare, as an instance of the reduction — is that we are, in our very being-in-the-world, suspended over an abyss capable of swallowing, or better eroding any ground we may project for ourselves — *and* that being-in-the-world must be therefore characterized as irreducibly finite. Here then is a thought without which contemporary philosophy of religion is virtually unthinkable: a proper understanding of ourselves, and by extension the very possibility of attending properly to truth, or for that matter goodness and beauty — in short, the very possibility of genuine thinking *awaits* and *responds to* a call that arrives, at least in its pure form, from beyond our world and everything in it. *At least in its pure form*: that is, specifically in the form of the encounter with nothing that is ascribed to the experience of anxiety.

One does not need to be reminded that in the philosophy of Heidegger "nothing" passes as a pseudonym of "being" in order to recognize it as the focal point for first philosophy. More than a founding concept, nothing, or being — being as nothing — also denotes a posture: henceforth, philosophy, when attending to its proper topic, always gets underway *in the wake* of the material it is given to work with. As the thinking of being, philosophy begins from the manner in which being discloses itself and thus also conceals itself, and then moves toward a meditation on the manner

---

[2]   M. Heidegger, "Was ist Metaphysik?," in *Gesamtausgabe*, vol. 9 (Frankfurt: Klostermann, 1976), p. 28. On this point, the essay on metaphysics seems rather more ambitious than *Sein und Zeit*: the nothing before which we are anxious must be defined with respect not only to the inner-worldly beings that we encounter (cf. *Sein und Zeit*, §40) but also with respect to the being of our world and finally of our very Dasein.

in which that unconcealment that is also a concealment comes to pass. Only thus, according to an attitude of attendance — of a certain openness and patience — does authentic thinking take place. But then fundamental ontology, to the degree that it depends on an analysis of Dasein, proves unsuited to the task originally assigned to it. Heidegger notes it himself, in his Nietzsche lectures: the attempt to free thinking from any prejudice for subjectivity that would move through a preparatory, self-interpretation of the subject's deeper condition as Dasein flirts with submitting the entire meditation on being to the limits of what Dasein can see and say about itself.[3] Are we then to repudiate the entire effort as a re-entrenchment of the subject after all? Heidegger's more prudent response has been to step back until capable of submitting it (i.e., the existential analytic) to close hermeneutical scrutiny. This makes an important difference: whereas previously he appears content to place fundamental ontology within the limits opened up by the self-interpretation of Dasein, his later tendency must be to consider it as an exercise in which thinking certainly did achieve new realization of its own dependence on being — and yet failed to fully understand what this implies for any future thinking. And if a fuller understanding would mean, principally, recognizing the radical priority of being over thinking, then in Heidegger's later philosophy thinking begins to recognize that its proper place is not simply in the world but perhaps at its margin, where the thinker can interpret the world against the background of what exceeds it.

All of this suggests that the philosophy of Heidegger not only represents a penetrating account of our this-wordliness, as has been noticed by any careful reader, but also proceeds to *problematize* it: or, more precisely, the former step is taken in the early works and the later works unmistakably proceed to the latter, and indeed, are arguably preoccupied with it. What joins these two figures of his philosophy is an increasing awareness to what certain transitional texts call "the essential poverty of thinking before its own topic." There is nothing immediately spiritual about this poverty: the thinking that knows itself to be dependent on the initiative of being, and has learned that both its question and the means available to pursue it are communicated by history, must relinquish the dream of suspending every historical condition imposed on its movement — must let go of the desire to leap over those conditions — and instead accept and indeed concentrate on the fact that being has abandoned us to them. The task of such thinking will then come down to a meditation on the truth of being, which is to say being insofar as accessible only through the conditions in which it is unconcealed. And this requires, in the final instance, that thinking entrust itself to being as it permits itself to be seen. In the final instance, then, the questioning of being, as the highest expression of thought, must ground itself in what can only be called, no doubt with certain qualifications, an act of *philosophical faith*.

If the appearance of a notion of "faith" in Heidegger's philosophy has anything to offer the Christian thinker, it cannot lie in the alleged prospect of convergence

---

[3] M. Heidegger, *Der Wille zur Macht als Erkenntnis* (Pfullingen: Neske, 1961), vol. I, pp. 194 *et seq.*

with a radical commitment to God — not least because "being" is not God, but also because the existential attitude of faith in God is one from which Heidegger never ceases to distance his thinking. One does, however, find in the recourse to even a "philosophical" faith the stimulating thought that our this-worldliness seems bound to discover *within itself* the fact that it can be justified only by a leap to conditions that transcend it.[4] But to what does Heidegger's thinker leap? If it is to the task of meditating on the truth of being and if being must be known as abyss, then the mood in which that task is to be conducted is quite clear: after the initial shock of having been dispossessed of any pretense to comprehension, thinking enters immediately into a disquiet that may be broken only by the modicum of serenity that comes with positive acceptance of one's condition.

We may add a few notes in passing. First, the disquiet of the thinker dispossessed of every claim to comprehension is the disquiet of one who finds himself to be not-at-home (*Unzuhause*). Precisely this is to be endured by the thinker, who thus has more in common with the tragic hero than with, as one may have thought a moment ago, Kierkegaard's knight of faith. To suppose that thinking must have faith in the truth of being as it is offered in a form that is always historically determined comes close to supposing that thinking must have faith in *finitude itself*, as the irreducible condition of our encounter with being. Such a faith would have to be contrasted with Christian faith in the God who is notably infinite. This makes it difficult to imagine that the serenity of the thinker who becomes a shepherd of being is quite the joy awaiting the believer who reaches intimacy with God.

Second, in the conception of philosophical faith in the truth of being, and in the experience of disquiet and then serenity at being not-at-home one finds the elements of an eschatology proper to the Heideggerian account of being. The thinker, after all, looks toward a truth of being that would become *fully* accessible only according to conditions that must remain beyond us mortals.[5] Heidegger rightly makes this a question of disposition, of fundamental mood: overcoming a previous disquiet, serene thinking attends to its topic, the truth of being. Can there be any agreement between this attitude and the Christian attitude of hope? Jean Greisch has given us a concise statement of the evident difference: serene attention would seem to be without the impatience, even the fever, of hope, which,

---

4   The *Beiträge* contain reflections on such a "leap" (*Sprung*) at §§ 117–20, 122, 124, 181.

5   Hence a first approach to the oracular talk of "the final god," *der letzte Gott*, who arrives from beyond the difference between faith and reason because from before the possibility of their difference. This notion cannot fail to evoke those other gods who, along with mortals, heaven and earth, meet in the Fourfold (*Geviert*). It is true that Heidegger never clearly distinguished the final god from them. It is also true, however, that he might have done so, since this final god is no more subject to the Fourfold than is the Christian God. Rather than enter into a comparative theology of God and god, the present essay approaches their possible difference as a question of attitude and attunement.

for its part, does not wish to reconcile itself with the conditions in which one finds oneself, but desires a happiness that would transcend or perhaps transform them.[6]

For Heidegger, the very fact that the eschatology of being displays no such desire goes hand-in-hand with the fact that the thinker aims above all at ceding every initiative to being. From that perspective, the Christian desire for perfect happiness, or for salvation, remains contaminated by an insistence on the primacy of our own initiative and by the deeper human interests that drive it. By definition, then, the attitude of serene attention will have freed itself of all such personal initiative interest. And as for the last god who may come to save us, the attitude of attention has thus abandoned all means to call to it, let alone make a claim on it.

A final thought on Heidegger: it is useless to contest the possibility of such attention, since in any case it has every appearance of coherence. It is also pointless to characterize it as *esoteric*, which after all says only very little, or else *gnostic*, which at least has the advantage of being etymologically correct. These charges are familiar enough. Quite apart from them, one is faced with the rather stark proposal, made in the name of phenomenology itself, that our being-in-the-world must be qualified simply as being not-at-home, without possibility of overcoming that condition. Such would be the philosopher's final word on our human condition — we are subject, evidently enough, to the rule of finitude: one either recognizes and accepts the singularity and errancy of being, or else flees from it into a consolation that can only be false. A high asceticism is commanded of the thinker, in whom our humanity will have reached its greatest expression. Love of wisdom, opening itself to the truth of being, takes the form of emptying oneself of every other form of knowing, and indeed comprehension itself, but without the grace of another, fulfilling love that might come to him in the form known to the believer: *from on high*.

The Eschatology of Love

There is no longer anything to prevent us from asking about the pertinence of Heidegger's philosophy, and perhaps especially its eschatology, for the thinking that takes place at the heart of Christian faith. Enough has already been said to rule out the idea that it may serve as a preamble to that faith, not only because God would cease to be God when submitted to the screen or filter of being but also, and first, because Heidegger requires us to think any and every notion of the divine through originary finitude. There is no room in Heidegger's philosophy to assign a positive meaning to what Stanislas Breton understood about the life of the believer: it is bathed in the element of the absolute. How may the phenomenologist see this difference in the distinct lives of the thinker and the believer? One approach appears in the movement of Heidegger's own thinking, where the life of the thinker no less than the life of the believer can be defined by the same three

---

[6]   J. Greisch, "La contrée de la sérénité et l'horizon de l'espérance," in R. Kearney and J.S. O'Leary (eds), *Heidegger et la question de Dieu* (Paris: Grasset, 1980), pp. 68–193.

virtues of faith, hope, and — one suspects — love. Of course, they are hardly the same in the two cases. What then distinguishes the theological virtues by which we are accustomed to define the life of belief from the corresponding virtues by which Heidegger would have us define the life of thinking?

On these points, the life of belief is precisely what the life of thinking is not: the faith of the Christian believer rests in a God who calls us to a peace that this world alone cannot provide, opening a hope that looks eagerly toward the perfect happiness thus held out to us, and — let us finish the thought — supporting a love by which we find ourselves capable of more than any selfish desire might produce. It would not be difficult to show that Heidegger almost certainly had these Christian definitions in mind, simply by reviewing the many instances when his own position becomes most intelligible precisely when negating them. However, in the present case, for once, it is especially useful to consider something that Heidegger does *not* seem to consider at any serious length: the promise that grounds the faith and structures the hope of the believer. If, unlike what Heidegger has said about attention, hope rests on a well-defined relation with what one hopes for, this is because hope, like faith itself, is already a response to a promise extended by God. The notion itself could hardly be more evident: one believes in salvation and one hopes for salvation only if one first binds oneself to it as a real possibility. This is already enough to yield a rather precise definition of the basic mood (*Grundstimmung, Grundton*) proper to Christian life: a believing Christian lives from a foretaste of salvation or, if one prefers, of perfect happiness, beatitude. It also outlines the Christian mode of being-*in*-the-world but not *of*-the-world in a manner that neatly distinguishes it from Heidegger's sense of being not-at-home: the believing Christian attends not to being as abyss or perhaps as irreducibly pluriform, but to what philosophers call the absolute. The counterpart of the serene errancy of Heidegger's *thinker* must be the joyful foolishness of St. Francis's *pilgrim* (and indeed, the holy fools of which he is only the most memorable figure).[7]

Is it certain that this joy, or even the hope that confidently longs for it, are, as Heidegger might insist, merely the projected satisfaction of deep personal interest? Let us take seriously what every reflective Christian will profess: the promise is offered already before one recognizes and embraces it. Where is this promise encountered? One might just as well ask where the Christian God is truly revealed: in Jesus Christ, who, as God become flesh, is at once the expression of God's love for all people and the way and the means for all people to love God. What can this mean? On one hand, the notion that Jesus Christ incarnates God's love for us illumines the radical nature of what he embodies and preaches; to "love the Lord your God with all your heart, and with all your soul, and with all your mind" (Mt 22:37) is, as the Theologian

---

[7]   On the theological significance of holy fools, the *locus classicus* is J. Saward, *Perfect Fools: Folly for Christ's Sake in Catholic and Orthodox Spirituality* (Oxford: Oxford University Press, 1979). The philosophical, even phenomenological importance of this phenomenon has been suggested first by Stanislas Breton, for example in *The Word and the Cross* (New York: Fordham University Press, 2002), pp. 31–46.

puts it,[8] to love God beyond all sin, which assuredly is also to say, beyond the innate conditions of our mortality. On the other hand, the sense of that extraordinary love thus seems to call for a notion of divine love without which, in this world, it would not be possible. It is to this that the believer entrusts himself. Jesus is first of all the *proposal* of God's love,[9] and it is the defining feature of faith to have accepted this proposal as the *promise* of a fulfillment that thus world alone cannot provide.

This would seem the moment to recall a point of great hermeneutical importance: the Christian believer does not love God as God, or God as such, so much as God insofar as revealed and proposed to us in Jesus Christ. This is less interesting as a matter of Christian distinctiveness — confirmed in its importance by the endless attempts to suppress or evade it — than as a rich definition of the very attitude of Christian faith. I will limit myself to two important and complementary implications.

1. To begin with, if Christian love of God is formed in and through a relation to Jesus Christ, then there is no evading the task of interpreting his flesh and blood presence. Or, more to the point, one must recognize and attend to the role of his physical body in the logic of faith in the Christian God. This is still a matter of simple phenomenology: if it is possible to know Jesus Christ as one among us, then his body is not incidental to his nature as proposal and as promise. Yet the matter is immediately complicated by faith in the ineffable, which opens itself not only to what is available to the senses but also God's withdrawal from them. Theology has its own way of understanding this: God has condescended all the way to becoming an object of the senses. For the later Feuerbach, this is decisive. It is thus a testament to both the glory and the mercy of God that God goes so far as to become available to us even by our senses, which the philosophers would have us consider to be least divine, even least human in us. It is initially and always, though of course not exclusively as sensuous (*sinnliches*) that Jesus appeals to us — initially and always as sensuous that the proposal of divine love elicits our desire and our trust.[10]

2. This is not the right time to develop the manner or degree to which this focus might serve as a useful corrective for an overt, alternative focus on abstract images or ideas, though it may serve the present purpose to at least

---

[8]   Thomas Aquinas, *Summa Theologica*, II–II, q. 44, aa. 4–5.

[9]   Jesus Christ as *proposal* of God's love is a theme of Kierkegaard's *Philosophical Fragments*. I have been alerted to the importance of the idea by J.-Y. Lacoste, "Dieu connaissable comme aimable. Par delà 'foi et raison'" in J.-Y. Lacoste, *La Phénoménalité de Dieu* (Paris: Cerf, 2008), pp. 87–110; English translation by J. Bloechl, in J. Bloechl (ed.), *Christian Thought and Secular Reason. Classical Themes and Modern Developments* forthcoming with the University of Notre Dame Press.

[10]   Cf. L. Feuerbach, *The Essence of Faith According to Luther* (New York: Harper and Row, 1967), pp. 64–5.

note the salient point: whereas there is always a danger that images or ideas alone may prove to have originated in the ego of the believer, in the body of Jesus Christ there opens a way to God that is *immediately* intelligible already before the generation of one's own images for God, and therefore already in the aid of the believer who watches against the idols of the mind.[11] Under these conditions, any claim for the greater appeal of things available to the senses is plainly, if one will permit the word, "existential": in the flesh and blood of Jesus Christ, the love of God becomes meaningful in the most familiar terms possible without, however, becoming strictly or purely comprehensible in our own solely human terms. And so, returning now to an earlier line of reflection, it appears that it would be first in the body of Jesus Christ, physical and historical, that one may encounter the proposal that life is founded *not* solely here in this world where we do not feel entirely at home, that is *not* destined to find its way between accepting that condition and coming to terms with it, and that life might accomplish *more* than the care-taking of being in its present epoch being (though this is no small thing).

3. Is it necessary to state that the intimacy with God made possible in and through Jesus Christ is far from assured even for the faithful? The greater appeal of a God who becomes available to the senses does not go all the way to offering complete or compelling certitude. The conversion proposed in and by Jesus Christ is not immediately matter of substance but first of attitude. A discipline is called for, and thus a perspective is implied. If it is by Jesus' flesh and blood that the proposal of God's love touches a person most deeply, it is by his spirit, his *pneuma*, that that proposal guides faith toward maturity. In what can maturity of faith consist if not progress in opening oneself to the promised advent of salvation? It is by love that one labors at the hope which is instilled in faith — the love embodied and modeled by Jesus Christ: love of God beyond all else, all the way to emptying oneself of every attachment that impedes movement toward God, or if one prefers, impedes openness to the coming of God. For evident reasons, Paul identifies the ready example of Jesus, and not the limited capacity of the faithful, as the necessary assurance for all of this. He develops the matter with characteristic severity: one is either *psychikos*, with life determined solely within this world (one is tempted to say by his "secularity"), or else *pneumatikos*, bound in faith to Jesus Christ and opened by the Spirit of the living God to receive truth and power from an age still to come:

The *psychikos* does not receive the gifts of the Spirit of God, for they are folly to him, and he is not able to understand them because they are spiritually discerned.

---

[11]   This insight lies at the heart of much of Jean-Luc Marion's earlier work: a proper understanding of the crucified Christ shows that it has always and already overcome every form of idolatry.

The *pneumatikos* judges all things, but is himself to be judged by no one. 'For who has known the spirit [*nous*] of the Lord so as to instruct him?' But we have the spirit [*nous*] of Christ. (1 Cor 2:16)

What is perfectly obvious about this passage is also what is essential: Paul is far from claiming that faith can achieve the fullness of Christ's own sense of the living God, but he does direct faith to an identification with Christ's "spirit" — that is, to Christ's attitude and understanding such as he communicates it in his life and preaching. The life of faith, I have suggested, is rooted in an acceptance of Christ as embodiment of proposal. It is nourished, I now hastily add, by an identification with Christ as hermeneutic of promise. The Christ made available even to the senses is also the Christ who remains available to instruct the soul — that is, the Christ who directs us in mind and attitude to the coming of the loving God from beyond all ordinary measure.

Having come at this late point to a conception of a faith that identifies with the *sensus Christi* evoked by Paul in 1 Corinthians 2, it may now be clear that a proper understanding of the Christian mode of being-in-the-world or indeed of the Christian *Grundstimmung* that animates it, depends finally on recognizing that it is love that determines hope rather than vice versa. Let me rehearse the steps: it is the unique and defining appeal of Jesus Christ to *propose* the love of God to us; faith accepts this proposal as a *promise* that that love will be fully realized from beyond the conditions prevailing in this life, whereupon the believer may take up the attitude properly called hope; this faith and this hope are focused by identification with Christ, who does not only express divine love for humanity but also instructs the faithful on its meaning. The same Christ who reveals God's love for us already in his presence among us, continues to reveal that love, and in a consistently identifiable form, in all his words and deeds — that is, in every manifestation of his spirit. It is by love and to love that the Christian is called, and Christ is the possibility of both of these movements at once.

I have been reflecting especially on the matter of eschatology. I have been developing the thesis, no doubt unremarkable for the theologian, that in the encounter and identification with Christ there emerges a specific form of eschatology that is determined by an experience of divine love. With Heidegger so close at hand, it is necessary to be quite precise about this. What must the hopeful Christian know? Surely not that the time of my desire is one and the same with the time of God's mercy. God's mercy comes in its own time, and for that matter — at least if the believer is honest about the modest conditions in which one lives, desires, worships — sometimes not at all. Faith is not promised a salvation or a beatitude one can see actually coming yet also not one whose coming is in complete doubt.[12] That coming is assured by a bond of love to love, and is therefore in some real sense personal. And love for another person, a careful phenomenologist will tell

---

[12]   This is a constant theme of J.L. Chrétien, *The Unforgettable and the Unhoped For* (New York: Fordham University Press, 2002), especially pp. 99–118.

us, must include a trust in the other as he or she truly is in his or her own freedom — that is, it must include a capacity to see and welcome a goodness that does not always answer immediately to one's own desires.

If it is no longer possible to avoid the conclusion, again theologically unremarkable, that Christian hope and thus Christian time is defined specifically by a relation with a personal God, or if one insists, with a God which it makes eminent sense to understand as personal, it is also no longer possible to postpone a return to Heidegger: *to Heidegger*, whose thinker, recall, refuses any ulterior support for his attitude of attention to being. Can the attitude of Christian hope be reduced to a false appeal to some such support? One easily understands the reasoning that might come to this conclusion: from a certain distance, the personal God of love looks all too much like a source of assurances granted, the believer insists, from the benevolent will of a superior being. Yet this is an oversimplification, and Heidegger himself would have been the first to recognize it. Whatever sense of "will" the believer attributes to God is itself an anthropomorphism formulated in response to something immeasurably greater. If identification with Christ has anything in particular to teach a person, it must assuredly include this. And while that can hardly be expected to satisfy the thinker, it does severely qualify any claim that the hope which knows its God will come *one day* therefore possesses that God, as it were, in advance. The operative distinction is still a matter of love, and of the freedom of the beloved: the hopeful Christian believes that God will fulfill his promise, but does not claim either the power to *know* that that will occur or the right to *insist* on it.

This, it seems to me, takes us directly to what is fundamentally at stake in the difference between an eschatology of being and an eschatology of love: the only remaining objection that Heidegger might raise against Christian hope must consist in showing that the very openness that defines it — while perhaps not a matter of power and right — is already evidence of an assumption and thus a pretense that only genuine thinking has been able to do without. The short form of the objection would contend that the true meaning of the openness belonging to hope is to be found in covert desire to be saved from one's own finitude. Even properly understood, hope would thus prove to be an idol of the subject.

And yet there is good reason to give the final word to the Christian believer. Indeed, Heidegger's own objection is of a sort that virtually calls for that possibility. After all, in making the debate a matter of overcoming the idols of our existence, Heidegger surrenders the right to exempt himself from the same interrogation. For the thinker, faith, hope and love are a means by which one permits oneself to say "it is possible that God may raise me from the conditions of this world in which I find myself." What will be the corresponding utterance of a thinker who claims to be free from such idolatry? Inevitably: "I know that no such God can touch me in this way, from beyond this, our finitude." It is not evident to me that this last certainty truly escapes the very charge it imputes to Christianity. Is the confidence that God cannot reach us the necessary passage from idolatry to thoughtful thinking, as Heidegger would have it, or is it, to the contrary, the subtlest idol of all?

PART IV

Phenomenology and Eschatology:
Historical Confluences

Chapter 8

"Hineingehalten in die Nacht": Heidegger's Early Appropriation of Christian Eschatology

Judith E. Tonning

In a letter to Elisabeth Blochmann from 12 September 1929, Martin Heidegger reflects on their impressions of a recent visit to the Benedictine Abbey St. Martin in Beuron, with which Martin was intimately familiar from his university days, when he had often used its library during the vacation. He and Blochmann spent a Sunday or holiday at the abbey, talked about religion, and attended two services: Solemn Mass and Compline.[1] In a previous letter, Heidegger mentioned how deeply impressed he was by the latter. This last and shortest of the community's daily liturgical prayers consists of three Psalms of trust and watchfulness (4, 91 and 134), the hymn *Te lucis ante terminum*, and a short reading from Jeremiah 14:9: "*Tu autem in nobis es, Domine, et nomen sanctum tuum invocatum est super nos; ne derelinquas nos, Domine, Deus noster.*"[2] Several other short verses and prayers, including the *Kyrie eleison* and the *Pater noster*, follow. A blessing by the Abbot and a Marian antiphon close the prayer, after which the monks maintain silence until the morning.[3]

In response to Blochmann's question how he can so "emphatically affirm" a liturgy whose religious foundations he does not share, Heidegger writes on 12 September that the real significance of the liturgy is not narrowly confessional, but philosophical and existential: It is a proclamation of the perpetual "immersion of existence into the night," and the "inner necessity of daily readiness" for this

---

[1]   Letter to Elisabeth Blochmann, in Joachim W. Storck (ed.), *Martin Heidegger/ Elisabeth Blochmann: Briefwechsel 1918–1969* (Marbach: Deutsches Literaturarchiv, 2nd ed., 1990), 32; cited and discussed in Bernd Irlenborn, *Der Ingrimm des Aufruhrs: Heidegger und das Problem des Bösen* (Vienna: Passagen Verlag, 2000), 99–103, and Johannes Schaber, "Te lucis ante terminum: Martin Heidegger und das benediktinische Mönchtum," in *Edith Stein Jahrbuch 8: Das Mönchtum* (Würzburg: Echter Verlag, 2002), 281–94; pp. 281–2.

[2]   "But you are in the midst of us, O Lord, and Your Holy Name is upon us; do not leave us, O Lord, our God" (Author's translation).

[3]   *Breviarium monasticum: Pro omnibus sub regula sanctissimi patris Benedicti militantibus*, vol. 1, 117–21.

night.[4] Only through this inner readiness (which Heidegger regards as almost entirely lost in his day) is an authentic life possible:

> In the prevailing hustle and its successes and results, we are fundamentally misguided in our search. We think that the essential can be produced, and forget that it only grows when we live *wholly*, and that means in the face of night and evil — according to our heart.[5]

The terminology of "night" and Dasein's "immersion" (*Hineingehaltensein*) in it — also used in his inaugural lecture in Freiburg on 24 July 1929, "Was ist Metaphysik?" — entered Heidegger's vocabulary a decade earlier, in his 1917–19 notes on Christian mysticism and his 1920/21 lecture series *Einführung in die Phänomenologie der Religion*.[6] The origin of this terminology in the Christian tradition is eschatological: "the night," for the Psalmists, the Evangelists, Paul, and their theological and literary heirs, is a symbol of the dark and death-filled world, in which the faithful presently find themselves, but to which (as "Sons of Light") they are not connatural. This night, however, will necessarily give way to the dawn of Christ's Coming, for which the faithful are called to watch and pray.

Throughout the 1910s and 1920s, the Christian eschatological tradition decisively shaped Heidegger's developing thought about authenticity, culminating in his vision of Dasein's perpetual, but ordinarily disregarded or forgotten, "immersion" in, or "face-to-facedness" with, "night" or "Nothing." This essay will trace central aspects of this influence in the 1910s, and discuss Heidegger's progressive reworking, in the early 1920s, of the eschatological thought of Paul, Luther and Augustine into an "eschatology without eschaton." I will conclude by raising (without here attempting to answer) the question whether Heidegger's a-theistic eschatology — most thoroughly realized in his paragraphs on "being-unto-death" in *Sein und Zeit*, and in his 1929 inaugural lecture, "Was ist Metaphysik?" — "overcomes" Christian eschatology or remains inadequate to it.

***

---

[4] "So ist ... die Complet [ein] Symbol ... des Hineingehaltenseins der Existenz in die Nacht u. der inneren Notwendigkeit der Bereitschaft für sie"; Storck (ed.), *Martin Heidegger/Elisabeth Blochmann*, 32. All translations from the German are my own.

[5] "Wir sind durch die herrschende Betriebsamkeit u. ihre Erfolge u. Resultate von Grund auf mißleitet in unserem Suchen — , wir wähnen das Wesentliche sei zu verfertigen u. vergessen, daß es nur wächst, wenn wir *ganz* u. d. h. im Angesicht der Nacht u. des Bösen — nach unserem Herzen leben"; loc. cit.

[6] Published in *Phänomenologie des religiösen Lebens*, ed. Matthias Jung, Thomas Regehly, and Claudius Strube (Frankfurt: Klostermann, 1995), 301–37 and 1–156, respectively. (This volume is hereafter cited as *GA* [= Gesamtausgabe] 60.)

Heidegger published his earliest essays and reviews between 1909 and 1911, when he was still training for the Catholic priesthood at the *Collegium Borromaeum* and the Catholic Faculty in Freiburg. Since his grammar school days — influenced, among others, by his rector Dr. Conrad Gröber and by the work of Carl Braig, J. Jørgensen, and F.W. Foerster[7] — he had participated fully in the anti-Modernist rhetoric of post-Vatican I Catholicism, and published his first, strongly polemical pieces in the local ultramontanist newspaper *Heuberger Volksblatt* and the conservative Catholic journals *Allgemeine Rundschau* and *Der Akademiker*.[8] Though the rhetoric of these pieces is largely conventional, the motivating force of Heidegger's condemnation of the Moderns is from the first a characteristic concern for authenticity, anticipating in many details his later censure of *das Man*. Here as later, Heidegger regards "authenticity" as dependent on a persistent willingness to reach beyond one's ordinary, contented, everyday life — a willingness to engage with the fact that Dasein never fully "coincides" with itself, but always exceeds the present *existentiell* realizations of its existential possibilities.[9] However, Heidegger's description of this "transcendence" undergoes a radical shift between these early texts and the more mature writings leading up to *Sein und Zeit*. In the early articles, he regards authenticity as dependent on an acknowledgment of the "truthfulness" (*Wahrhaftigkeit*) of one's "desire ... for completed, completing answers to the final questions of being."[10] In the late 1910s and the 1920s, by contrast,

---

7   See "Lebenslauf (Zur Habilitation 1915)," first published in *GA* 16, 37–9; p. 37. On the ultramontanist Gröber, later Archbishop of Freiburg, see Wilhelm Friedrich Bautz, "Gröber, Conrad," in idem (ed.), *Biographisch-Bibliographisches Kirchenlexikon*, 18 vols. (Hamm: Traugott Bautz Verlag, 1990); vol. 2, cols. 353–4.

8   The *Heuberger Volksblatt*, founded in Heidegger"s hometown Meßkirch in 1899, was a Catholic daily associated with the Baden Centre Party and publicly opposed to the liberal daily *Oberbadischer Grenzbote* (founded 1872). *Der Akademiker* acted as the official organ of "Catholic German Academics" student association (Katholischer Deutscher Akademikerverband). It strongly supported Pius X's interpretation of Vatican I and also attracted such contributors as Romano Guardini and Oswald von Nell-Breuning (see Hugo Ott, *Martin Heidegger: Unterwegs zu seiner Biographie* [Frankfurt: Campus, 1988], 63). The *Allgemeine Rundschau* was a "weekly for politics and culture" edited by the controversial Catholic intellectual Dr. Armin Kausen. It continued from 1904 to the eve of the accession of the NSDAP, and was directed particularly against what the editor perceived as Modernist "immorality in life and art" (Klemens Löffler, "Periodical Literature [Germany]" tr. Douglas J. Potter, in *Catholic Encyclopedia*, vol. 11 [1911], 677–80; p. 679). Heidegger continued to write for these journals until 1913, but the tenor of his contributions (as we shall see) changed after 1910.

9   See *Sein und Zeit* (Tübingen: Max Niemeyer Verlag, 18th ed., 2001), esp. §§40–41; cf. Stephen Mulhall, *Heidegger and Being and Time* (London: Routledge, 2nd ed., 2005), xii and 112.

10   "Das Verlangen ... nach abgeschlossenen, abschließenden Antworten auf die Endfragen des Seins"; "Zur philosophischen Orientierung für Akademiker," *Der Akademiker* vol. 3, no. 5 (March 1911), 66–7; rpt. *GA* 16, 11–14; p. 11. "Zimmermann, O.,

he comes to understand authenticity as dependent precisely on a renunciation of such answers — or, more specifically, of the assumption that such answers could coherently be given in the form in which religious systems must necessarily offer them. This change is reflected in Heidegger's shifting terminology: in the earliest texts, "authenticity" is marked by *Entselbstung* (offering-up of self); in the mature texts, by *Eigentlichkeit* (mine-ness). The trajectory of Heidegger's earliest thought, leading up to this shift, bears closer investigation — an investigation aided by the recent publication, in the *Gesamtausgabe* and by Alfred Denker and others, of a large number of previously unavailable early Heideggerian texts.[11]

Heidegger's earliest known publication, a lyrical short story about the dramatic conversion of a young atheist on All Souls' Day ("Allerseelenstimmungen," November 1909), opens with a description of the urban "Moderns" as unable to hear God's judgment call, sounded by the church bells on All Souls' morning. This inability is rooted in their "desire [for] lust," which they willingly mistake for "intelligence" and "freedom," turning (in a remarkably early allusion to Nietzsche) "into 'blonde beasts' when you dare to doubt the logic of their passions."[12] Heidegger likens this self-delusion to an inability to distinguish the "black, agonising night" from sunlight. His young atheist moves towards conversion when he recognizes the ephemerality of the "wild," "intoxicating" night, and receives the dawning, white light of divine revelation and mercy.

In a May 1910 review of the moral philosopher Friedrich Wilhelm Foerster's essay *Autorität und Freiheit: Betrachtungen zum Kulturproblem der Kirche* (1910), and a number of related articles, Heidegger extends this general criticism to the ideal of scientific liberty and impartiality. He argues that while the Modernists demand "free scientific enquiry and free thought,"[13] true freedom of thought and joy of life require above all a habit of self-discipline. "Truly *free* thinking," in the words of Foerster, "presupposes an heroic act of moral self-liberation."[14] Heidegger echoes

---

S.J., Das Gottesbedürfnis," Review, *Akademische Bonifatius-Korrespondenz*, vol. 26, no. 4 (May 1911), 214; rpt. in *Reden und andere Zeugnisse eines Lebensweges*, ed. Hermann Heidegger (Frankfurt: Klostermann, 2000), 15. (This volume is hereafter cited as *GA* 16.)

[11]   See esp. the "Dokumentationsteil" of Alfred Denker, Hans-Helmuth Gander and Holger Zaborowski (eds), *Heidegger-Jahrbuch I: Heidegger und die Anfänge seines Denkens* (Freiburg: Karl Alber Verlag, 2004), 13–93, containing a number of early articles and letters not previously published or reprinted, as well as contemporary reviews of Heidegger's qualifying thesis *Die Kategorien- und Bedeutungslehre des Duns Scotus* (Tübingen: Mohr Siebeck, 1916). (This volume is hereafter cited as *HJB*.)

[12]   "Und 'blonde Bestien' können sie werden, die 'Herrenmenschen,' wagst du es, an der Logik ihrer Leidenschaften zu zweifeln"; *Heuberger Volksblatt*, 5 November 1909; rpt. in *HJB* 18–21; pp. 18–19.

[13]   "*Per mortem ad vitam*: Gedanken über Jörgensens 'Lebenslüge und Lebenswahrheit,'" *Der Akademiker*, vol. 2, no. 5 (March 1910), 72–3; rpt. in *GA* 16, 3–6; p. 3.

[14]   "Wirklich *freies* Denken setzt einen heroischen Akt der sittlichen Selbstbefreiung voraus"; Foerster, *Autorität und Freiheit*, 28; quoted in Alfred Denker, "Heideggers Lebens-

this conviction almost *verbatim*: "Strict logical thinking that hermetically seals itself off from all affective influences of the emotions, all *truly* presupposition-less scholarly work, requires a certain fund of ethical power, the art of self-collection and self-emptying."[15] Such self-liberation, however, according to Foerster, can only be achieved through obedience to the Catholic Tradition: "Not *I* should judge the highest Tradition from my perspective, but I should learn to evaluate myself in a wholly new way from *its* perspective: That is true emancipation."[16]

Intellectual honesty or objectivity is here coextensive with personal truthfulness or "Wahrhaftigkeit." Church doctrine is authoritative precisely because it contains not only factual truth but also the "light of truth" that enables an authentic life. Heidegger echoes this idea in the conclusion of his Foerster review, borrowing the language of the Judeo-Christian Wisdom tradition — a genre that inflects the classical ideal of knowledge with a specifically moral and spiritual emphasis culminating, for the Christian, in the Incarnation of the "Wisdom of God" (1 Cor 1.24):

> To him who has never set foot on straying paths and has not been blinded by the deceptive dazzle of the modern spirit; who can dare to walk through life in the radiance of truth, in true, deep, well-grounded offering-up of self; to him, this book bears tidings of great joy, and conveys again with startling clarity the high joy of possessing the truth.[17]

***

Heidegger's understanding of authenticity as *"Entselbstung"* towards a truth independently revealed, metaphorically expressed in the conventional terms of a stark dichotomy between "darkness" and "light," was deeply unsettled in the years following Pius X's *motu proprio Sacrorum antistitum*, promulgating the Oath against Modernism, in September 1910. In February 1911, Heidegger was forced

---

und Denkweg 1909–1919," *HJB* 97–122; p. 104.

[15]   "Zum strengen logischen Denken, das sich gegen jeden affektiven Einfluss des Gemüts hermetisch abschliesst, zu jeder *wahrhaft* voraussetzungslosen wissenschaftlichen Arbeit gehört ein gewisser Fond ethischer Kraft, die Kunst der Selbsterraffung und Selbstentäusserung;" "Zur philosophischen Orientierung für Akademiker," *GA* 16, 11.

[16]   "Nicht *ich* soll von mir aus die höchste Tradition richten, sondern ich soll von *ihr* aus mich selber ganz neu beurteilen lernen: das ist wahre Emanzipation"; Foerster, *Autorität und Freiheit*, 58, quoted in Denker, "Denkweg," 104.

[17]   "Wer den Fuß nie auf Irrwege setzte [cf. Ps 1.1; Prov 1.15, 2.18, 4.14] und sich nicht blenden ließ vom trügerischen Schein des modernen Geistes, wer in wahrer, tiefer, wohlbegründeter Entselbstung im Lichtglanz der Wahrheit sich durchs Leben wagen darf [Wis 9.11], dem kündet dieses Buch eine große Freude [Lk 2.10], dem bringt es wieder überraschend klar das hohe Glück des Wahrheitsbesitzes zum Bewußtsein;" *Der Akademiker*, vol. 2, no. 7 (May 1910), 109–10; rpt. in *GA* 16, 7–8; p. 8.

to break off his studies due to a violent outbreak of his nervous heart disease, and only re-entered university in October 1911, now as a student of mathematics and philosophy. In a *curriculum vitae* of 1922, he attributes this change of direction to his "inability" to "take upon himself" the then mandatory Anti-Modernist Oath — a reluctance aroused by his recent discovery of the critical writings of Franz Overbeck and Albert Schweitzer, and the research of the Protestant "history of religion" school (particularly Gunkel, Bousset, Wendland and Reitzenstein).[18] This retrospective account is not entirely reliable; yet there is no doubt that Heidegger's engagement with Overbeck and other Protestant writers in the early 1910s exercised a crucial influence on his theological and philosophical development.[19]

An important aspect of this development was the (re-)discovery of early Christian eschatology through the Protestant scholarship mentioned above. Gunkel and Bousset focused on a tradition-historical interpretation of early Christian apocalyptic material, which they regarded as defining for the shape and direction of primeval Christian belief.[20] This emphasis was shared by Schweitzer, who drew a sharp distinction between early Christian eschatological fervour and the subsequent development of institutionalized liturgical forms, ethical teaching,

---

[18]   This *curriculum vitae* was submitted upon request to Professor Georg Misch, formerly of Marburg and then of Göttingen, in 1922. The passage reads in full: "Das Bestreben, über das Gebotene hinauszusehen, führte mich auf die kritischen Untersuchungen von Franz Overbeck und machte mich überhaupt mit der protestantischen dogmengeschichtlichen Forschung bekannt. Entscheidend wurde für mich, daß die modernen religionsgeschichtlichen Forschungen von Gunkel, Bousset, Wendland und Reitzenstein und die kritischen Arbeiten von Albert Schweitzer in meinen Gesichtskreis kamen. Im Verlauf der ersten Semester hatte mein theologisch-philosophisches Studium eine solche Richtung genommen, daß ich im Frühjahr 1911 auf dem Konvikt austrat und das theologische Studium aufgab, da ich den damals zur ausdrücklichen Forderung erhobenen 'Modernismuseid' nicht auf mich nehmen konnte;" "Vita (1922)," first published in *GA* 16, 41–5; p. 41.

[19]   Heidegger gives a very different account in a *curriculum vitae* submitted to the Catholic Philosophy Department in Freiburg in 1915 as part of his application for a license to teach philosophy; see "Lebenslauf (Zur Habilitation 1915)," first published in *GA* 16, 37–9.

[20]   See esp. Hermann Gunkel, *Schöpfung und Chaos in Urzeit und Endzeit: Eine religionsgeschichtliche Untersuchung über Gen 1 und Apk Joh 21* (Göttingen: Vandenhoeck & Ruprecht, 1895); Wilhelm Bousset, *Der Antichrist in der Überlieferung des Judentums, des Neuen Testaments und der alten Kirche* (Göttingen: Vandenhoeck & Ruprecht, 1895); *Die jüdische Apokalyptik: ihre religionsgeschichtliche Herkunft und ihre Bedeutung für das neue Testament* (Berlin, 1903); *Die Offenbarung Johannis: Kritisch-exegetischer Kommentar über das Neue Testament* (Göttingen: Vandenhoeck & Ruprecht, 3rd ed., 1906).

For the Göttingen "history of religion" school more generally, see W.G. Kümmel, *Das Neue Testament: Geschichte der Erforschung seiner Probleme* (Freiburg: Karl Alber Verlag, 1958), chapter 5; see also Johannes Schaber, "Martin Heideggers 'Herkunft' im Spiegel der Theologie- und Kirchengeschichte des 19. und beginnenden 20. Jahrhunderts," *HJB* 159–84; pp. 180–81.

and theology. In his view, these religious sensibilities were not merely different, but fundamentally incompatible: the second could only arise out of the failure of the first.

In this claim, Schweitzer was preceded by Franz Overbeck, whose *magnum opus Über die Christlichkeit unserer heutigen Theologie* (1873, 2nd edition 1903) Heidegger described in 1970 as "establish[ing] the world-denying expectation of the end as the primary feature of the primordially Christian [*das Urchristliche*]."[21] Here, Overbeck posits an absolute contrast between the ascetic apocalypticism of the earliest Christians, which for him represented a radical rejection of any hope of salvation within temporal existence, and the subsequent secularization (*Verweltlichung*) and historicization (*Vergeschichtlichung*) of Christianity, effected by the development of a Christian theology and (political) establishment. Overbeck's assumption is that any such development is fundamentally misguided, because it assumes the possibility of intellectually analyzing or grounding faith, and of achieving within history what can only be attained by its End.

These inquiries redirected Heidegger's thinking both methodologically and topically. By integrating early Christianity into a wider historical picture of human religions, the Protestant theologians implicitly advanced a conception of religion as an essentially human (rather than a supernatural) phenomenon, and highlighted the irreducible historical dimension of any manifestation of religious beliefs and practices. Further, Overbeck, Schweitzer, and others emphasized the eschatological character of early Christian spirituality as a kind of immediate, intuitive religious experience inherently resistant to ("metaphysical") systematization. While to Schweitzer or Johannes Weiss, this spirituality did not imply an imperative for contemporary Christianity (but was rather an aberration to be left behind), to Overbeck and Heidegger, it constituted the paradigm of "authentic" Christian experience, and as such formed the basis of a radical critique of "metaphysicizing" neo-Scholasticism. The task emerging from these inquiries, for Heidegger, was both a religiosity marked by such aboriginal experience, and a theology appropriate to it. Such a theology, it seemed to him, had to give expression to Christian experience from within, rather than impose upon it an objectivized system which must, by its very nature, thwart the phenomenon it sought to describe.[22] This required, among

---

[21]   In a 1970 "Vorwort" to the 1927 lecture "Phänomenologie und Theologie" published under the same title as *GA* 9, Friedrich-Wilhelm von Herrmann (Frankfurt: Klostermann, 1988), 45–6 (followed by the lecture, 47–78). In the lecture itself, "Christlichkeit" is distinguished from "Christentum" as the proper subject of theology — "das, was Christentum allererst zu einem ursprünglichen geschichtlichen Ereignis werden läßt" (p. 52). Together with Overbeck's *Über die Christlichkeit unserer heutigen Theologie*, Heidegger mentions his friend Nietzsche's *Unzeitgemäße Betrachtungen* as a further "still unseasonable" text, "für die wenigen Denkenden unter den zahllosen Rechners bedeutend, weisend in das sagend, fragend, bildende Verharren vor dem Unsagbaren" (p. 46).

[22]   See esp. the conclusion of Heidegger's qualifying thesis, *Die Kategorien- und Bedeutungslehre des Duns Scotus*, where he calls for a "philosophy of the living spirit, of

other things, a sensitivity to the inherent historicity of religious belief, that is, its determination by the historical situation and development — by the "facticity" — of its practitioners.[23]

***

This developing perspective necessarily distanced Heidegger from the orthodox neo-Scholasticism of his time, which he increasingly outspokenly criticized for its unwillingness to approach philosophical and other problems "as problems".[24] Drawing on his developing phenomenological method, he devoted much of the years 1915 to 1922 to the attempt to formulate a more authentic Christian theology, moving as an *exitus/reditus* from and to "factic life experience."[25] In this effort, Heidegger turned, among others, to the Protestant sensibilities of Luther, Kierkegaard, and Schleiermacher.[26] Particularly in Schleiermacher, he felt that he

---

active love, of reverent piety [*Gottinnigkeit*]," wrought by engagement with the insight that "the living spirit is as such essentially historical spirit in the widest sense of the word" (*GA* 1, 189–411; pp. 407, 410–11).

[23] For Heidegger's development of the term "facticity," see Theodore Kisiel, *The Genesis of Heidegger's Being and Time* (Berkeley: University of California Press, 1995), 496. Heidegger's developing appreciation of history during the years 1911–1913 is chronicled in his *curriculum vitae* of 1915 (first published in *GA* 16, 37–9; p. 39) and in the "Acknowledgements" of his qualifying thesis (*GA* 1, 191).

[24] "Lebenslauf (1915)," *GA* 16, 38; see also "*Kant und Aristoteles* von Charles Sentroul" (review), *Literarische Rundschau für das katholische Deutschland*, vol. 40, no. 7 (1914), cols. 330–32; rpt. in *GA* 1, 49–53; esp. pp. 50, 53.

[25] See esp. *Einleitung in die Phänomenologie der Religion*, *GA* 60, 9–14; and compare his 19 August 1921 letter to Karl Löwith, in which he affirms his commitment to his own "facticity," which involves being "a Christian theo*logian*" ("Drei Briefe Martin Heideggers an Karl Löwith," ed. Hartmut Tietjen; in *Zur philosophischen Aktualität Heideggers*, vol. 2, ed. Dietrich Papenfuss and Otto Pöggeler [Frankfurt: Klostermann, 1990], 27–38; p. 29).

[26] Cf. Heidegger's reminiscence in his 1923 lecture series *Ontologie: Hermeneutik der Faktizität*: "Begleiter im Suchen war der junge Luther und Vorbild Aristoteles, den jener haßte. Stöße gab Kierkegaard, und die Augen hat mir Husserl eingesetzt" (published under the same title as *GA* 63, ed. Käte Bröcker-Oltmanns [Frankfurt: Klostermann, 1988]; here p. 5).

Heidegger began reading Kierkegaard between 1910 and 1914 (see Heidegger's "Antrittsrede" upon election to the Heidelberg *Akademie der Wissenschaften* (1957); rpt. in *Frühe Schriften*, ed. Friedrich-Wilhelm von Herrmann (Frankfurt: Klostermann, 1978), 55–7; p. 56. [This volume is hereafter cited as *GA* 1.]). He read Luther (it now appears) as early as 1908 (see Otto Pöggeler, "Heideggers Luther-Lektüre im Freiburger Theologenkonvikt", *HJB* 185–96). He first engaged with Schleiermacher in depth in 1917, when he held a private lecture entitled "Das Problem des Religiösen bei Schleiermacher" on the occasion of Elfriede Heidegger's birthday, 1 August 1917 (remembered in two letters by Heinrich Ochsner, dated 2 and 5 August 1917; noted in "Schriftenverzeichnis (1909–2004)," compiled by Chris Bremmers, *HJB* 419–598; p. 469).

had found a proto-phenomenological conception of religion as a "disposition" or "form of experience" (*Erlebnisform*), which overcame the traditional conflation of religion with "metaphysics."[27] In 1917, he defined religion (after Schleiermacher's Second Speech on Religion, "Über das Wesen der Religion") as "the specific religiously intentional, emotional [*gefühlsartige*] relation of every experiential content to an infinite whole as [its] originary sense [*Grundsinn*]."[28]

This "infinite whole," for Schleiermacher, is not the God of traditional theism, who is prior to and independent of the world, but that world itself in its infinite variety (for which "God" is one appropriate "auxiliary means of representation"[29]). "Religion" is the recognition of every finite being as a "part," a "cut-out," an "imprint," or a "representation" of that whole, and the consequent liberation of the "believer" to "love the World Spirit and joyfully observe its work."[30] (Thus, Heidegger excerpts, "*History*, in its most proper sense, is the highest object of religion; with [history] it begins and ends."[31])

For Heidegger, one of the most important implications of this conception of religion is the dependence of the object of religious experience on the act of intuition: "*Mysterious* moment of unstructured unity between intuition [*Anschauung*] and feeling," he notes. "[T]he former is nothing without the latter. The noetic moment is itself constitutive of the noematic content [*Gesamtgehalt*] of the experience."[32] This experienced co-originality of *noesis* and *noema* sharply distinguishes authentic religious feeling and its object (which are not transferable or delegable) from conventional religiosity, which, by merely appropriating the

---

[27] "Zu Schleiermachers zweiter Rede 'Über das Wesen der Religion'" (1917), in *Die philosophischen Grundlagen der mittelalterlichen Mystik* (notes towards an ultimately cancelled lecture series by that name, which Heidegger intended to deliver in 1918/19), *GA* 60, 301–37; pp. 319–22.

[28] "Die spezifische religiös intentionale, gefühlsartige Beziehung jedes Erlebnisgehaltes auf ein unendliches Ganzes als Grundsinn ist Religion"; *GA* 60, 322. (*Dasein* here probably still means simply "existence.")

[29] "Alle Begebenheiten in der Welt als Handlungen eines Gottes verstehen, das ist Religion, es drükt ihre Beziehung auf ein unendliches Ganzes aus, aber über das Sein dieses Gottes vor der Welt und außer der Welt grübeln, mag in der Metaphysik gut und nöthig sein, in der Religion wird auch das nur leere Mythologie, eine weitere Ausbildung desjenigen, was nur Hülfsmittel der Darstellung ist"; Friedrich Schleiermacher, *Über die Religion: an die Gebildeten unter ihren Verächtern*, ed. Günter Meckenstock (Berlin: Walter de Gruyter, 2001), 82–3.

[30] Ibid., 80–82, 92.

[31] "*Geschichte* im eigentlichsten Sinne ist der höchste Gegenstand der Religion, mit ihr hebt sie an und endigt mit ihr;" *GA* 60, 322, citing Schleiermacher, *Über die Religion*, 100 (emphasis added by Heidegger).

[32] "*Geheimnisvoller* Augenblick der ungegliederten Einheit von Anschauung und Gefühl, die eine ist ohne das andere nichts. Das noetische Moment ist selbst konstitutiv für den noematischen Gesamtgehalt des Erlebens"; *GA* 60, 322, referring to Schleiermacher, *Über die Religion*, 89–90 (emphasis added by Heidegger).

experiences, thoughts and precepts of others, inherently falls short of what is "living" and "holy."[33]

This co-originality, for Heidegger, is most aboriginally realized in early Christian eschatology. In his 1920/21 lecture series *Einführung in die Phänomenologie der Religion*, in which he seeks to prepare the ground for an "original [or aboriginal] way of approach to the Christian religion,"[34] Heidegger expounds on what he regards as the "factic" centre of Paul's First Epistle to the Thessalonians, namely his exhortation regarding the Coming of Christ in Chapter 5:

> Now concerning the times and the seasons [of Christ's return], brothers and sisters, you do not need to have anything written to you. For you yourselves know very well that the day of the Lord will come like a thief in the night. When they say, "There is peace and security", then sudden destruction will come upon them, as labour pains come upon a pregnant woman, and there will be no escape! But you, beloved, are not in darkness, for that day to surprise you like a thief; for you are all children of light and children of the day; we are not of the night or of darkness. So then, let us not fall asleep as others do, but let us keep awake and sober.[35]

For Heidegger, the phenomenological significance of this passage lies in the fact that Paul's expectation of the *parousia* is not controlled by speculation about the exact time of Christ's return but, on the contrary, effects a complete transformation of his experience of time or temporality (*Zeitlichkeit*) as such. It calls forth a subjective experience of time "without order and fixed spots, which cannot be grasped by any objective notion of time," and thus gives rise to eschatological "affliction" (*Bedrängnis*), characterized by an existential insecurity or uncertainty which arouses an intense and undelegable "watchfulness."[36] Heidegger's gloss on the passage (reconstructed from students' transcripts) is worth quoting in full:

> For the Christian life there is no security; constant insecurity [or uncertainty] is also the characteristic of the basic meaningfuls of factic life. The uncertain is not coincidental, but necessary. This necessity is not logical or merely natural. To see clearly here, we have to recollect our own life and its practice. Those "who speak of peace and safety" ([1 Thess.] 5:3) pour themselves out into that which

---

[33]   *GA* 60, 307, 336. Cf. Schleiermacher, *Über die Religion*, 90.

[34]   "Das Eigentümliche des religionsphänomenologischen Verstehens ist es, das Vorverständnis zu gewinnen für einen ursprünglichen Weg des Zugangs"; *GA* 60, 67.

[35]   1 Thess. 5:1–5. This is itself a central text for the composition of the Benedictine Compline, with which it shares its confrontation with "night." (The post-Vatican II Compline is even more explicitly eschatological than the Roman one; cf. the Scripture readings for Sunday evening [Rev 22.4–5], Monday [1 Thess. 5:9–10], and Thursday [1 Thess. 5:23].) All biblical citations are taken from the *New Revised Standard Version*.

[36]   Einleitung in die Phänomenologie der Religion, *GA* 60, 98 and 104.

life brings their way, occupy themselves with any random tasks of life. They are absorbed by that which life offers; they are in the dark as far as self-knowledge is concerned. The faithful, by contrast, are sons of light and of the day. Paul's answer to the question of the "when" of the *parousia*, then, is the exhortation to watch and be sober. This implies an attack on the enthusiasm, the compulsive speculation, of those who pursue and speculate about questions like that of the "when" of the *parousia*. They are only concerned with the "when," the "what," the objective determination; they have no actual [or authentic] personal interest in it. They remain stuck in the worldly.[37]

In Heidegger's Overbeckian reading, this experience soon gave way in the history of Christianity to dispersion, hustle, and dogmatism. Consequently, Christianity today presents itself most commonly as a closed system of "answers" precluding rather than opening existential uncertainty or questioning.[38]

This reading of the history of Christianity throws light on Heidegger's continuing attraction to the abbey at Beuron. The life of the monks, in its daily self-exposure to the darkness of night, ready to watch and pray, remains for him a testimony to the earliest, authentic Christianity, and thus also a universally meaningful practice. Thus, he writes to Blochmann after their 1929 visit:

> Contemporary Catholicism and everything like it — Protestantism no less — must remain to us a horror. And yet "Beuron," if I may use this as shorthand,

---

[37] "Für das christliche Leben gibt es keine Sicherheit; die ständige Unsicherheit ist auch das Charakteristische für die Grundbedeutendheiten des faktischen Lebens. Das Unsichere ist nicht zufällig, sondern notwendig. Diese Notwendigkeit ist keine logische oder naturnotwendige. Um hier klar zu sehen, muß man sich auf das eigene Leben und dessen Vollzug besinnen. Die, 'welche Friede und Sicherheit sagen' (5:3), geben sich aus an das, was das Leben ihnen bringt, beschäftigen sich mit irgendwelchen Aufgaben des Lebens. Sie sind aufgefangen von dem, was das Leben bietet; sie sind im Dunkel, angesehen auf das Wissen um sich selbst. Die Gläubigen dagegen sind Söhne des Lichtes und des Tages. Die Antwort des Paulus auf die Frage nach dem Wann der *parousia* ist also die Aufforderung, zu wachen und nüchtern zu sein. Hierin liegt eine Spitze gegen den Enthusiasmus, die Grübelsucht derer, die solchen Fragen, wie der nach dem 'Wann' der *parousia*, nachspüren und darüber spekulieren. Sie kümmern sich nur um das 'Wann,' das 'Was,' die objektive Bestimmung; sie haben kein eigentliches persönliches Interesse daran. Sie bleiben im Weltlichen stecken"; *GA* 60, 105.

[38] Thus, Heidegger, asserts in his 1935 lecture series, *Einführung in die Metaphysik*: "Wem z.B. die Bibel göttliche Offenbarung und Wahrheit ist, der hat *vor allem Fragen* der Frage 'Warum ist überhaupt Seiendes und nicht vielmehr Nichts?' schon die Antwort: das Seiende, soweit es nicht Gott selbst ist, ist durch diesen geschaffen" (emphasis added); published under the same title as *GA* 40, ed. Petra Jaeger [Frankfurt: Klostermann, 1983]; here p. 5. Compare Heidegger's famous remark, in a letter to Engelbert Krebs dated 9 January 1919, that certain "epistemological realisations" have made the "*system* of Catholicism" "unacceptable" to him (author's emphasis); cited in Ott, *Martin Heidegger*, 106.

will unfold as the seed of something essential. This is already apparent in your attitude to Compline, which *had* to give you more than Solemn Mass ... Decisive is this elementally forceful *negative*: putting *nothing* in the way of the depth of existence. It is this which we have to concretely learn and *teach*; only thus will we force the turn of the age from the depths.[39]

***

Both texts (from 1920/21 and from 1929) are interested primarily in a *Befindlichkeit* — a "*gestimmtes Sichbefinden*" or intuitive, situated "attunement" within and to the world.[40] Heidegger labels this disposition "eschatological" affliction; yet his etymological understanding of *Befindlichkeit* (influenced by Schleiermacher[41]) as a function precisely of human situatedness *in* a world resists the inclusion of the traditional Christian object of this disposition, namely the anticipated irruption into the world from without of Christ's *parousia*, as a term of the analysis. Consequently, the object of eschatological "care" or "affliction" is no longer (as for Paul) the dark and death-filled world *inflected by* its imminent "solicitation" by Christ, but only that world in its transience.

It is important to note that although Heidegger presents this as a phenomenologically precise representation of Paul's eschatology, which he has stripped only of its heuristic appeal to a specific object of anticipation (the *parousia*), his "phenomenological reduction" in fact causes him to misidentify Paul's basic eschatological *Befindlichkeit*, which is not affliction but hope. Paul offers his discourse on the *parousia* to increase the hope of the faithful (1 Thess. 5:13), and closes it with an appeal, "therefore," to persevere in faith, love and

---

[39] "Der heutige Katholizismus u. all dergleichen, der Protestantismus nicht minder, [muß] uns ein Greuel bleiben — und doch wird 'Beuron' wenn ich es kurz so nenne — als Samenkorn für etwas Wesentliches sich entfalten. Das zeigt schon Ihre Stellung zur Complet, die Ihnen mehr geben *mußte* als das Hochamt.. Entscheidend ist dieses urgewaltige *Negative*: *nichts* in den Weg legen der Tiefe des Daseins. Dies ist es, was wir konkret lernen u. *lehren* müssen; nur so werden wir die Wende des Zeitalters aus der Tiefe erzwingen." Letter from 12 September 1929; in Storck (ed.), *Martin Heidegger/Elisabeth Blochmann*, 33.

[40] See *Sein und Zeit*, §29; "attunement" is Stephen Mulhall's (Cavellian) translation of "*Befindlichkeit*" (see his *Heidegger and Being and Time*, 116). The German *Befinden* (from the verb *sich befinden*), from which *Befindlichkeit* is developed, means both "residing" or "being situated" and "condition" or "disposition."

[41] Theodore Kisiel also cites Schleiermacher's "felt intuition" as a precursor and model of Heidegger's *Befindlichkeit*, which enters his vocabulary in the 1919/20 lecture series *Grundprobleme der Phänomenologie*, a series which grew partly out of his engagement with Schleiermacher and medieval mysticism (compare his 1917–19 notes in *GA* 60, 301–37). In his 1924 lecture series *Grundbegriffe der aristotelischen Philosophie* (published under the same title as *GA* 18, ed. Mark Michalski [Frankfurt: Klostermann, 2002]), Heidegger identifies the term as an equivalent of Aristotle's "*diathesis*." See Kisiel, *Genesis*, 492.

hope (5:8–11).[42] Nor is this misreading accidental. On the contrary, "hope" (alone among the three theological virtues) is entirely absent from Heidegger's writings on the phenomenology of religion. The reason may be that Christian hope, as Alexander Jones puts it, "is to be confident of receiving the eschatological gifts" — in other words, is inherently directed towards that which exceeds the "naturally" human, and is gratuitously bestowed on Dasein by Another.[43] What is more, Paul identifies precisely this hope as the "ownmost" calling (*Beruf*) of the faithful, thus suggesting, paradoxically, that what is most proper to a person is also beyond his or her natural capacity — which is bounded by death — and must be received from Christ through his Resurrection and Return.[44] Heidegger's early phenomenology is fundamentally at odds with such a vision.

This contrast continues to develop in Heidegger's engagement with Augustine and Luther during the following year. In a reading of *Confessiones* X in his 1921 lecture series *Augustinus und der Neuplatonismus*, Heidegger frames Augustine's marveling discovery that the memory exceeds the grasp of the conscious spirit as a proto-phenomenological insight: "'*Penetrale amplum et infinitum*.' All this belongs to myself, and yet I do not grasp [or contain] it myself. The spirit is too narrow to possess itself."[45] For Heidegger, this non-coincidence of the self is at the root of Augustine's central insight into human facticity, "*inquietum est cor nostrum*."[46] It enables and perpetuates *curare* or *Bekümmertsein*, the existential *Befindlichkeit* which he describes as eschatological affliction in the *Einführung in die Phänomenologie der Religion*, and as *Sorge* in *Sein und Zeit*.

However, for Heidegger this "eschatological" affliction is radically compromised by Augustine's actual eschatological vision. For Augustine, one central aspect of the discovery that the memory exceeds the human grasp is that it contains an implicit knowledge of "the happy life" (*vitam beatam*): "Is not the happy life that which all desire, which indeed no one fails to desire? But how have they known about it so as to want it? Where did they see it to love it?"[47] To turn to Christ is to

---

[42] Parallels can be found in all Pauline Epistles. See, among many other examples, Rom 5:2, 8:18–23; 1 Cor 15:19f; Gal 5:5; Eph 1:17f; Col 1:5, 1:27; Titus 1:2, 2:13.

[43] In his note to Rom 5:2 in the *New Jerusalem Bible* (London: Darton, Longman & Todd, 1994), 1873.

[44] See the verses listed above, especially 1 Cor 15:19f. For the most influential formulation of this Christian position, see Thomas Aquinas, *Summa Theologiae*, Ia–IIae q. 114 a. 2 ad 1. (*Beruf* is a favourite Heideggerian term, though he does not, of course, apply it to this context.)

[45] "'*Penetrale amplum et infinitum*.' All das gehört mir selbst, und ich fasse es nicht selbst. Um sich selbst zu haben, ist der Geist zu eng"; *Augustinus und der Neuplatonismus*, first published in *GA* 60, 157–299; p. 182 (commenting on *Confessiones* X. xvii [26]). Cf. Philippe Capelle, "'Katholizismus,' 'Protestantismus,' 'Christentum' und 'Religion' im Denken Martin Heideggers: Tragweite und Abgrenzungen," *HJB* 346–71; p. 362.

[46] *Confessiones* I. i (1).

[47] *Confessiones* X. xx (29).

recognize this *anamnesis* as the presence of God in the human soul; for the happy life is nothing other than enjoyment of God, the *summum bonum*.[48] However, this presence in a sense does not alleviate but only concentrates the restlessness of the human heart, because it is not the presence-at-hand of an object, but the presence "*magis intimum cuilibet*" of the One who is both Maker and Other, at a depth of the believer's heart which (as Augustine has just emphasized) is beyond her own grasp.[49] In other words, it is a perpetual reminder that the believer is not "self-contained," but made in the image of, and in relation to, God: "*fecisti nos ad te*." This implies that she is not even tendentially self-identical, but can only come to herself in the enjoyment of another — "*et inquietum est cor nostrum, donec requiescat in te*."[50]

By contrast to this reading of Augustine's eschatology as distinctively "Christian" — where the human being is ultimately not self-reflexive but "God-reflexive," and therefore can never find rest in herself, but only in an eternal, "face to face" encounter with God[51] — Heidegger regards this eschatology as reducible to Neo-Platonism. For him, Augustine's "beatific vision" is merely a version of the Neo-Platonic notion of *theoria* or *contemplatio*, a static contemplation of God as a metaphysical object.[52] But this passive vision of a God thus understood is inherently incompatible with the living experience of the holy which Heidegger has defined as authentic religion. Specifically, unlike the inherently "unfulfilled" character of human willing (which is always directed to something it "does not yet have" or "not yet is"), contemplation of God as "*das Seiende selbst*" "no longer points beyond itself, [but] is fulfilled in itself."[53] Thus, it betrays the existential experience of eschatological "affliction" or "care" to which both Paul and Augustine himself have testified.

One of the sources of disagreement between Heidegger and Augustine regarding the question of what constitutes human "facticity" (and, consequently, what falls within the purview of phenomenological analysis) is their divergent understanding of the *diastasis* or *distensio* of human existence. Both Heidegger and Augustine (the latter after Plotinus) understand time most importantly as "temporality", that is, as a "distension" of the soul.[54] But for Augustine, this "distension" is caused by

---

[48]   "Gaudere de te, ad te, propter te"; *Confessiones* X. xxii (32); see also X. xxvii (38).

[49]   Thomas Aquinas, *Summa Theologiae*, Ia. q. 8 a. 1 co.; cf. *Confessiones* X. xx (29).

[50]   *Confessiones* I. i (1).

[51]   Cf. *Confessiones* I. v (7), where Augustine quotes 1 Cor 13:12. Cf. also 2 Cor 3:18; Col 3:3–4; 1 John 3:2.

[52]   See *GA* 60, 199–203.

[53]   In the 1925/26 lecture series *Logik. Die Frage nach der Wahrheit*; published under the same title as *GA* 21, ed. Walter Biemel (Frankfurt: Klostermann, 2nd ed., 1995), 122. I owe the reference to *GA* 21 to John van Buren, *The Young Heidegger* (Bloomington: Indiana University Press, 1994), 187.

[54]   See *Sein und Zeit* §§65–71; *Confessiones* XI. xxvi (33). Cf. Plotinus, *Enneads* 3.7.11 (cited in Henry Chadwick (trans. and ed.), *Saint Augustine: Confessions* (Oxford:

the fact that, while we are within time, we strain towards eternity. Echoing Paul's commitment to "stretching forward" (*epekteinomenos*) towards the "prize of the upward call of God in Christ Jesus" (Phil 3:13–14), he writes:

> "Because your mercy is more than lives" (Ps 62:4), see how my life is a distension in several directions. "Your right hand upheld me" (Ps 17:36; 62:9) in my Lord, the Son of man who is mediator between you the One and us the many, who live in a multiplicity of distractions by many things; so "I might apprehend him in whom also I am apprehended" (Phil 3:12–14), and leaving behind the old days I might be gathered to follow the One, "forgetting the past" and moving not towards those future things which are transitory but to "the things which are before" me, not stretched out in distraction but extended in reach, not by being pulled apart but by concentration. So I "pursue the prize of the high calling" where I "may hear the voice of praise" and "contemplate your delight" (Ps 25:7; 26:4) which neither comes nor goes. But now "my years pass in groans" (Ps 30:11) and you, Lord, are my consolation. You are my eternal Father, but I am scattered in times whose order I do not understand. The storms of incoherent events tear to pieces my thoughts, the inmost entrails of my soul, until that day when, purified and molten by the fire of your love, I flow together … into you [*in te confluam*].[55]

For Heidegger, by contrast, *diastasis* is conditioned by *diathesis*: like Schleiermacher's religious feeling (which reveals Dasein as part of the world as an "infinite whole", and thus cannot extend to "the being of God before the world and outside the world"), the "thrown projection" ("*Geworfenheit/Entwurf*") characterizing (authentic) Dasein necessarily moves within the horizons of this world and this time.[56]

Accordingly, for Heidegger, death and not eternal life becomes the authentic object of eschatology. Here, too, he is preceded by Overbeck, with whose work (not coincidentally) he engaged intensely in the early nineteen-twenties. Heidegger particularly approved of Overbeck's "Christian scepticism."[57] This "scepticism" is

---

Oxford University Press, 1992), 240 n. 27).

[55]   *Confessiones* XI. xxix (39); Chadwick's translation. There is no doubt about the Neo-Platonic influence on this passage; nevertheless, it is not reducible to Neo-Platonism. Cf. also Gregory of Nyssa's mystical appropriation of *epektasis*, curiously absent from Heidegger's catena of mystical sources.

[56]   Cf. Schleiermacher, *Über die Religion*, 82. Heidegger does not use the terminology of "*Geworfenheit*" and "*Entwurf*" until *Sein und Zeit*; however, he expresses a similar concept from 1919 onwards. In the 1924 lecture series *Grundbegriffe der aristotelischen Philosophie* (*GA* 18), he thematizes this issue in relation to *Befindlichkeit* (see Kisiel, *Genesis*, 498).

[57]   Hans-Georg Gadamer, Heidegger's student in Marburg, recalls that in the discussion following a guest lecture by Eduard Thurneysen in 1923, Heidegger energetically invoked

expressed most systematically in Overbeck's sense that at the heart of Christianity lies its "eschatology," which he interprets as nothing other than a self-reflexive *memento mori* — in other words, an acknowledgement of the mortality of all things, which must necessarily include even the transience of Christianity itself. "The highest wisdom" of Christianity, Overbeck writes, is found "in [its] eschatology, that is, its *doctrine of the future* or *of death*. For Christianity is nothing other than the wisdom of death. It teaches us exactly what death teaches us, not more nor less."[58]

Heidegger developed the implications of this shift in his reading of Luther. In his notes towards the 1921/22 lecture series *Phänomenologische Interpretationen zu Aristoteles: Einführung in die phänomenologische Forschung*, he notes as a motto for the series a quote from Luther's Lectures on Genesis: "*Statim enim ab utero matris mori incipimus.*"[59] The passage from which this sentence is taken is Luther's commentary on Genesis 3.15, which prophesies the striking of the serpent's head by the "seed of the woman." This prophecy incites Luther to speak about the promise of eternal life:

> This … is the text that made Adam and Eve alive and brought them back from death into the life which they had lost through sin. Nevertheless, the life is hoped for rather than one already possessed. Similarly, Paul also often says (1 Cor 15:31): "Daily we die."[60] Although we do not wish to call the life we live here a death, nevertheless it surely is nothing else than a continuous journey toward death [*perpetuus cursus ad mortem*]. Just as a person infected with a plague has already started to die when the infection has begun, so — because of sin, and

---

Franz Overbeck, whose "radical self-doubt" he related to the "true task of theology", namely to "search for the word which was capable of calling to faith and sustaining in faith"; Gadamer, "Marburger Theologie" (1964), in idem, *Heideggers Wege: Studien zum Spätwerk* (Tübingen: J.C.B. Mohr, 1983), 29–40; p. 29.

[58] "In der christlichen Eschatologie, das heisst seiner *Zukunfts*- oder *Todeslehre*, [liegt die] höchste Weisheit [des Christentums]. Denn etwas anderes als Todesweisheit ist das Christentum nicht. Es lehrt uns dasselbe wie der Tod, nicht mehr noch weniger"; from the unpublished "Kirchenlexikon" (collection of several thousand index cards), index card series entitled "Christentum Eschatologie Allg.", 2–3; quoted in Rudolf Wehrli, *Alter und Tod des Christentums bei Franz Overbeck* (Zürich: Theologischer Verlag, 1977), 229. Cf. Franz Overbeck, *Christentum und Kultur*, ed. C.A. Bernoulli (Darmstadt: Wissenschaftliche Buchgesellschaft, 1963), 297–8.

[59] "Right from our mother's womb we begin to die"; in Martin Luther, *In Genesin Enarrationum*, vol. 42 of *D. Martin Luthers Werke* (Weimar: Hermann Böhlaus, 1883–), p. 146; quoted in Heidegger, *Phänomenologische Interpretationen zu Aristoteles. Einführung in die phänomenologische Forschung*, ed. Walter Bröcker and Käte Bröcker-Oltmanns (Frankfurt: Klostermann, 2nd ed., 1994), 182. (This volume is hereafter cited as *GA* 61.) I owe the source reference to *GA* 61 to van Buren, *The Young Heidegger*, 175.

[60] This proclamation comes in the centre of Paul's great discourse on eschatology (1 Corinthians 15).

death, the punishment for sin — this life can no longer properly be called life
after it has been infected by sin. Right from our mother's womb we begin to
die.[61]

Heidegger's term *Vorlaufen zum Tode*, in *Sein und Zeit* and other texts, is a
direct German translation of Luther's *cursus ad mortem*; but its use depends
on a bracketing of Luther's aetiology of that condition, namely that human life
tends towards death because it is infected with sin, and that Christ's conquest
of sin and death proleptically overcame this predicament, opening the way to
eternal life (which is man's "ownmost" vocation).[62] The human being who is,
like Heidegger's Dasein, no longer inherently directed towards eternity is also
no longer "condemned" to die, but naturally, and at the deepest level, mortal. It is
the paradoxical situation of a being that is utterly contingent, and yet responsible
for its own existence as long as it continues, which becomes the focal point of
Heidegger's "fundamental analysis" in *Sein und Zeit* and contemporary texts.

The culmination of this eschatological trajectory in Heidegger's early thought
are his sections on "being-unto-death" in *Sein und Zeit* (§§46–53) and his 1929
inaugural lecture at Freiburg, "Was ist Metaphysik?"[63] In that lecture, which
incorporates ideas associated with Heidegger's and Blochmann's summer visit
to Beuron, his private description of Compline as "a symbol of the immersion
[*Hineingehaltensein*] of existence into the night" appears as "Being-there means:
immersion [*Hineingehaltenheit*] into the Nothing."[64] Nothingness is revealed to
Dasein in the experience of Angst, in which the totality of that-which-is (*das
Seiende im Ganzen*) "slides" or "slips away" from Dasein.[65] This experience,
paradoxically described as "the bright night of the Nothing of Angst,"[66] is what
first gives rise to "the original openness of that which is as … something that *is*
— i.e. is not nothing."[67] By "soliciting" or "making to tremble" that-which-is in its
totality (to borrow a Derridean term), the Nothing is "the condition of possibility

---

[61]   *Luther's Works, Volume I: Lectures on Genesis Chapters 1–5*, ed. Jaroslav Pelikan,
tr. George V. Schick (Saint Louis: Concordia Publishing House, 1958), 196.

[62]   The alternative term *Sein zum Tode* is, of course, modelled on Kierkegaard's
"sickness unto death" (in the German translation, *Krankheit zum Tode*), to which it bears a
similar relationship as *Vorlaufen zum Tode* to *cursus ad mortem*.

[63]   The date of the visit is uncertain; Rüdiger Safranski's opinion that the lecture (given
on 24 July 1929) is a "paraphrase of the experience at the night prayer in Beuron" must
thus remain speculative (*Ein Meister aus Deutschland: Heidegger und seine Zeit* [Vienna,
1994], 216; cited in Schaber, "Te lucis", 283).

[64]   "Da-sein heißt: Hineingehaltenheit ins Nichts;" *Was ist Metaphysik?* (Bonn:
Friedrich Cohen, 1929); rpt. in *GA* 9, 1–41; p. 35.

[65]   "Das Seiende im Ganzen … entgleitet"; *GA* 9, 34.

[66]   "Die helle Nacht des Nichts der Angst"; loc. cit.

[67]   "In der hellen Nacht des Nichts der Angst ersteht erst die ursprüngliche Offenheit
des Seienden als eines solchen: daß es Seiendes ist — und nicht Nichts"; loc. cit.

of the revealedness, to human Dasein, of that-which-is *as* being [*seiend*]."[68] It is only by countenancing the "solicitation" of the Nothing, and thus allowing itself to experience its own immersion into the Nothing, that Dasein "transcends" that-which-is. But "to transcend" (for Heidegger as for scholastic thought) means not only "to surpass" but also "to gather up": by acknowledging its own "ownmost and deepest finitude,"[69] Dasein also leads all other beings to themselves: "Only in the Nothing of Dasein does that-which-is come to itself according to its ownmost possibility, i.e. in a finite way."[70]

Christian eschatological practice as a conscious "immersion into the night" both resembles and radically diverges from this vision. Christ unfailingly reiterates that because his listeners are chosen and called by God, Angst has become an inadequate gauge of their condition, and must give way to faith, hope and love. As "Sons of Light" and "adopted children of God," their presence within the "night" of corruption is a prophetic presence which identifies the darkness of the world precisely as *night* — a transient state in which the coming dawn is already implicit.[71] In this way, the vigilant faithful transcend and so "gather up" all things — not merely in an acknowledgement of their finitude, but in a more radical acknowledgement that that finitude has itself been "solicited" (here in the double sense of "made to tremble" and "demanded") by its Maker. In other words, they direct the world not to its own merely natural possibility, but to God's promise of renewed life, which the faithful grasp by "partaking" of Christ in faith and hope:

> For the creation waits with eager longing for the revealing of the children of God; for the creation was subjected to futility…in hope that [it] will be set free from its bondage to decay and will obtain the freedom of the glory of the children of God.[72]

This reading of the biblical and liturgical texts, which also claims to be a reading of the phenomenological horizon of the believer, implicitly queries Heidegger's argument, in "Phänomenologie und Theologie" (1927), that phenomenology is logically prior to theology because it lays bare the existential structures of which specifically Christian experiences or concepts are only particular *existentiell* outworkings.[73] For what the believer asserts is precisely an ontological transformation of Dasein's relation to the Nothing or, put differently, an eschatological transformation of the Nothing itself through the divinely enabled

---

[68]　"Das Nichts ist die Ermöglichung der Offenbarkeit des Seienden als eines solchen für das menschliche Dasein"; *GA* 9, 35.

[69]　"Die eigenste und tiefste Endlichkeit"; *GA* 9, 38.

[70]　"Im Nichts des Daseins kommt erst das Seiende im Ganzen seiner eigensten Möglichkeit nach, d.h. in endlicher Weise, zu sich selbst"; *GA* 9, 40.

[71]　Cf., for example, Ps 57:8; Ps 130:6; Ps 134; 1 Thess. 5:6.

[72]　Rom 8:18–22.

[73]　See *GA* 9, 64.

"transcendence" of man. Thus, Compline and 1 Thessalonians do not instantiate but potentially subsume Heidegger's interpretation of "the night."

Heidegger's readings of the Christian tradition are "strong misreadings,"[74] which close to the theologian a simple return to the pre-critical positions echoed in Heidegger's own earliest writings, but compel him or her, in turn, to a more profound re-reading of the texts involved, allowing these texts to respond to and point beyond Heidegger's reductions. The Christian counterposition emerging from this re-reading no doubt requires a rigorous phenomenological account of the experiences central to it, which may, in turn, involve a rethinking of the scope and capacity of the phenomenological method as such. This essay can do no more than to encourage such an endeavor.

---

[74] See Harold Bloom, *The Anxiety of Influence: A Theory of Poetry* (New York: Oxford University Press), 1973.

Chapter 9
Phenomenology and Eschatology in Michel Henry

Jeffrey Hanson

For Michel Henry the question "Can the truth be learned?" is as much an *aporia*[1] as it was for Meno.[2] According to Henry, this question belongs to two separate fields: it is a question for phenomenology inasmuch as the issue of the truth is phenomenology's proper concern, and not just propositional content or quotidian facts about the world but saving truth, the truth that is appropriate to human beings and makes their lives worth living.[3] Though phenomenology on its own is actually unable to grasp the truth understood in this elevated sense. The question "Can the truth be learned?" also belongs to life itself, a domain of experience that is alien to that of phenomenology and to philosophic thought in general, wherein human beings do actually inhabit the truth, that is, what Henry will call the Parousia. So as in Plato's classic formulation, for Henry we can only learn the truth by recognizing we are already in it, but unlike in the *Meno*, this is a realization that cannot be accomplished by philosophy but only within the invisible dynamic of life itself, which remains utterly foreign to, and impenetrable by, thought.

This essay examines Henry's argument that we cannot learn the truth from phenomenology, that phenomenology always comes "too late" as he puts it, to attain the essential truth. Then we will see how, in Henry's work, phenomenology is supplemented by — and even surpassed by — a realized eschatology that discloses

---

[1]   This is not my term but Henry's own, which occurs in the context of the more explicitly theological analogue to the thesis I am exploring here but seems just as appropriate in this context. The passage is from page 93 of *I Am the Truth*, where Henry calls it a phenomenological *aporia* that Christ cannot show himself in the world as Christ. Henry, Michel, *I Am the Truth: Toward a Philosophy of Christianity*, trans. Susan Emmanuel (Stanford: Stanford University Press, 2003). Hereafter *IT*. Page numbers to the French edition are provided in square brackets. Henry, Michel, *C'est moi la vérité: Pour une philosophie du christianisme* (Paris: Seuil, 1996).

[2]   Plato, *Meno*, trans. G.M.A. Grube. Second edition (Indianapolis: Hackett, 1976).

[3]   On the very first page of *I Am the Truth* Henry announces that "what will be in question here is *what Christianity considers as truth* — what kind of truth it offers to people, what it endeavors to communicate to them, not as a theoretical and indifferent truth but as the essential truth that by some mysterious affinity is suitable for them, to the point that it alone is capable of assuring them salvation" (*IT*, 1/[7]).

truth not at the end of a phenomenological process or after the work of reduction, but at the beginning, serving as the presupposition of all philosophic work. Finally we will conclude by entertaining the possibility that Henry's realized eschatology actually endangers one of his other frequent themes, namely the idea that there are two truths, one equivalent to hetero-affective experience of transcendent objects in the world, wherein I experience something else, and the other equivalent to the auto-affective experience of immanent life, wherein I experience myself and nothing other than myself.

In order to come to an understanding of why Henry denies phenomenology the power to grasp essential truth we must examine his account of the nature and limits of phenomenology as a philosophic discourse. Phenomenology is often explained as a method, an approach that seeks the description of phenomena, of what appears to consciousness. Henry maintains however that phenomenology's ostensible concern with method is almost immediately absorbed by its objects, the "what" of our experience, the phenomena that present themselves.[4] Extending a suggestion by Heidegger,[5] Henry points the way, not to the phenomena themselves but to phenomenality, the condition of the phenomena that makes them phenomena and allows them to appear to consciousness, or the "how" of experience as opposed to the "what." This "how" is the true object of phenomenology to Henry. In the essay "Material Phenomenology and Language" he writes: "This object does not designate the set of phenomena, but what makes each phenomenon what it is, that is, the phenomenon's phenomenality considered as such — its appearance, its manifestation, its revelation or yet the truth understood in an originary sense" (*MPL*, 343).

So for Henry phenomenology is not a method of investigating subject matter or pursuing an inquiry into some determined set of phenomena, of things that show themselves to consciousness or even the sum total of every thing that shows itself or could show itself to consciousness. It is instead an inquiry into the showing itself, the revelation or manifestation of phenomena. Phenomenality, as he puts it, "constitutes our access to the phenomenon; in its very phenomenalization, phenomenality opens the path which leads right up to the phenomenon," and

---

4   Henry, Michel, "Material Phenomenology and Language (or, Pathos and Language),"
trans. Leonard Lawlor, *Continental Philosophy Review*, 32.3 (1999): 343–65. Hereafter
MPL. See especially 343–9.

5   Found in the definitive §7 of *Being and Time*. Heidegger, Martin, *Being and Time*,
trans. John Macquarrie and Edward Robinson (New York: Harper & Row, 1962). Hereafter
BT. "The expression 'phenomenology' signifies primarily a *methodological conception*.
This expression does not characterize the what of the objects of philosophical research
as subject-matter, but rather the *how* of that research" (*BT*, 50). Heidegger proceeds to
join rigor of method with the "how" of phenomenological investigation, but for Henry
genuine focus on the "how" of phenomenality precludes method, as classical methodology
is incapable of capturing phenomenality.

for this reason phenomenality is the real object of phenomenology (*MPL*, 344).[6] Phenomenality is "the truth understood in an originary sense," and thus the original, essential truth has nothing to do with the things that show themselves or even the totality of things that show themselves but to do with what makes them showing themselves possible in the first place.[7]

Unfortunately though, according to Henry's analysis, "phenomenology has left this question which is crucial for it in the dark" (*MPL*, 345). The question of the "how" has been eclipsed by the "what" because one particular mode of appearing has become identified with the meaning of all appearance as such. What type of phenomenality is it that has become confused with all phenomenality? "It is the conception of phenomenality which is borrowed from the immediate perception of mundane objects; at the end of the account, it is borrowed from the appearing of the world itself. This disastrous confusion of the appearing of the world with the essence of all conceivable appearing overtakes phenomenology as a whole ..." (*MPL*, 346). So what has happened without exception in the history of phenomenology — and even before, all the way back to ancient Greece (*EM*, 74/[91]) — is that the phenomenalization of phenomena in the world, the way that ordinary objects appear to consciousness, has become tacitly identified with phenomenality as such.

This tendency of phenomenology to conceive of all appearance on the model of the appearance of things in the world to consciousness is what Henry calls "ontological monism,"[8] and we must be clear here that the monism he condemns is not a monism of substance, the idea that there is only one reality (in fact, Henry

---

[6] "Phenomenology is the science of phenomena *in their reality*. Its object is not the ensemble of phenomena with their structures and, as a result, with their specific domains, but the essence of the phenomenon as such." Henry, Michel, *The Essence of Manifestation*, trans. Girard Etzkorn (The Hague: Martinus Nijhoff, 1973), 53/[64]. Hereafter *EM*. Page numbers to the original French edition are provided in square brackets. Henry, Michel. *L'Essence de la manifestation* (Paris: PUF, 1963).

[7] The explicit connection between truth and phenomenality is by no means to be found only in *I Am the Truth* and "Material Phenomenology and Language"; it is established early in Henry's career and recurs continuously in the later works. See *EM* §35. Henry frequently refers to phenomenality in the language of "how" as opposed to the "what" of phenomena. See also the crucial pages of *EM* §8, entitled "The Clarification of the Essence of the Phenomenon: The Central Task of Phenomenology" and arguably readable as a response to *Being and Time* §7: "Phenomenology allows itself to be guided by its object. The 'how' of its approach is subordinate to the 'how' of the reality which it approaches, reality which is the 'how' itself ... Does not the manner in which this reality comes before us regulate the manner with which we receive it and in which we open ourselves to it? Or rather, is not the 'how' of our reception necessarily the same as the 'how' of the arrival of the absolute in us?" (*EM*, 57/[69]). And again: "*How* such a revelation takes place must still be understood. *The revelation of the content of this original receptivity is not to be dissociated from this 'how' since revelation is this 'how' as such*" (*EM*, 251/[312]).

[8] The term is introduced and explained in *EM* §8–16.

arguably endorses a version of this view); what he condemns is a monism of phenomenality, a way of thinking that affirms only one mode of appearance as decisive. The dominant mode of appearance is one of "distance" where a thing "out there" appears by standing out from a transcendent horizon or the backdrop of the world, to consciousness. So the assumption is that I have to form a relationship with something out there in order for it to appear to me, and knowledge consists in this relationship.[9] Ontological monism is a problem though if there are forms of appearance that are unnecessarily excluded by this model.

The most important form of appearance that ontological monism obscures is the mode of appearance of the self to itself, self-awareness or self-consciousness, or even better, what Henry will most frequently call self-affection, not the self's *knowledge* of itself but the self's *feeling* of itself, which is also nothing other than the feeling of, and the truth of, life itself. Western philosophy and science as well traditionally have viewed the appearance of the self to itself as the appearance of just another object to consciousness and in so doing neutered life, rendering abstract and dead the self's feeling of itself in its active and dynamic living.[10] Because of the pervasive influence of ontological monism we are disposed to think that if we are to grasp the meaning of the self, then we must relate ourselves to ourselves at that metaphorical "distance," in the same way we come to know anything else out there in the world, thereby reducing the mystery of life to an inert object.

The Essence of Manifestation makes this point well and suggests a new possibility. "As long as philosophy remains prisoner to the idea of a transcendent horizon of human knowledge, the relationship of the ego to itself cannot be understood except as a particular case of a transcendental relationship of Being-in-the-world ... The problem of the knowledge of self is placed on a completely new basis when in the light of the problematic of immanence this knowledge ceases to be looked upon as a 'relationship'" (*EM*, 45/[57–8]). Henry maintains throughout his career that self-awareness cannot be understood as just another kind of object-awareness in general.

If phenomenology is to discuss phenomenality, essential truth, or self-affection then it must do so in a new way that does not regard self-awareness as analogous to or reducible to our awareness of objects in the world and does not articulate self-affection, the self's feeling of itself, as a kind of relationship between myself as subject of my experience and myself as object of my experience simultaneously. For Henry, the way to do this is to account for the awareness that the self has of itself in terms of sheer immanence. That self-awareness takes place in the sphere of immanence means that the self appears to itself not as a transcendent object out there in the exteriority of the world. "Where there is no transcendence, there is neither horizon nor world. Far from being a universal structure of all manifestation, and consequently, of constituting the essence of the latter, the horizon of the world

---

9   *EM* §9.
10   *IT*, chapter 3.

is, on the contrary, excluded from this essence considered in itself. A comparable exclusion is that of all intramundane reality in general" (*EM*, 281/[349–50]).

If the truth of immanence excludes everything in the world and the world itself and its horizon, against which objects in the world show themselves to us, then how can the truth of immanence be learned? How do we grasp this truth of immanence if it never appears as an object at a distance for us to be aware of? Because this truth does not appear in the world it is in an important sense "invisible"[11] (*EM*, 41/[53]). As an invisible form of phenomenality, then, it is hard to see how we can either know or speak of this essential truth. Before addressing this difficulty it should be noted that he does name this invisible phenomenality and that name is life. Within the immanence of the self he says the essential "... *rejoices concerning itself, has the experience of itself, reveals itself to itself in that which it is, such as it is. That which has the experience of self, that which enjoys itself and is nothing other than this pure enjoyment of itself, than this pure experience of self, is life*" (*EM*, 285/[354]).

To understand what Henry means by the self's experience of itself, the meaning of what he calls life, it is critical to understand the vast difference between the kind of appearance that is appropriate to life, to immanence, to self-awareness, and the kind of appearance that belongs to the world, to transcendence, and to awareness of objects of experience. Truth and affection are equivalent terms, but there are two forms of affection and thus two forms of truth. Henry explains this straightforwardly but at some length in a passage from *I Am the Truth* worth examining in full:

> Affection generally implies a manifestation. If a being of the world affects me, it makes itself felt by me, shows itself to me, gives itself to me, enters into my experience in some way or other. The concept of affection, designating any affection whatever and thus any manifestation (that affects me via a sound that I hear, an object that I see, an odor I smell, or else that affects my mind via an image or any other representation), contrasts sharply with the concept of self-affection. In self-affection what affects me is no longer anything foreign or external to me who am affected, and consequently no object belonging to the world or the world itself. What affects in the case of self-affection is the same as what is affected. But this extraordinary situation in which what affects is the same as what is affected occurs nowhere except within life. And such a situation occurs there absolutely, such that it defines the essence of this life. (*IT*, 105/[133–4]).

---

[11] Henry places this term prominently in the title of section III in *The Essence of Manifestation*: "The Internal Structure and the Problem of Its Phenomenological Determination: The Invisible" (*EM*, 279). See also Zahavi, Dan, "Michel Henry and the Phenomenology of the Invisible," *Continental Philosophy Review* 32.3 (1999): 223–40.

What defines life is that it does not appear by entering into relationship with me from out there in the world. The experience of life is auto-experience, where what is affecting is just the same as what is affected. Life, the experience of self-awareness, as something that is not intuited like an object in the world, in the mode of hetero-affection, as an invisible phenomenon, cannot be known or seen like objects in the world. Because it does not appear in the world and has nothing in common with things in the world, nothing in the world is a clue to life, and nothing in the world provides a path to it. Life "*... can be neither thought nor understood, that which speaks in it has no meaning and cannot receive one. It ... cannot be understood by thought and expects no response from it*" (*EM*, 552/[690–91]). The language of the world, the way we typically talk about things that appear to us, is incapable of addressing or expressing life. We are left then with our *aporia*: Can the truth be learned? or put another way, Where do we hear the words of life? Henry reminds us that it is not foreign to us, not outside, not in the transcendence of the world nor in exteriority but the truth of our immanent being. "We are always already in life; always already life is given to us by giving us to ourselves in the pathos of its Speech" (*MPL*, 364). So perhaps the real question is this: How do I know I am already in life? If words of phenomenology are an example of the human voices that Henry says drown out rather than amplify the words of life, then he is perfectly consistent to conclude as he does that "Material phenomenology neither uncovers nor reveals life. The task of making life advent to itself is really beyond its powers; in order to accomplish this, philosophy truly comes too late" (*MPL*, 364). So one might very well ask based on this conclusion what phenomenology is good for if it does not uncover or reveal life and thus like all other language of the world is incapable of expressing or transmitting essential truth on its own. Henry concludes, "Material phenomenology exercises in complete lucidity the power to think *après coup*, to meditate on life (this power that we have also received). Then it is capable of *founding the phenomenological method by proceeding to its radical critique*" (*MPL*, 364).

So phenomenology cannot reveal the essential truth, but it can "meditate" on it after the fact. Not even Henry's own books can reveal the essential truth; all they are is a set of retrospective meditations on a language of life that no words on paper can articulate. Phenomenology, while animated by the desire for essential truth, though taking as its proper task the exploration of phenomenality itself, can only proceed by critiquing the deficient phenomenologies of the past, those that bought into the error of ontological monism.[12]

---

[12]   It is worth mentioning if only briefly that for Henry theology and even the words of Scripture do not fare any better than phenomenology in delivering the essential truth, despite the fact that later in his career Henry is closely attentive to the message of the Gospels, particularly that of John. If as Henry makes abundantly clear "God is Life — he is the essence of Life, or if one prefers, the essence of Life is God" (*IT*, 27/[40]) then we can know this only "in and through Life itself" (*IT*, 28/[40]). This essential identity is taught by Scripture according to Henry. "The content of Scripture is divine revelation, but this

But this somewhat anticlimactic conclusion is not the end of the story. The relative futility of phenomenology is supplemented in Henry by a realized eschatology: If phenomenology can only make us aware that life is a *fait accompli*, then how can the truth be learned? By acknowledging that I already inhabit the essential, or to use a more properly eschatological term, that the Parousia is not a figure of unimaginable futurity but an immemorial past and an abiding present.

The term "parousia" is a well-known one to students of Scripture, where it appears in the apocalyptic passages of Matthew 24, 2 Peter 3, James 5, and the letters to the Thessalonians, where (laying to one side the plenitude of possible interpretations as to the particulars of these passages) it is clearly yoked with the full revelation or sheer presence of God. The concept notably finds its way into phenomenological discourse via the early studies of primitive Christianity undertaken by Heidegger, the residua of which are detectable in *Being and Time*.[13] Early in *Being and Time* Heidegger associates παρουσία with the history of Being as understood from its origin in the "problematic of Greek ontology" which finds its fundament in an understanding of Being "oriented towards the 'world' or 'Nature' in the widest sense ... in terms of 'time'" (*BT*, 47). Ancient ontology's orientation toward temporality is configured in part by its "treatment of the meaning of Being as παρουσία or ουσία, which signifies, in ontological-temporal terms, 'presence.' Entities are grasped in their Being as 'presence'; this means that they are understood with regard to a definite mode of time — the 'Present'" (*BT*, 47). Henry himself responds to Heidegger's analysis of Greek ontology in terms of Parousia and attempts to exceed that analysis. According to Henry, "The 'world's

---

revelation is made to people in the language that is their own" (*IT*, 217/[271]). As such Scripture is an example of language, of speech, just like any other and just as powerless by itself to evoke the truth of life. We only see that Scripture has for its content divine self-revelation not because we hear its words, which are just more human words, but because we hear a different word, the word of life, the word we hear in and through life, which does not originate with an actual speaker and is not directed to any hearer who exists before or without this word (*IT*, 217/[271]). So like phenomenology, the words of Scripture, theology, are "too late," the exact same two-word charge he laid against phenomenology. Hearing the words of life "has no freedom at all with respect to what it hears" because as living I am unavoidably already thrown into life, immersed in it. Hearing this word is not like receiving a letter from God; it is identification with God's self-revelation, it is revelry in life itself. "It is not the hearing of a call to which the person has license to respond or not. To be able to respond to the call, to hear it in an appropriate listening, but equally to turn away from it — it is always too late for all that" (*IT*, 227/[285]). Too late because the truth is already within. Theological speech, even the speech of the Gospels, is subject to the same limitations as phenomenological speech: to thematize its real object, the essential truth, only after the fact. Both phenomenology and theology are therefore *ad hoc* vocabularies for speaking of the same thing, the truth that cannot be learned, only lived, and more specifically, they speak of the relation between this truth and its opposite, the truth of the world.

[13]   See 190–202 in van Buren, John, *The Young Heidegger: Rumor of the Hidden King* (Bloomington: Indiana University Press, 1994).

truth' is nothing other than this: a self-production of 'outsideness' as the horizon of visibility in and through which every thing can become visible and thus become a 'phenomenon' for us" and like Heidegger, he contends that "Nature as conceived by the Greeks was undoubtedly no different from this self-production of 'outsideness' as the original truth of the world" (*IT*, 17/[27]). Henry couples this self-production with "another name that we know still better: it is called time" (*IT*, 17/[27]). For Henry, however, the problematic nature of time in Greek ontology is not confined to its privileging of the present but pertains to the false, illusory nature of the world itself, which is inextricably joined with time, and time as traditionally understood as a function of transcendental horizonality, in turn, is just as alien to life as the world.[14]

The centrality of the theme of Parousia is indicated by its placement at the very beginning of the large section from *The Essence of Manifestation* entitled "Transcendence and Immanence," which takes as its task the further clarification of the very notion of phenomenality. This essay opened with the claim that in Henry's thinking phenomenology, while motivated by the search for essential truth, is "too late" to grasp the essential and is supplemented by a kind of realized eschatology that does grasp the essential but has nothing therefore to do with philosophy; the hinge of this phenomenological *aporia* runs through what Henry himself designates as the introductory portions (§17–21) of this section. It is no accident that the very final words of §17–21 are: "It is not philosophical knowledge that matters. Philosophy always comes along too late because what is says was at the beginning" (*EM*, 169). The sections that end with these words are devoted to substantiating this claim.

Henry begins §17 with a recapitulation of his conclusions thus far: "The first result of the clarification of the concept of phenomenon, however, was to make evident the necessity of effecting a dissociation between this work of clarification which, on the one hand, defines the task of phenomenology and, on the other hand, the reality of the concept which forms its object, namely, the bursting forth of the essence in the effectiveness of its phenomenal condition" (*EM*, 137). Here we find expressed in different words the same notion that phenomenology, the "work of clarification of the concept of phenomenon," is simultaneously occupied with its task and hopelessly divided from its object. Phenomenology therefore fails on its power to achieve its own animating task.[15] If the essence is attained, it is not thanks to the work of the philosopher. *"The manifestation of Being, far from being able to be a simple consequence of the methodological work of clarification of phenomenology, is rather its condition, as it is the condition of all possible*

---

[14]   Instead, Henry interprets time as a function of immanent self-affection. See *EM* §24 and §52.

[15]   Henry forthrightly calls phenomenology "impotent" throughout §29 of *The Essence of Manifestation*, which he titled "The Making Evident of the Ontological Motif for the Impotence of the Problematic at Building a Phenomenology of the Foundation and Giving a Content to the Idea of the Formal Structure of Autonomy" (*EM*, 218/[268]).

manifestation of any being in general. The manifestation of Being, therefore, does not realize itself in the 'finally' of the accomplished task of phenomenology, but in the 'already' of its primitive condition which, as such, is absolute … 'Already' means not merely as a presupposition for this work itself, but as the absolutely universal condition of all activity of natural consciousness in general" (*EM*, 137/[166]).

Phenomenology rests upon the same foundation as all consciousness and the activities that belong to consciousness, the foundation that consciousness is incapable of itself bringing to consciousness. This foundation Henry here calls "absolute," thereby designating the essential not as the omega point of the philosophic project's arrival but as the alpha of its departure point. Henry articulates this thesis against Heidegger's claim (which Henry calls ambiguous) that "to be able to understand the essential determination of this being through Being, the determining element itself must be understood with sufficient clarity" (*EM*, 137–8/[166]).[16] Like Heidegger, Henry regards Being itself as the question, not beings, and he thinks taking account of some being or group of beings is inadequate to the task of comprehending Being itself. According to Henry's analysis, it is true that Being must be clarified as the determining element of all beings, but he disagrees with Heidegger as to how this is to occur: "The manifestation of Being understood as the determining element of a being … is here interpreted as having to occur in the future" (*EM*, 138/[166]). Hence the dimension of Heidegger's thought that reflects his interpretation of primitive Christian temporality as not merely presence but futurity; the absolute is obtained only in a postponed "to come."

Heidegger's mistake is that this clarification does not *produce* Being in its clarity in the future; Being in its clarity is *assumed* by the work of clarification as a past and ever-present accomplishment. "*The determination of a being by Being, however, realizes itself anteriorly to the understanding of this determination by the philosopher; this determination anterior to all philosophical understanding presupposes, nevertheless, the manifestation of Being insofar as it is actually nothing other than this manifestation itself*" (*EM*, 138/[166]). Like self-affection as described in the long passage from *I Am the Truth* cited above, the manifestation of Being manifests itself and nothing but itself, an auto-disclosure presupposed by all other disclosure, and while all manifestation rests on self-manifestation, the two orders remain completely alien to each other. "The determination of a being by Being expresses the dependence of that which appears with regard to the act of appearing considered in and for itself. In pure appearing, the determination finds the origin of its destiny: this destiny, which is its own, is foreign to it" (*EM*, 138/[167]).

Call this sentence another way of phrasing the phenomenological *aporia*. Phenomena assume phenomenality, but they have nothing to do with it. Phenomenality cannot appear in the world of phenomena. Life is not in the

---

[16]   Quoted from 230 in Heidegger, Martin, *Kant and the Problem of Metaphysics*, trans. James S. Churchill (Bloomington: Indiana University Press, 1960).

world. The only solution to the *aporia* then is to contend that *consciousness is not in the world either*. "That its own proper destiny is foreign to the content of the determination does not mean that it is also foreign to natural consciousness which lives in the presence of this content ... *Being manifests itself to natural consciousness*" (*EM*, 138/[167]).[17] Because Being, the essential truth, does not have to venture into the world to be grasped, its comprehension need not be postponed, since natural consciousness already dwells in the self-manifestation of being presupposed by philosophy, and this dwelling is the Parousia. "The absoluteness of the absolute is the Parousia. Once it has entered into relationship with a being, natural consciousness must maintain itself in the Parousia; it is already absolute knowledge ..." (*EM*, 138/[167]).

Several qualifications are in order, particularly as Henry's account of the Parousia unfolds against the backdrop of both Hegel's Introduction to *The Phenomenology of Spirit* and Heidegger's commentary thereupon, "Hegel's Concept of Experience,"[18] both of which he references throughout these pages. Given this context, Henry must surely intend to make an amusing inside joke when he quips, "This is why there can be no introduction to phenomenology" — because "*Consciousness is itself and as such the manifestation of Being*. For this reason, it does not have to be drawn to the place wherein this manifestation takes place" (*EM*, 139/[168]). There can be no introduction to phenomenology because the work of phenomenology is already over before it has begun. The first feature of the Parousia to note is that it is original, and it requires no special effort on the part of consciousness to maintain itself therein. "The habit whereby natural consciousness remains in the Parousia is not an acquired habit, rather it designates the *immediate* condition of consciousness" (*EM*, 139/[168]). Unlike in Hegel's realized eschatology,[19] for Henry there is no dialectical progression required to arrive at the absolute, for consciousness to realize itself (*EM*, 139–40/[169]).

---

[17]   The same contention is presented in *I Am the Truth*, in the same passage cited above where Henry calls this structure a phenomenological *aporia*. "The phenomenological aporia whereby it is impossible for Christ to show himself in the world *as Christ*, as the Word of God, destroys any possibility of man having access to Christ, of knowing him as Christ and thus knowing God, as long as man himself continues to be understood as a Being of this world" (*IT*, 93/[119]). A fascinating study could be undertaken by placing this notion of man as excluded from the horizon of being-in-the-world with Jean-Yves Lacoste's similar line of argument in *Experience and the Absolute: Disputed Questions on the Humanity of Man*, trans. Mark Raftery-Skehan (New York: Fordham University Press, 2004). See especially chapter 2.

[18]   Heidegger, Martin, "Hegel's Concept of Experience" in *Off the Beaten Track*, trans. and ed. Julian Young and Kenneth Haynes (Cambridge: Cambridge University Press, 2002).

[19]   On the appropriateness of applying this term to Hegel, see chapters 2A and 2B in Westphal, Merold, *History and Truth in Hegel's* Phenomenology, third edition (Bloomington: Indiana University Press, 1998); and "Laughing at Hegel" in *Overcoming Onto-Theology: Toward a Postmodern Christian Faith* (New York: Fordham University Press, 2001).

Second, while dwelling in the Parousia is categorized by Henry as knowledge, it is a fundamental knowing that has nothing in common with hetero-affective experience of things in the world, the structure of ontological monism. Consequently, the Parousia belongs not to the world but to life, so again, unlike in Hegel, the achievement of the Parousia is not the outcome of a speculative exercise, the apotheosis of Reason, but the feeling of life. "Far from arising merely in a determined mode of the life of consciousness, the Parousia constitutes the very essence of this life and, as such, the condition of all determinations which this life is capable of assuming. The Parousia is not the fact of true knowledge; it is its presupposition, just as it is the presupposition of the non-true knowledge of natural consciousness which limits itself to a being" (*EM*, 144/[174]).

As the presupposition of all activity, including all philosophical activity, and of all knowledge, both the genuine knowledge that belongs to life's auto-affectivity and the "non-true knowledge" that belongs to hetero-affectivity, the Parousia marks the division in Henry's thought between the two forms of truth referred to above. The mode of disclosure exercised by consciousness in the world is entirely different from, though always already wholly dependent upon, the self-manifestation of Being, that is, the Parousia. It is for this reason that Henry argues for two different forms of truth. Being does indeed show itself, the essential truth can be known, but this happens in a way foreign to the ordinary mode of hetero-affectivity. "That natural knowledge does not attend to Being, therefore, means *not that Being does not manifest itself to natural consciousness in this original self-manifestation which is the Parousia itself*, but simply that it does not manifest itself to this consciousness under the form of an object given in the act of grasping" (*EM*, 147/[178]).

We can see on the basis of this examination that for Henry the Parousia is an effective presence that makes of eschatology not a mere complement to phenomenology but its inauguration and fulfillment.[20] Ultimately though one might wonder whether this structure undercuts Henry's frequent insistence that there are two truths, one of life, the Parousia, the truth of immanence on the one hand and one of transcendence, the world, on the other. Despite this distinction, it

---

[20]   A stimulating point of contrast is provided to this point by Jean-Yves Lacoste, who repeatedly insists that despite the fact that man's being exceeds the strictures of being-in-the-world, while inhabiting the world man nevertheless does not experience the Parousia. See *Experience and the Absolute*, 143: "Liturgy imitates the Parousia while acknowledging the nonparousiacal presence of God, and no experience that necessarily figures in liturgical grammar will annul what separates us, in the world, from the Parousia" and especially 90: "If the truth be known, the concept of the Parousia can reveal itself to be singularly inadequate to think what unites the originary and the *eschaton* — the noninterpositioning of 'world' or 'earth' between God and me — and what separates them — the infinite journey that marks the relation of man to an always greater God, and which prevents us from conceiving the eschatological reality of this relation as [the possibility] of enjoying possession of an omnipresence in which God would cease to dwell in an 'inaccessible light.'" See also 58, 61–2, 68, and 84–5.

is arguable that for Henry there is not really an opposition between two truths but only one truth deserving of the name. Phenomenology can only fail to address the truth if it is in fact totally unrelated to the truth of eschatology, which it turns out, is the only truth that matters. There is thus only one thing to know, the essential itself, which is disclosed by the Parousia. There is no other truth, but if there is only one truth to know, then Henry's theory of two truths, the truth of life and the truth of the world, is in question. If the essential is the only truth, disclosed in the Parousia, then it is not in competition with another truth at all. Anything else claiming to be truth can only be a sham, an illusion, and it is comparatively rarely that Henry underscores this.

In Chapter 11 of *I Am the Truth*, entitled "The Paradoxes of Christianity," Henry returns to his familiar theme of two truths, according to which, as he puts it, "Everything is double" (*IT*, 195/[245]): On the one hand, there is life in its self-affecting truth, and on the other is the truth of the world. "[B]ut if what is double — what is offered to us in a double aspect — is in itself one and the same reality, then one of its aspects must be merely an appearance, an image, a copy of reality, but not that reality itself — precisely its double. Two eventualities are then offered: that this double, this exterior appearance, corresponds to reality, or that it does not correspond to it. In the second case, appearance is a trap" (*IT*, 195[245]). So far from there being a legitimate truth of the world in paradoxical tension with the truth of life, there is in fact only the truth of life, and therefore the truth of the world, which does not correspond to reality, the one and only reality of life, is a trap, or as he goes on to say in the following two pages, "counterfeit" (*IT*, 197/[247]) "flimsy and empty" (*IT*, 197/[247]) and a "simple appearance" (*IT*, 196/[247]). Surely Henry is most consistent when he writes not that there are two truths but when he writes, "reality is real only once" (*IT*, 196/[246]).

This conclusion truly explains why phenomenology as "truth" is always too late to disclose the essential. Reality is real only once, and the Parousia excludes everything foreign to it. It is not then the case that phenomenology is too late because it offers only a partial or belated truth; its truth is truth in name only. Recall that the intuition that motivated much of Henry's work was his rejection of what he called ontological monism, the implicit supposition that only one kind of appearance is the meaning of all appearance. Has not Henry himself come dangerously close to enshrining a kind of monism, only now with the terms reversed,[21] privileging the Parousia and its self-affective mode of phenomenality and its truth, over the phenomena and their pseudo-truth? This criticism is bolstered by two considerations: first, Henry characterizes the Parousia not merely as a mode of disclosure, a "how," but is itself a content, a "what"; second, Henry

---

[21]   This possibility is suggested by the "ethical" principles outlined in chapter 10 of *I Am the Truth* and referred to at *IT* 197/[247].

repeatedly calls both of these contents "truths" rather than designating them by different terms.[22]

Consider this statement from *I Am the Truth*: "What, then, is a truth that differs in no way from what is true? If truth is manifestation grasped in its phenomenological purity — phenomenality and not the phenomenon — then what is phenomenalized is phenomenality itself. The phenomenalization of phenomenality itself is a pure phenomenological matter, a substance whose whole essence is to appear" (*IT*, 25/[36]). Henry claims that phenomenality is not just the condition of the appearance of phenomena, not merely the "how" that underpins the "what" of phenomena, but here he claims that it is itself a "matter," a "substance whose whole essence is to appear" (*IT*, 25/[36]). The seeds of this striking conclusion were already sown in *The Essence of Manifestation*: "The revelation of the content of this original receptivity is not to be dissociated from this 'how' since revelation is this 'how' as such" (*EM*, 251/[312]). Phenomenality is not just the way phenomena phenomenalize themselves, it is itself a phenomenon. Finally, from "Material Phenomenology and Language": "Pathos designates the mode of phenomenalization according to which life phenomenalizes in its originary self-revelation ... In this pathos, the 'how' of revelation becomes its content; its *Wie* is a *Was*" (*MPL*, 353).[23]

A tension thus emerges between Henry's frequent references to two truths and his contention that phenomenality is itself a substance or content. Henry devotes two separate chapters to the truth of the world and to the opposed truth of Christianity at the very beginning of *I Am the Truth*. The opening words of the former chapter are "There are many kinds of truths" (*IT*, 12/[21]). Almost immediately thereafter, however, he qualifies this generalization with the words, "If it is in the very essence of truth — in the sense of a pure manifestation, of a pure revelation — that the fact of self-showing consists, then everything that shows itself is true only in a secondary sense" (*IT*, 13/[22]). The confusing aspect of these competing formulations is that both are called "truths," from the most pedestrian contingent truth of what the weather is like and necessary truths of geometry (*IT*,

---

[22]   It might be clearer and more consistent for example to call the empty, illusory substance of the world "truth" if one wanted thereby to grant it some relative legitimacy (or condemn it with a more disparaging term) and call the essential truth of life something else to illustrate its supremacy over the true and its fundamentally different character.

[23]   Numerous other passages could also be cited: "... how is the essence of manifestation capable of receiving this ontological content which is not different from it; how can it represent it to itself, not as a foreign reality, but as this reality which it itself is? Precisely because to receive such a content constituted by it means that the essence represents the content to itself ..." (*EM*, 237/[294]). Again: "If the manifestation of the essence, in turn finds its possibility in the return to itself of the act of appearing, it is because the concept of auto-affection is neither formal nor empty, but rather yields as content that which assures the ultimate and final possibility of such a manifestation" (*EM*, 234–5/[290]).

12/[21]) to the self-manifestation that is as "indifferent to what shows itself as is the light to what it illuminates" (*IT*, 13/[22]).

But only ten pages later, Henry seems to associate the name "truth" only with the latter, decisive truth of life: "The fact of self-showing, appearing, manifestation are pure phenomenological concepts precisely because they designate phenomenality itself and nothing else. Other equivalent terms, already mentioned because they are those of Christianity, are 'apparition,' 'truth,' and 'revelation'" (*IT*, 23/[34–5]). The more consistent claim that Henry could or should be making[24] then is that only self-manifestation is the truth. In the following passage Henry actually unites the contention that self-manifestation is a content in its own right with the stronger argument that it is the only content that matters: "The world, too, reveals and makes manifest, but within the 'outside,' casting a thing outside itself, as we have seen, in such a way that it never shows itself as other, different, external, in its setting of radical exteriority that is the 'outside-itself' of the world. Hence it is doubly exterior: external to the power that makes it manifest — and this is where the contrast between Truth and what it makes true intervenes — and also exterior to itself. It manifests itself only in its own exteriority to itself, emptied of its own substance, unreal ..." (*IT*, 29/[42]). The capitalization of "Truth" in this crucial sentence is surely noteworthy and is original in the French.[25] As this excerpt shows, self-manifestation is not merely a means of appearance but is a content, not just a "how" but also a "what" that produces the untruth of the world precisely by evacuation of that content, an evacuation that generates a "truth" that is ultimately unreal. If the "how" of phenomenality excludes the "what," as it is clear that it does, or if the "how" is itself a "what," then there is only one eschatological truth that matters.

---

[24]   Naturally I disregard the question of whether this change in formulation would be an overall improvement or whether this change would precipitate its own further problems.

[25]   See Henry, *C'est moi la vérité*, p. 42. In this work Henry capitalizes "Truth" when he is referring to the truth of life, a move that supports my reading and suggests an intensification of his feeling that the world is not just incapable of grounding itself but is false and illusory toward the end of his career.

Chapter 10
"Without World":
Eschatology in Michel Henry

Kevin Hart

Michel Henry subtitles, *C'est moi la vérité* (1996), the first book of his trilogy on Christianity, "pour une philosophie du christianisme."[1] In its most general form, the first question I want to ask is simply this: What does "philosophy of Christianity" mean here? And the second question is just as straightforward: Is this philosophy of Christianity persuasive?

What Henry proposes is not Augustinian in inspiration; it does not follow the rhythm of believing in order to understand and understanding in order to believe.[2] Nor does it promote a sense of philosophia as ascesis or self-mastery. Christianity is a practice, he says, and yet the philosophy of Christianity is not itself a guide to spiritual exercises.[3] Nor does Henry develop a "Christian philosophy" such as Etienne Gilson finds when defending the thought of the Middle Ages against the attacks of Emile Bréhier, and as Jacques Maritain, Maurice Blondel and Henri de Lubac support to varying extents and in their own ways.[4] Christian philosophy requires the preservation of the two formal orders of reason and revelation. Yet Henry discounts all natural theologies and, at least in *C'est moi la vérité*, hardly can be said to accept dogma as regulative.[5] The main thrust of his later

---

[1]   I wish to thank Jean-Yves Lacoste, Claude Romano and Alain Toumayan for comments on an earlier version of this essay.

See Michel Henry, *I am the Truth: Toward a Philosophy of Christianity*, trans. Susan Emanuel (Stanford: Stanford University Press, 2003).

[2]   See St. Augustine, Letter 120, *Letters, 100–155*, ed. Roland J. Teske (Hyde Park, NY: New City Press, 2002), 131.

[3]   See Henry, "Christianisme et phénoménologie," *Auto-donation: Entretiens et conférences* (Paris: Beauchesne, 2004), 139.

[4]   Emile Bréhier presented three lectures entitled "Y-a-t-il une Philosophie Chrétienne?" in Brussels in 1928, which were published in the *Revue de Métaphysique et de Morale*, 38:2 (1931), 133–62. Etienne Gilson replied in a discussion that he inaugurated at the Société française de philosophie. See "La notion de philosophie chrétienne," *Bulletin de la Société française de philosophie*, 31 (1931), 37–85.

[5]   See Gilson, *The Spirit of Medieval Philosophy*, trans. A.H.C. Downes (New York: Charles Scribner's Sons, 1936), ch. 1. On the question of Christian philosophy in general, from patristic times to the twentieth century, see Maurice Nédoncelle, *Is There a Christian*

thought is to take New Testament revelation as essentially indistinguishable from phenomenological manifestation. In hearing that claim we doubtless recall Henry Duméry who argued that "the life of Christ is theophany in action because it 'shows' itself."[6] At the same time one must acknowledge Henry's originality in arguing that phenomenology and Christianity are both to be understood as the self-revelation of life. Only if one figures Henry's trilogy as depending on the historical existence of the Christian faith would Gilson's expression be at all appropriate. And yet it is precisely the Christian faith in its historical development that Henry brackets.

If Henry's understanding of "a philosophy of Christianity" does not accord with what "Christian philosophy" describes, nor does his work contribute to the project that Gilson inaugurates with the same words. There is no attention given to the metaphysics of *esse*, the immortality of the soul (as an incorporeal substance), let alone any interest shown in the writings of St Thomas Aquinas. For Henry, all these things, including those that Aquinas discusses, occur in the sphere of ecstatic intentionality whereas his task is to elucidate an enstatic, non-intentional phenomenology and to establish its priority with respect to intentional consciousness. If Christian philosophy is a "round square," as Heidegger says, Henry has no brief to straighten it out by viewing it from another perspective or by doing it in the order of exercise in preference to the order of specification.[7] Finally, nor is Henry's philosophy of Christianity a critical inspection of the faith that seeks to strip away doctrinal and ritual accretions, to downplay revelation and determine the faith's true center in ethics, such as one finds in Kant's *Religion within the Limits of Reason Alone* (1793) and those from Fichte to Derrida who follow him, closely or at a distance.[8] In fact Henry is resolutely anti-Kantian both

---

Philosophy?, trans. Illtyd Trethowan (New York: Hawthorn Books, 1960). For the debate of 1931, also see Alexandre Renard, *La Querelle sur la possibilité de la philosophie chrétienne: essai documentaire et critique* (Paris: Ecole et Collège, 1941). On Christian philosophy accepting dogma as regulative, see Gilson, *Christian Philosophy: An Introduction*, trans. Armand Mauer (Toronto: Pontifical Institute of Medieval Studies, 1993).

   [6] See Henry Duméry, *Phenomenology and Religion: Structures of the Christian Initiation*, trans. Paul Barrett, Hermeneutics, vol. 5 (Los Angeles: University of California Press, 1975), 76, and Henry, *I am the Truth*, 23, and *Incarnation: Une philosophie de la chair* (Paris: Seuil, 2000), 37.

   [7] See Martin Heidegger, *An Introduction to Metaphysics*, trans. Ralph Manheim (New York: Anchor Books, 1961), 6. Also see Jacques Maritain, *An Essay on Christian Philosophy*, trans. Edward H. Flannery (New York: Philosophical Library, 1955), 11.

   [8] Fichte's *Versuch einer Kritik aller Offenbarung* appeared in 1792, a year before Kant's *Die Religion innerhalb der Grenzen der blossen Vernunft* (1793), yet it was so indebted to Kant's critical philosophy as to be taken by its first readers to be by Kant. Jacques Derrida formulates his late philosophy of religion with respect to *Die Religion*. See his "Faith and Knowledge: The Two Sources of 'Religion' at the Limits of Reason Alone," trans. Samuel Weber, in Derrida and Gianni Vattimo (eds), *Religion* (Cambridge: Polity Press, 1998), 1–78.

in his account of the subject and in his prizing of revelation over ethics. As he says, "Everywhere in Christianity, the ethical is subordinated to the order of things."[9]

It is this "order of things" that Henry attempts to describe, and in doing so to bring forth his philosophy of Christianity and advocate its superiority over earlier attempts to link philosophy and faith. Description and philosophy converge here, for the thought at issue is a phenomenology, albeit a very unusual one. Three things about it need to be remarked at the outset. First, description is restricted on principle to what shows itself in its appearing. Second, for Henry appearing is not only self-appearing but also appearing to the self. And third, this self-manifestation is what Henry calls "life." The word "life" is used in an unusual sense, and since it is central to Henry's philosophy in general, as well as his philosophy of Christianity, I will take some time to clarify it.

First of all, "life" for Henry is not to be understood as *bios*, or able to be expressed in terms of a physical-chemical process. (An autobiography for Henry, assuming we can bracket the reference to *bios*, would be a record of invisible moments of joy and suffering, and would doubtless resemble a series of lyric poems more than a prose narrative. Biography would be strictly impossible for him, for nothing can be said about another's life.[10]) Neither is this life as Aristotle conceives it in *De Anima* 413a–b or *Nichomachean Ethics* 1098a where there are three types of life (plant, animal and human). Nor is this life as Kant stipulates it, "the faculty of a being by which it acts according to the laws of the faculty of desire." Life, for Henry, is primary, and does not constitute "the reality of the objects" that are posited by the ideas of the faculty of desire.[11] And nor is Hegel at the root of Henry's concept. "*Life*," Hegel says, "is the highest to which nature drives in its determinate being, but as merely natural Idea, life is submerged in the irrationality of externality …".[12] For Henry, life contrasts radically with externality, and it has nothing to do with biology. Rather, life is unitary, considered only in terms of humans and God — there is no talk of animals or plants — and is to be distinguished unequivocally from every worldly category. Henry calls *la vie* — his *maître-mot* — absolute phenomenological life, by which he means the unconditioned inner manifestation of non-intentional states, both what reveals and what is invisibly revealed, "that which is moved from within by itself," as Meister Eckhart puts it.[13]

---

[9]   Henry, *I am the Truth*, 26

[10]   See Henry, "Indications biographiques: Entretien avec Roland Vaschalde," *Michel Henry, l'épreuve de la vie*, eds Alain David and Jean Greisch (Paris: Cerf, 2001), 489.

[11]   Kant, *Critique of Practical Reason*, trans. and intro. Lewis White Beck (Indianapolis: Bobbs-Merrill Educational Publishing, 1956), 9, n. 7.

[12]   G.W.F. Hegel, *Philosophy of Nature*, trans. and intro. Michael John Petry, 3 vols (New York: Humanities Press, 1970), I, 209.

[13]   Meister Eckhart, *Sermons and Treatises*, trans. and ed. M.O'C. Walshe, 3 vols (Longmead, Dorset: Element Books, 1979), I, 111.

Attending to what abides within the subject, Henry's thought is governed in precisely the same measure by the preposition "without." His philosophy turns on immanence without transcendence, of life "without world" and without any relation between them; it is, as he says, "without thought, without representation, without imagination, without perception, without conception, without being preceded in any way, and without wanting, without showing itself in any world."[14] Far from being a figure of poverty, though, "without" functions for Henry as a secret abundance, as the very essence of Christianity, as new life in Christ, life that "knows itself without knowing itself" (240), consequent upon the birth of "Self without Self, without image of itself ... Self without face" (231). If we think that we are dealing with another *Lebensphilosophie* we will be mistaken. This thought is not a pendant to Friedrich Schlegel's *Vorlesungen über die Philosophie des Lebens* (1827) or a continuation of the Neo-Kantian understanding of "la vie intérieure," or kin to Henri Bergson's or Jean-Marie Guyau's vitalism. Nor is it continuous with Hans Jonas's *The Phenomenon of Life* (1966): there is neither a "philosophy of the organism" offered by Henry nor a "philosophy of mind," let alone an interlacing of the two.[15] If Henry's thought looks back to the "expérience intérieure" of François-Pierre Maine de Biran, it has nothing to do with the "expérience intérieure" of Georges Bataille, which, far from being a state of immanence, is an anguished exposure to exteriority.[16] As Henry tells us himself, his thought is best approached as a reversal of Husserlian and Heideggerian phenomenology: the phenomenon is sought by way of originary phenomenality rather than by looking for its appearing within horizons supplied by intentionality.[17] For Henry, it is the self-revelation of life that supplies the abiding ground of phenomenology, thereby making non-intentional analysis anterior to intentional analysis.

Thus stated we have what is by any reckoning an original philosophical system: a phenomenology that denies the primacy of intentionality; an understanding of the flesh that is wholly subjective; an account of subjectivity that makes it an object, rather than a supposition, of phenomenology; a non-classical dualism; and a shift of attention from transcendence to immanence that puts itself in the service of theism, not atheism. The position is reached by an immanent critique

---

[14]   Henry, *The Essence of Manifestation*, trans. Girard Etzkorn (The Hague: Martinus Nijhoff, 1973), 40, §34, 671, and "Speech and Religion: The Word of God," *Phenomenology and the "Theological Turn": The French Debate*, trans. Bernard G. Prusak (New York: Fordham University Press, 2000), 227.

[15]   Hans Jonas, *The Phenomenon of Life: Towards a Philosophical Biology*, foreword Lawrence Vogel (Evanston: Northwestern University Press, 2001), 1.

[16]   See François-Pierre Maine de Biran, *Essai sur les fondements de psychologie*, ed. F.C.T. Moore, 2 vols, in *Oeuvres*, 13 vols (Paris: J. Vrin, 2001), VII. 1, 15, and Georges Bataille, *Inner Experience*, trans. and intro. Leslie Anne Boldt (Albany: State University of New York Press, 1988).

[17]   See *Incarnation*, Part I. Also see "La méthode phénoménologique," *Phénoménologie matérielle* (Paris: Presses Universitaires de France, 1990), esp. 121–35.

of Husserl and Heidegger, especially their methodologies, and is then unfolded in a long, expository text, *L'Essence de la manifestation* (1963). Presented without close attention to argument or the consideration of counter-examples, the system generates all manner of questions, and it will be useful to clarify some of these and to identify criticisms that would come to mind when engaging the more narrow concern of this essay but that would ultimately distract us from it.

1. First, one might question the distinction between the non-intentional and the intentional as Henry draws it. From the beginning, Henry sets himself against Husserl in affirming the importance of self-affect, although it must be said that Husserl devotes attention to non-intentional sensations, the pain of burning oneself, for example, in the fifth of the *Logical Investigations*.[18] Be that as it may, Henry certainly rejects Brentano's second thesis, that intentionality is the mark of the mental, but not by way of a reduction of the mental to the physical. For Henry, there are non-intentional states — joy, pain, and unspecified anxiety, for example — and these are prior to intentional states such as perceiving, desiring, and so on. Let us put the issue of priority to one side for the moment. Can the distinction between the two be quite as sharp as Henry says it is? There is reason to doubt it. After all, one might argue that perceptual states have non-intentional properties — *qualia* — and that the non-intentional cannot always be severed from the intentional.[19] And one might also argue, from another direction entirely, that all supposed non-intentional states have internal objects and are therefore intentional.[20]

2. Second, pressure might be put on the distinction between life and world, which converges exactly with that between the non-intentional and the intentional. What seems to be a radicalization of Husserl's *Lebenswelt* is asserted to be prior to it. Not only is the world of science separated from life but also life is said to be without a world, a horizon of horizons. Henry's motivation is clear: Husserlian intellectualism is to be rejected along with Galilcan reductionism.[21] Husserl will insist that there is no clear borderline between life and world: "I can enter no world other than the one that gets its sense and acceptance or status [*Sinn und Geltung*] in and from

---

[18] See Edmund Husserl, *Logical Investigations*, trans. J.N. Findlay (London: Routledge and Kegan Paul, 1970), 2 vols, II, 572–8.

[19] See, for example, Sydney Shoemaker, "Qualities and Qualia: What's in the Mind?" in his *The First-Person Perspective and Other Essays* (Cambridge: Cambridge University Press, 1996).

[20] See, for example, Tim Crane, "Intentionality as the Mark of the Mental" in Anthony O'Hear (ed.), *Current Issues in the Philosophy of Mind* (Cambridge: Cambridge University Press, 1998), 5.

[21] See Henry, *La Barbarie* (Paris: Grasset, 1987).

me, myself," he says in the first of the *Cartesian Meditations*.[22] Yet there is no border precisely because of the intentional structure of consciousness. Against this thesis Henry will define "life" by reduplication, life *as* life, by which he means that life in its essence is self-affect. Henry's definition may well strike us as unreasonably narrow. Believing, desiring, fearing, hating, hoping, judging and loving would therefore not be part of life as life, nor would experiences of cold, fatigue, hunger and warmth. The criticism can be addressed by observing that Henry is specifying the essence of life, not its many ventures into the sphere of representation. It is this life that we experience as anguish or joy even when entertaining false representations of the world (as in dreams, for example).[23]

3. Third, we might ask on what basis Henry can assert the priority of the non-intentional (life) with respect to the intentional (world). Such priority is not unfamiliar in phenomenology: Husserl argues that with the reduction we pass from transcendent time to subjective time, which is constituted in absolute timeless consciousness, itself unconscious and immanent.[24] Henry's claim is that "in the phenomenality which is not phenomenalized in exteriority resides the phenomenological possibility of the phenomenality of exteriority itself."[25] It is clear that "phenomenality" is being given a broader sense than we are used to, both in Husserl (for whom it is the objectness of objects) and in Heidegger (for whom it is *Vorhandenheit*, *Zuhandenheit* or another modality of being). Phenomenality, here, is the pathos of self-affect; and it appears to me in its very self-appearing, there being no distinction between the two. This non-intentional state can be regarded as the ground of intentionality because it presents the subject as a phenomenon, and therefore, Henry argues, rescues phenomenology from a major philosophical embarrassment: the claim that everything is open to phenomenological investigation except God and the constituting subject.

---

[22] Husserl, *Cartesian Meditations: An Introduction to Phenomenology*, trans. Dorion Carins (The Hague: Martinus Nijhoff, 1977), 21.

[23] On several occasions Henry refers us to Descartes' "The Passions of the Soul" §26: "although we may be asleep, or dream, we cannot feel sad or moved by any other passion without its being very true that the soul actually has this passion within it," *The Philosophical Works of Descartes*, 2 vols, trans. Elizabeth S. Haldane and G.R.T. Ross (Cambridge: Cambridge University Press, 1972), I, 343–4. See, for example, Henry, "The Critique of the Subject," trans. Peter T. Connor, in *Who Comes after the Subject?* eds Eduardo Cadava et al. (New York: Routledge, 1991), 161.

[24] See Husserl, *On the Phenomenology of the Consciousness of Internal Time (1893–1917)*, trans. John Barnett Brough (Boston: Kluwer, 1991), A, third section, and Appendix VI to the second part.

[25] Henry, *The Essence of Manifestation*, 266.

The exclusion of God is defensible for Husserl but not so the subject, since that gesture sets an infinite regress in motion.[26]

Several objections immediately present themselves. To begin with, it is hard to know how to square Henry's insistence that the non-intentional precedes and grounds the intentional with his equal insistence that there is no relation between life and world. It is also not clear why, in becoming aware of a flow of primal self-affect, I do not make that pathos into an intentional object in the same way that transcendent objects are. Such seems to be the impact of Henry's favored expression "self-phenomenalizing of phenomenality." Finally, I might agree with Henry that a primal upsurge of life is indisputably felt, but also hold that this judgment does not give me the warrant to say that this non-intentional life is absolutely primary. I might argue that life itself started eons ago as a chemical process and that my self-affect is consequent upon that process but that it is revealed only in scientific reflection subsequent to the identification of self-affect.

4. Fourth, it must be asked what follows from establishing the priority of the non-intentional over the intentional. Henry takes himself to abolish the subject of representation, as installed by Kant, in order to affirm the subject that Descartes intuited but that has been misunderstood by philosophers ever since, Heidegger chief among them.[27] On his account, "I represent" is not basic to the "I," or, if you like, the qualitative character of experience is not reducible to its representational content. The subject that is revealed is a phenomenon without the light of the world, and in affirming its priority with respect to the world Henry marks the deep truth, which, as Shelley's Demogorgon says, is "imageless."[28] More important than this, however, is that Henry's subject is eminently capable of divine revelation. This is not a revelation that comes from outside or beyond the self, but from within, an immanence that is without meaning or *telos*. It is a revelation that coheres with and justifies iconoclasm.

These preliminary concerns about Henry's overall position will impinge on all that follows, even though I do not propose to examine the more narrowly metaphysical of them in any detail. My concern is with what happens when this complex position becomes a "philosophy of Christianity." That occurs only when the Christian God, the Father of Jesus, is identified with Life, the *zōē* of John's gospel, the sheer

---

26   See Husserl, *Ideas Pertaining to a Pure Phenomenology and to a Phenomenological Philosophy, First Book: General Introduction to a Pure Phenomenology*, trans. F. Kersten (Boston: Kluwer Academic Publishers, 1983), §58.

27   See Henry, *The Genealogy of Psychoanalysis*, trans. Douglas Brick (Stanford: Stanford University Press, 1993), ch. 1.

28   P.B. Shelley, "Prometheus Unbound," II. iv. 116, in his *Poetical Works*, Thomas Hutchinson (ed.), corrected by G.M. Matthews (Oxford: Oxford University Press, 1970), 238.

power to reveal itself that is eternally present and that cannot be overcome, even by death. There is reason to pause here, for in the fourth gospel it is the Son, rather than the Father, who is seen as Life; and we are alerted to Henry's tendency to read Scripture quickly rather than slowly. At any rate, for Henry this *zōē* is prior to being — being can *be* only as life — a view that renders him sympathetic to the Jean-Luc Marion of *Dieu sans l'être* (1982).[29] Henry does not say that God is the cause of life, as one finds in *The Divine Names* of Pseudo-Dionysius, but that God is Life, thereby orienting his philosophy of Christianity around the divine name of Life and arguing that it not only has precedence over Being but also excludes it altogether.[30] And yet in general Henry is committed to the quite different view that the essence of Life is God.[31] His philosophy has always been attuned to life, and it becomes a philosophy of Christianity only when the minuscule becomes a majuscule and Life is described as divine. The standpoint resembles Eckhart's *esse est deus* more than Aquinas's *deus est ipsum esse subsistens*.[32] Resemblance is not the same as identity, however: "God's being is my life," says Eckhart; God's Life is my life, says Henry.[33] Unlike Aquinas and Eckhart, though, the Father is conceived by Henry as Arch-Passibility, a theologoumenon to which I shall return, while simply noting now that the relation "Father" is not one in which a hypostasis or person subsists.

Before then, however, it needs to be noted that Henry's is a philosophy of Christianity in two senses. Christianity is the object of a philosophy that was elaborated in its own terms, mostly without reference to religion; also, as Henry presents it, Christianity — taken solely as New Testament revelation, if not simply as Johannine revelation — discloses its own philosophy, which turns out to be Henry's as elaborated in *L'Essence de la manifestation*. Henry argues against Hegel from time to time, especially against his notion of experience, yet there is a strong impulse to comprehend as well as clarify the faith philosophically that

---

[29]	See Henry, *I am the Truth*, 281 n. 2, and "Speech and Religion," 228. Yet Marion modifies his position quite considerably with respect to Aquinas. See his essay "Thomas Aquinas and Onto-theo-logy" in *Mystics: Presence and Aporia*, eds Michael Kessler and Christian Sheppard (Chicago: Chicago University Press, 2003), 38–74.

[30]	See Pseudo-Dionysius Areopagite, *The Divine Names*, ch. vi, in his *The Divine Names and Mystical Theology*, trans. John D. Jones (Milwaukee: Marquette University Press, 1980), 174. Henry, *I am the Truth*, 54. Janicaud is not quite correct in saying that Henry denudes God of all the divine attributes. Life and eternity are retained, and perhaps simplicity also. See his essay in *Phenomenology and the "Theological Turn*,*"* 74.

[31]	See Henry, *I am the Truth*, 27, 104.

[32]	See Eckhart, *Parisian Questions and Prologues*, trans. and intro. Armand A. Maurer (Toronto: Pontifical Institute of Medieval Studies, 1974), 85.

[33]	Eckhart, *Sermons and Treatises*, II, 134. In *Le Fis du roi*, we hear, "L'œil par lequel nous voyons les choses, lui dis-je, n'est autre que œil par lequel Dieu nous voit. Celui qui voit cet œil voit Dieu lui-même … ," 194.

should not be overlooked.[34] The impulse derives less from Hegel's dialectic, or his inversion of the world, than from Schelling's idea of a "philosophical religion" that separates doctrine and history, eschewing the literal, *wörtliche* teaching of revealed theology, and that seeks the content of the faith and remains uninterested in historical witnesses to it.[35] Henry relies on John's gospel, especially the proem and the farewell discourse. His remarks turn on the gospel's *Sache* not its *Lehre*, as Schelling would say, and shows no interest in arguments about the different editorial strata of the text. For what is important in the gospel is Christ Himself, not the events of his life as represented by the evangelists.[36]

* * *

What does Henry mean by "the order of things"? In the first place, as already noted, it is revelation. In general, this is the self-revelation of life, which in the trilogy becomes the self-revelation of God. By "Father" Henry understands "the movement, which nothing precedes and of which nobody knows the name, by which Life is cast into itself in order to experience itself."[37] The Father, then, is Life as Life; and "this Father eternally engenders the Son within himself, if by the latter we understand the First Living in whose original and essential Ipseity the Father experiences himself" (57). Have we passed from life as originary phenomenality, self-affect, to something else — an absolute phenomenality? Certainly Life is regarded as distinguishable (but not distinct) from my life, and if it is irreducible to all living beings then Henry is making a metaphysical claim. If it cannot be separated from them, he is affirming pantheism.

Even if we accept that "Life's generation cannot come about without generating within itself this Son as the very mode in which this process takes place" (57–8), it is doubtful that this statement can stand as a viable account of the relations between the Father and the Son. It bespeaks a process theology without theodicy, a binatarian doctrine of God in which the Son is a mode of the Father. If Life is God, rather than (or as well as) the other way around, we lose all sense of agency in the deity and all sense of the *kairos* of the Incarnation. Also, we might wonder if this doctrine of the Christ can be brought into accord with the two natures of Christ,

---

[34] See Henry, *The Essence of Manifestation*, §20.

[35] See Manfred Schröter (ed.), *Schellings Werke, Nach der Original in neuer Anordnung, Münichner Jubilämsdruck* (Munich: C.H. Beck'sche Verlagsbuchhandlung, 1927–46), VI, 710. For the claim that Henry's reversal of phenomenology recalls Hegel's inversion of the world, see Jean Greisch, "'Le monde à l'envers': Quel renversement de quelle phénoménologie?," *Phénoménologie et Christianisme chez Michel Henry: Les derniers écrits de Michel Henry en débat*, ed. Philippe Capelle (Paris: Cerf, 2004), 56–9.

[36] See *Schellings Werke*, VI, 620f. Needless to say, perhaps, Henry is also close to Kierkegaard here. See the latter's *Concluding Unscientific Postscript*, trans. David F. Swenson and Walter Lowrie (Princeton: Princeton University Press, 1941), Book 1, ch. 1, §1.

[37] Henry, *I am the Truth*, 57.

as the Council of Chalcedon specifies. Since Henry rejects all worldly categories, his Christology — the center of his philosophy of Christianity — inclines sharply towards Monophysitism.[38] I put these problems aside, although they will return of their own force, and turn to several matters consequent on Henry's conception of the divine life.

The first of these is that Henry proposes a very high Christology. This may be unusual in modern theology but not in the Catholic and Orthodox traditions as a whole. What makes it peculiar is that this descending Johannine Christology is never integrated with a synoptic ascending Christology. This "Christology from above" is not all that presses on his religious thought, however. The philosophy is at heart Neoplatonic in its emphasis that reality has the structure of *exitus* and *reditus*, although the basic principle is Life, not the Good, and is regarded as phenomenality and not noumenon. Also, Henry's philosophy of Christianity is deductive rather than inductive, closer to St. Bonaventure's *Breviloquium* (1257) than to anything by his contemporaries Levinas and Derrida. "Now our thought would not be the most elevated if we did not believe that God could communicate himself in the most complete way, and it would not be the most loving if, believing him so able, we thought him unwilling to do so. Hence, if we are to think of God most loftily and most lovingly, faith tells us that God totally communicates himself by eternally having a beloved and another who is loved by both."[39] Until we reach the reference to the Holy Spirit, and with reservations about the use of the words "love" and "faith," all of which I will touch on a little later, Bonaventure could be seen as summarizing an important dimension of Henry's philosophy of Christianity.

In the second place, the order of things means truth. Not truth in Husserl's sense of the word, the fulfilling of an empty intention by *Evidenz* or a modification of it, since that construes truth as an intentional relation with the world. And not in Heidegger's sense, either — *alētheia*, or the unconcealment of beings, *Unverborgenheit* — for that too links truth to our being in the world. For Henry, the strict distinction between life and world that is fundamental to his thought requires him to reject any correspondence theory of truth. On his understanding, two distinctions are required before we can speak clearly of truth. A line is drawn between truth of life and truth of the world; the former is enstatic (and primary), while the latter is ecstatic (and secondary). And another line is drawn between self-showing as such, and what shows itself in any given situation. In developing a

---

[38]   See Henry, *I am the Truth*, 99. Xavier Tilliette evokes the specter of "crypto-docetism" in his "Le Christ du philosophe," in "Dossier sur le livre de Michel Henry," *Communio*, 21:5 (1996), 98. In general, Tilliette assimilates Henry (and Maine de Biran) to the teaching of the "Verbe intérieur" and to the tradition of philosophical Christology. See his *Le Christ des philosophes: Du Maître de sagesse au divin Témoin* (Namur: Culture et Vérité, 1993), ch. 8, and *Le Christ de la philosophie: Prolégomènes à une christologie philosophique* (Paris: Cerf, 1990).

[39]   St. Bonaventure, *Breviloqium*, ed. Dominic V. Monti, *Works of St. Bonaventure*, vol. 9 (St. Bonaventure, NY: Franciscan Institute Publications, 2005), 30–31.

philosophy of Christianity Henry is concerned not with what actually showed itself in first-century Palestine, events such as the Transfiguration and the Resurrection that, people say, could be determined as historical or unhistorical, but with something irreducible to history, namely, that Jesus Christ is not a phenomenon in and of the world but the self-manifestation of not just originary but absolute phenomenality, the disclosure of Life to the living. Once again, Henry agrees with Eckhart who, explicating the verse "God sent His only-begotten Son into the world" (1 John 4:9), says, "You should not take this to mean the external world, as when he ate and drank with us, but you should understand it of the inner world."[40] A philosophy of Christianity will orient itself exclusively by reference to this self-showing that cannot be brought before any tribunal because it is self-attesting. The truth of Christianity, Henry maintains, does not turn on anything that Jesus did or did not do but on the rightness of the messianic claim, the theme of the Farewell Discourse in the fourth gospel (John 13:31–17:26), that Jesus is indeed the Christ, that He is Life itself (John 14:6). The order of things for Henry is Johannine in structure; and to the extent that the Farewell Discourse is a fulfilling of the farewell discourses of Moses, Samuel and David, among others, and is spoken by Jesus from the perspective of eternity, the order of things is eschatological.

In the third place, when Henry evokes "the order of things" he has in mind a philosophy of the flesh. Here we turn to the second volume of his trilogy, *Incarnation* (2000), which has as subtitle, "Une philosophie de la chair." Once again Henry had broadly established the philosophical position in question long before attending to the specific issue of how the Word became flesh. We read *Incarnation* in the wake of two works: the study that Henry wrote first (but published second), *Philosophie et phénoménologie du corps* (1965) and an important essay, "Le concept d'âme a-t-il un sens?" (1969). The thesis at issue is more extreme than the better-known one of Husserl developed in *Ideas II* (1952) in which there are two manifestations of the body, the material body or *Körper*, which is objective, and the psycho-organic [*leiblich-seelichen*] strata that make up the subjective body. In the subjective body we have sensual feelings such as pleasure and sadness that are non-intentional, but the material body makes up "a fundamental component of the real givenness of the soul and the Ego."[41] Rather, following Maine de Biran, Henry argues that the subjective body precedes the material body, and that a true material phenomenology is also non-intentional, attending first and foremost to self-affect.[42] Auto-affection precedes hetero-affection; it is life itself as it moves

---

[40]   Eckhart, *Sermons and Treatises*, I, 117.

[41]   Husserl, *Ideas Pertaining to a Pure Phenomenology and to a Phenomenological Philosophy, Second Book: Studies in the Phenomenology of Constitution*, trans. Richard Rojcewicz and André Schuwer (Boston: Kluwer, 1989), 165. Also see his *Phenomenological Psychology: Lectures, Summer Semester 1925*, trans. John Scanlon (The Hague: Nijhoff, 1977), 147–53.

[42]   See Henry, *Philosophy and Phenomenology of the Body*, trans. Girard Etzkorn (The Hague: Martinus Nijhoff, 1975), 179.

between the poles of suffering and joy. The life into which I am born, Henry says, is absolutely subjective. At issue are not my subjective preferences, whether I choose coffee over tea, or listen to Bach rather than Beethoven, but the subjectivity of life itself, the invisible stream of self-affect that remains immanent. My experience of suffering and joy — my flesh, as Henry calls it — is what enables me to feel and know my body. Flesh, then, is a phenomenalizing of radical phenomenality understood as self-affect. And yet there is a theological counter-movement that needs to be taken into account. For it is a "phenomenology of the flesh" that returns us "invincibly to a phenomenology of the Incarnation," he says.[43] And he adds, "the phenomenology of the Incarnation should logically precede that of the flesh" (179). In other words, we grasp the meaning of our flesh only by recognizing that we are sons and daughters of God in and through the Arch-Son, Jesus Christ.

There is a great deal to say about this circular movement of flesh and incarnation, both in Christology and in the theology of religions. Henry may be able, at least to his satisfaction, to indicate the eternal generation of the Son by the Father, but he has no satisfactory answer to the question that the monk Boso poses in St Anselm's *Cur Deus Homo*: "I desire that you should discover to me, what, as you know, many besides myself ask, for what necessity and cause God, who is omnipotent, should have assumed the littleness and weakness of human nature for the sake of its renewal?"[44] More generally, Henry disassociates history and eschatology, including the *historia salutis* and the *ordo salutis*, so completely as to risk becoming Marcionite.[45] That the incarnation takes place in Jewish flesh is overlooked completely. Indeed, the exclusionary distinction between life and world frustrates any attempt to develop a thick description of the events remarked in the New Testament, and tends to skew any understanding of the Jewish context in which Jesus lived and taught. Torah, for instance, is figured wholly in worldly terms.[46] I will confine myself to just one remark that comes from within this circle of flesh and incarnation and that sounds my main theme again. The body for Henry as for Maine de Biran is not primarily objective or even organic but subjective.[47]

Of course, Maine de Biran did not entirely reject the physiological psychology of Pierre Cabinis and the other *idéologues* but asterisked the importance of the

---

[43]   Henry, *Incarnation*, 179.

[44]   St. Anselm: *Proslogium; Monologium: An Appendix on Behalf of the Fool by Gaunilo; And Cur Deus Homo*, trans. Sidney Norton Deane (1926; rpt. Chicago: The Open Court Publishing Company, 1903), Book 1, ch. 2.

[45]   Henry mentions Marcion in *I am the Truth*, 3.

[46]   See Henry, *I am the Truth*, 178.

[47]   Henry, *Philosophy and Phenomenology of the Body*, 207. Also see Maurice Merleau-Ponty's lectures on Maine de Biran in his *The Incarnate Subject: Malebranche, Biran, and Bergson on the Union of Body and Soul*, pref. Jacques Taminiaux, trans. Paul B. Milan, ed. Andrew G. Bjelland Jr and Patrick Burke (Amherst: Humanity Books, 2001). For a detailed consideration of the relation of flesh and body, see Emmanuel Falque, "Y-a-t-il une chair sans corps?," *Phénoménologie et Christianisme chez Michel Henry*, 95–133.

self's experiences of its own internal modifications. It is this subjective body, the flesh, and solely this body (or, as Henry and Maine de Biran would have it, this soul), that is to be raised in the resurrection. "For it is only if our body is, in its original being, something subjective that the brief allusions made by dogma with regard to its metaphysical destiny can be anything other than extravagant conceptions," he writes in *Philosophie et phénoménologie du corps*.

> Actually, they necessarily had to appear as extravagant in the eyes of the Greeks, such as the one which makes the resurrection of the body a dogma. This is why the Corinthians started to sneer when St Paul claimed not to reserve to the soul the privilege of this resurrection. Rather it is clear that if this original being of our body is something subjective, then, like the 'soul', it falls under the category of things which are liable to be revived [or repeated: the French is *répété*] and judged.[48]

Without the metaphysics of *esse*, Henry's philosophy of Christianity is also without a Thomist or Cartesian metaphysics of the soul, which he and Maine de Biran agree is a bare abstraction.

***

No sooner has Henry boldly claimed that in Christianity ethics is subordinated to revelation, truth, and the flesh, than he focuses on Jesus's notion of the *basileia*, and offers a challenging interpretation of its meaning, one that is very far from Albrecht Ritschl's in his revival of the theology of the *basileia*.[49] "'Kingdom' does not mean a sort of domain across which divine power extends," Henry writes, "a terrain reserved for its action. It is the very essence of Christ as identified with 'the Revelation of God', with His absolute self-revelation, that is designated foreign to the world: 'even as I am not of [the world]' (John 17:14)" (26). To enter the *basileia* is to forego the world and grasp life. Here, if nowhere else, the inspiration is as much Augustinian as Fichtean. "Do not go abroad. Return within yourself. In the inward man dwells truth," Augustine writes in *De vera religione*.[50] Now to explicate the meaning of the *basileia*, no easy thing, is to engage in eschatology; and it needs to be underlined, if it is not already apparent, that Henry's philosophy of Christianity is eschatological through and through. Let me be perfectly clear. Of course the Christianity that Henry describes is eschatological but so is his *philosophy* before it is a philosophy of Christianity. We have already sensed it in his comments on the resurrection of the flesh, in the appropriation of the

---

[48]   Henry, *Philosophy and Phenomenology of the Body*, 208–9.

[49]   See Albrecht Ritschl, "Instruction in the Christian Religion," §5, in Philip Hefner (ed.), *Albrecht Ritschl: Three Essays* (Philadelphia: Fortress Press, 1972), 22.

[50]   Augustine, "Of True Religion," in *Augustine: Earlier Writings*, trans. and introd. John H.S. Burleigh, *The Library of Christian Classics* (London: SCM Press, 1953), xxix. 72.

eschatological statements in Jesus' Farewell Discourse, and in the real distinction between "life" and "world."

It is perhaps no surprise to find Henry's philosophy interlaced with eschatology; it was a trait of French philosophy in the 1960s. At the start of *Totalité et infini* (1961) Lévinas evokes eschatology as referring to a state beyond totality. "The eschatological, as the 'beyond' of history, draws beings out of the jurisdiction of history and the future; it arouses them in and calls them forth to their full responsibility."[51] And in *Le Conflit des interprétations* (1969) Ricoeur observes that, "the phenomenology of religion" is grounded "in an eschatology."[52] Yet Henry's eschatology is neither a matter of judgment, as it is for Levinas, nor a question of existential function, as it is for Ricoeur. The theme of the eschaton is announced as early as *Philosophie et phénoménologie du corps,* as already noted, and plays a part in the system of *L'Essence de la manifestation*:

> The existence of consciousness in its universal essence is absolute knowledge because the essence of consciousness is existence, the self-manifestation of Being, the Parousia. Far from arising merely in a determined mode of the life of consciousness, the Parousia constitutes the very essence of this life and, as such, the condition of all determinations which this life is capable of assuming. The Parousia is not the fact of true knowledge; it is its presupposition, just as it is the presupposition of the non-true knowledge of natural consciousness which limits itself to a being. Because the presupposition of the true knowledge of philosophical consciousness and of the non-true knowledge of natural consciousness is the Parousia, this presupposition is not a foundation hidden behind the life of consciousness, *it is conscious life itself as such*, it is the life of philosophical consciousness as well as that of natural consciousness.[53]

"Parousia" comes from *pareimi*, "to be present" or "to come," and those are its usual meanings in Greek. In the New Testament, however, the word is shaded differently and with varying intensity by the gospel writers and by Paul but generally in reference to the coming of the glorified Christ.[54] The first *parousia* was both fulfilled and unfulfilled, and further distinctions were to be drawn. Medieval theologians spoke of the *adventus triplex,* namely, *adventus ad homines, in homines, contra homines.* We might suppose that we should distinguish a

---

[51]   Emmanuel Levinas, *Totality and Infinity: An Essay on Exteriority*, trans. Alphonso Lingis (The Hague: Martinus Nijhoff, 1979), 23.

[52]   Paul Ricoeur, "Existence and Hermeneutics," trans. Kathleen McLaughlin, in *The Conflict of Interpretations*, ed. Don Ihde (Evanston: Northwestern University Press, 1974), 23.

[53]   Henry, *The Essence of Manifestation*, 144.

[54]   See the entry on Parousia in Gerhard Kittel et al. (ed.), *Theological Dictionary of the New Testament*, 10 vols (1967; rpt. Grand Rapids, MI: Wm. B. Eerdmans Publishing Co., 1999), V, 858–71.

religious and a philosophical sense of "parousia" or even "eschatology," but as we shall see it is difficult to do so with Henry, especially in his last works.

In the context of *L'Essence de la manifestation* "parousia" is a word that Henry borrows from Heidegger who uses it in his explication of Hegel's understanding of *Erfahrung*, experience.[55] Hegel takes the starting point of modern philosophy to be Descartes' demonstration that consciousness of self gives us an absolute knowledge, and takes as his own project the thinking of the absolute character of that knowledge. The knowledge of self is absolute in that it has absolved itself from all objects of knowledge and has become aware of itself as knowing: *cogito, ergo sum*. Absolute knowledge is therefore not of an object but of self-manifestation. Heidegger moves quickly to claim that Hegel wishes to present experience as being yet cannot quite do so because his thought is mired in a philosophy of subjectivity. The interpretation forces Hegel along a Heideggerian path.[56] If we put that large issue to one side, though, we can focus on what is important to Henry in Heidegger's reading of Hegel.

For Heidegger, the absolute is the presence of manifestation, which he calls parousia. Hegel speaks of the presentation of manifestation as "the path of the soul, which is traversing the series of its own forms of embodiment, like stages appointed for it by its own nature, that it may possess the clearness of spiritual life when, through the complete experience of its own self, it arrives at the knowledge of what it is in itself."[57] Heidegger warns us that this image of the mind's *itinerarium mentis in Deum* could be misleading. Our problem, he says, is not "to arrive at the parousia from somewhere outside it, as people think; rather, it is a matter, from within the parousia and therefore from out of the parousia, of bringing forth our relationship to it before it."[58] Henry agrees, although he makes a half-twist in Heidegger's words as he does so, since for him the life of consciousness is itself the parousia before any relationship is formed between consciousness and the world. Parousia is wholly immanent, certainly not transcendent or a future event. Henry's is a "hidden God," more like Fichte's than Hegel's. He likes to quote from the former's *Die Anweisung zum Seligen Leben* (1806). Glossing the great proem of John's gospel, Fichte writes, "In him, in this immediate Divine Existence [*Daseyn*], was Life, — the deepest root of all living, substantial Existence, which

---

[55] Heidegger had discussed the parousia in relation to 2 Thesselonians in his seminar for the Winter Semester of 1920–21. See his "Introduction to the Phenomenology of Religion," *The Phenomenology of Religious Life*, trans. Matthias Fritsch and Jennifer Anna Gosetti-Ferencei (Bloomington: Indiana University Press, 2004), §26.

[56] See Theodore W. Adorno's correction of Heidegger in his essay "The Experiential Content of Hegel's Philosophy" in his *Hegel: Three Studies*, trans. Shierry Weber Nicholsen (Cambridge, MA: MIT Press, 1994), 53.

[57] Hegel, *Phenomenology of Mind*, trans. J.B. Baillie, intro. George Lichtheim (New York: Harper and Row, 1967), 135.

[58] Heidegger, "Hegel's Concept of Experience," *Off the Beaten Track*, ed. and trans. Julian Young and Kenneth Haynes (Cambridge: Cambridge University Press, 2002), 104.

nevertheless remains for ever concealed from view."[59] As might be expected, he does not continue the quotation to the end of the sentence: "and in actual men this Life is Light, or conscious Reflexion; and this one, eternal, primitive Light shines for ever in the Darkness of the lower and obscure grades of Spiritual Life, maintains these in existence, itself unseen, and the Darkness comprehends it not" (388). For Henry, the divine existence is untroubled darkness, not light.[60]

Distant as the passage by Henry that I have just explicated seems to be from the gospels and from the epistles of Paul, it is closer than one might think, and it leads us directly to the deep concerns of *C'est moi la vérité* and the other parts of the trilogy. The parousia is a central motif of the synoptic tradition. In the earliest of the canonical gospels Jesus says that "the Son of man" will be ashamed of those who are ashamed of him "when he cometh in the glory of his Father with the holy angels" (Mark 8:38), and later, at the Last Supper, Jesus says directly after he has accepted the title of the Christ, "ye shall see the Son of man sitting on the right hand of power, and coming in the clouds of heaven" (Mark 14:62). In later gospels we are told in the parable of the ten virgins to watch, "for ye know neither the day nor the hour wherein the Son of man cometh" (Matt. 25:13), and, while speaking of the *basileia*, Jesus tells his disciples, to be "like unto men that wait for their lord, when he will return from the wedding; that when he cometh and knocketh, they may open unto him immediately" (Luke 12:36). If the synoptic tradition parses the parousia in terms of the future and hope, the Johannine tradition is quite different since for John the parousia is the granting of eternal life here and now. Jesus says, "He that heareth my word, and believeth on him that sent me, hath everlasting life, and shall not come into condemnation; but is passed from death unto life" (John 5:24). Peter asks Jesus, "to whom shall we go?," a rhetorical question that he answers by saying, "thou hast the words of eternal life" (John 6:68). Jesus prays to the Father, and says, "this is life eternal, that they might know thee the only true God, and Jesus Christ, whom thou hast sent" (John 17:3). As early as *L'Essence de la manifestation*, Henry's eschatology is Johannine in its main lines, not synoptic.

Yet this is only part of the story. Two theological threads are knotted together in Henry's eschatology. The first comes from Eckhart. "We are wholly transformed into God and changed," he says in sermon sixty-five, quoting 2 Cor. 3:18, before giving the verse an original interpretation:

> It is just the same as when in the sacrament bread is changed into our Lord's body: however many pieces of bread there were, there would still only be one body ... I am converted into Him in such a way that He makes me *one* with His being, not *similar*. By the living God it is true that there is no distinction.[61]

---

[59] J.G. Fichte, "The Way Towards the Blessed Life or The Doctrine of Religion," *The Popular Works of Johann Gottlieb Fichte*, intro. Daniel Breazeale, 2 vols (1889; rpt. Bristol: Thoemmes Press, 1999), II, 388. See Henry, *The Essence of Manifestation*, 382.

[60] However, see Henry, *I am the Truth*, 86.

[61] Eckhart, *Sermons and Treatises*, II, 135–6.

For Henry, we enter the divine Life in passing from the world to life, not *in specie aliena* but as ourselves. The second thread is more modern; it comes from the Karl Barth of *Romans* (1922), and says that the parousia has no real relationship with time.[62] It presses on us at each and every moment. And for Henry it means that the world has already passed away. So his eschatology is at once over-realized (it has always and already happened) and under-realized (it has no decisive relation to Christ's Resurrection and to Pentecost).

***

Eschatology is usually regarded as the doctrine of consummation, the movement from emptiness to fullness of life, from the old being in Adam to the new being in Christ. At least since St. Athanasius's *Life of Anthony* (*c.* 356) and the *Historia Monachorum* (*c.* 405), and with support from the New Testament, it is associated with fleeing from the world either in order to participate more fully in the eternal life of God or to prepare for the coming of Christ. *Metanoia*, conversion, is commonly figured as a passage from "the world" to new life in Christ. For Henry, though, there can be no abandoning of the world, since living has never been possible there in any case. To be sure, this puts Henry at odds with most contemporary Christian eschatology, and first of all the Neo-Hegelian eschatologies of Wolfhart Pannenberg and Jürgen Moltmann.[63] If we think of Fritz Buri's suggestion that eschatology stimulates a reverence for life in all its fragility, we come nowhere close to Henry, for life is not revealed by the eschaton but is the eschaton itself.[64] A brief contrast with Karl Rahner will bring Henry's difference from most post-Vatican II Catholic eschatology into focus.

Like Henry, Rahner affirms that God performs a transcendental function in human subjectivity. Our knowledge of God, he says, "is not the kind of knowledge in which one grasps an object which happens to present itself from outside." Not at all: "It has rather the character of transcendental experience. Insofar as this subjective, non-objective luminosity [*subjekthafte, ungegenständliche Erhelltheit*] of the subject in its transcendence is always oriented towards the holy mystery, the knowledge of God is always present unthematically and without name and not just when we begin to speak of it."[65] Rahner argues that transcendental

---

[62]   See Karl Barth, *The Epistle to the Romans*, trans. Edwyn C. Hoskyns (1933; rpt. Oxford: Oxford University Press, 1968), 314.

[63]   See Wolfhart Pannenberg, *Systematic Theology*, 3 vols, trans. Geoffrey W. Bromiley (Grand Rapids, MI: William B. Eerdmans, 1998), III, ch. 15, and Jürgen Moltmann, *The Coming of God: Christian Eschatology*, trans. Margaret Kohl (Minneapolis: Fortress Press, 1996).

[64]   See Fritz Buri, *Christian Faith in Our Time*, trans. E.A. Kent (New York: Macmillan, 1966), 124–6.

[65]   Karl Rahner, *Foundations of Christian Faith*, trans. W.V. Dych (London: Darton, Longman and Todd, 1978), 21.

experience is experience of transcendence, and thereby makes a leap from immanence to transcendence, darkness to light. Henry refuses any movement from the transcendental to transcendence, while maintaining that transcendence must be grounded in the transcendental. The two agree that any hermeneutics of eschatological assertions must take place in the context of a Christology, but disagree over the orientation of this Christology. Where Rahner insists that the eschaton remains in the future, even if it informs the present, Henry regards the eschaton as having taken place in an immemorial past.[66] The immanent consummation that Rahner sees as a final outcome, joined with transcendent consummation, is for Henry a misunderstanding of immanence.[67] Where Henry insists on eschatology as being an eternal presence, Rahner seeks to integrate both the synoptic and the Johannine views into a whole. Similarly, where Henry speaks of eschatology solely in individual terms, Rahner attempts to take the individual and the social in tandem in forming a more balanced doctrine of the last things.

We can get an even better fix on Henry if we shift our attention from Rahner to Hans Urs von Balthasar. For him too Christ is "the governing center" of eschatology.[68] Christ's is the primary eschatology, Balthasar will say, for His Passion determines — that is, "realizes" — the sense and direction of human history, the secondary eschatological dimension of which is ours to live in a hope that is as yet unrealized. Both Rahner and Balthasar seek to integrate the synoptic and Johannine eschatologies, but whereas Rahner grants a tacit privilege to the synoptics in declining to regard a future judgment as mythological in Rudolf Bultmann's sense, Balthasar goes in another direction, one in which demythologizing does not feature. His prizing of the fourth gospel as offering a vertical ("eternally present") eschatology that enfolds the horizontal ("futurist") eschatology of the synoptic gospels with its teaching of the *basileia*, brings him closer to Henry, as does his emphasis on the possibility of the Father. As Balthasar observes, the possibility of the personae of the Trinity becomes possible once one discharges the assumption that God is absolute being. Where Henry differs from Balthasar is in his bypassing of the Passion as central to eschatology, and in the soteriological significance of the Passion. To under-realize eschatology to this extent is to detach it from the Christianity that Balthasar brings into view. It is also to erase the sacramental dimension of Christian life: baptism as the regeneration of life, and the Eucharist as the foretaste of eternal life.

---

[66]   See Rahner, "The Hermeneutics of Eschatological Assertions," *Theological Investigations*, IV: *More Recent Writings*, trans. Kevin Smyth (New York: The Seabury Press, 1974), 336.

[67]   See Rahner, "Immanent and Transcendent Consummation of the World," *Theological Investigations*, X: *Writings of 1965–67*, vol. 2, trans. David Bourke (New York: Herder and Herder, 1973), 277.

[68]   See Hans Urs von Balthasar, *Theo-drama*, 5 vols, V: *The Last Act*, trans. Graham Harrison (San Francisco: Ignatius Press, 1998), Introduction A, 1.

Another point of difference between the two — or between the three, I should say, since Henry differs from both Balthasar and Rahner here — is over the status of creation and its role in eschatology, and here we glimpse another profound problem with Henry's philosophy of Christianity. Balthasar may not hold that God is absolute being, and may argue from Scripture and the Fathers that God is pained by human acts, but he does not doubt that creation is qualitatively different from the Creator. Not so for Henry: he nowhere talks of creation, only of generation. Certainly he admits that the relation between God and human beings is asymmetrical. "God could just as well live eternally in his Son and the latter in his Father without any other living ever coming to Life," he says, reprising precisely what Aquinas argues in the *Summa theologiæ*, *De potentia* and *De veritate* about the asymmetric relations of God and creation: our relations with God are real, His relations with us are unreal.[69] Yet Henry does not draw the consequence that follows from what Aquinas teaches, that God's otherness is other than any relation of self and other in the world. When we say, "God is Life" we have little idea what "Life" means; whatever similarity a divine Life that consists of actual knowing, *ejus intelligere*, has to human life, even what we take to be pure phenomenological life, is diminished by being situated in a far greater dissimilarity between the two.[70] The divine life is incomprehensible to us, though it is not incomprehensible in itself.

I return to eschatology. As Balthasar points out, the "I am" [*ego eimi*] statements in John are themselves fulfillments of the Lord God's "I am" utterances in Ezekiel and Deutero-Isaiah.[71] In concentrating exclusively on those statements in *C'est moi la vérité* Henry is not only underlining the self-showing of the truth in Christ but also doing so in an eschatological mode. Unlike Balthasar, however, who ventures a theocentric understanding of eschatology, Trinitarian in its emphases, Henry develops an anthropological eschatology, one that is developed wholly in terms of the immanence of the subject. One of Balthasar's constant targets throughout the *Theo-Drama* is the distinction between the Jesus of history and the Christ of faith, especially as deployed by Bultmann. Unlike Balthasar, Henry does not wish to rejoin Jesus and Christ in quite this way; the Jesus of history falls out of focus for him by dint of philosophical methodology and our relation with Christ is more surely aligned with gnosis than with faith. There are times when Henry's *zōē* recalls the divine life of the Gnostics more strongly than it does the eternally present life of John.[72] The very fact that Henry figures God as Life makes

---

[69]   See St. Thomas Aquinas, *Summa theologiæ*, I, q. 13 art. 7, c; I, q. 28, art. 1, ad 3; I, q. 45 art. 3, *De potentia dei*, I, q. iii, iii, and *De veritate*, q. 4, art. 5, c.

[70]   See Aquinas, *Summa theologiæ*, I, q. 18, art. 4. For a discussion of life in Aquinas, see Carlo Leget, *Living with God: Thomas Aquinas on the Relation between Life on Earth and "Life" after Death* (Leuven: Peeters, 1997), esp. 2.2. For Henry, the phenomenality of God and the self are exactly the same. See "Speech and Religion," 224.

[71]   See Ezekiel 37:1–14 and Isaiah 43.

[72]   On this topic, see Jad Hatem, *Le Saveur et les viscères de l'être: Sur le gnosticisme et Michel Henry* (Paris: L'Harmattan, 2004), ch. 5.

it well nigh impossible for him to think of the Father as a person in the Trinity; and indeed throughout the trilogy there is little evidence that the doctrine of the Holy Spirit is of any use to Henry, for whom the deity is seen in binatarian terms, as Father and Son.[73] And, as already noted, how and why Life, self-affectivity without personhood and certainly without *telos*, can phenomenalize itself in the Incarnation remains obscure.

In *C'est moi la vérité* revelation is confined almost exclusively to the Johannine messianic utterances. The reference to the *basileia*, to which I alluded earlier, is not solitary but is the only one that is significant. At first blush, this is peculiar, since the telling of the parables is the very site of the revelation of the *basileia*, and it is even more puzzling that Henry talks of parables in the fourth gospel, something done by few if any modern exegetes of the New Testament. If we read "Parole et religion: la Parole de Dieu" (1992), however, both oddities disappear if only to re-appear at another level, namely that of the abstract distinction between life and world. Henry distinguishes cleanly between two words in Scripture, the Word of the World and the Word of God, the Greek *logoi* and the Johannine *ho logos*. The former is found in all human speech and writing; it is a system of signs, based on the intentional structure of consciousness. Images of phenomena are presented, and take the place of the phenomena themselves. It is what Plato in *The Statesman* calls "the bottomless abyss of unlikeness" (273d). Henry speaks of the Word of the World as "content without content" [*un contenu sans contenu*] (183), and observes that in the world "I" ultimately means "I am dead" (182). It is no accident that his language recalls that of Blanchot and Derrida, for intentionality yields the world of difference. Derrida would surely say that Henry's system of absolute phenomenological life divides precisely in the moment it is written, in his sense of the word *écriture*, and Henry would respond that his written texts are testimony to Life, which is immanent.

The Word of God, the other understanding of language according to Henry, is non-linguistic; it is the self-revelation of the Logos that "speaks" to us incessantly of joy and suffering. "Life has one word," he says; it is a "Parousia without memory and without project," and this parousia is our transcendental birth (199). Now only the Word of God, abiding in the unending darkness of our subjectivity, gives us a hermeneutical key to unlock Scripture. But what it prizes in Scripture is precisely the Johannine statements of messianic self-description. These eschatological statements are themselves parables of the Word of God, and if we think (as Henry seems to do for the most part, at least in *C'est moi la vérité*) that the synoptic

---

[73]   Dominique Janicaud objects to Henry's evocation of a Trinitarian life in God in the context of phenomenology. See his *Phenomenology "Wide Open": After the French Debate* (New York: Fordham University Press, 2005), 6. However, the relevant passage (*I am the Truth*, 90–91) speaks only of the Father and the Son. Yet see Francesco Gaiffi, "La dimension trinitaire dans la philosophie du Christianisme de Michel Henry," in *Colloque international de Montpellier, Michel Henry. Pensée de la vie et culture contemporaine* (Paris: Beauchesne, 2006), 149–65.

parables are examples of Jesus expressing the truth to the world, then it is evident why he is largely uninterested in them. They are more concerned with revelation than self-revelation, in inaugurated rather than realized eschatology, in ethics rather than revelation.[74] The beatitudes speak more of self-revelation than the synoptic parables. The parable — the word given in John 10:6 is *paroimian* — to which Henry devotes the most time is John 10:6–18 ("Verily, verily, I say unto you, I am the door of the sheep"), which is a parable of self-revelation. For Henry, as for Origen, Christ is *autobasileia*, Himself the Kingdom that He proclaims.[75]

Even so, Henry talks of synoptic parables in *Paroles du Christ* (2002), the third volume of the trilogy where charges of Gnosticism would be least well founded. Parables, he admits there, "establish an analogy between two universes, that of the visible and that of the invisible, that of the finite and that of the infinite, in such a way that a series of events produce in the first universe incite us to conceive the second, the kingdom of God."[76] Oddly enough, it is in the earlier volume, *C'est moi la vérité*, that Henry discusses two synoptic parables, that of the Good Samaritan and that of the Prodigal Son, and I will conclude by examining his treatment of the latter. Why this parable? Because it is here, if anywhere, that Henry can explain how human beings can fall away from God and find Him again, or, in his terms, how "Life [can know] itself without knowing itself' [*La vie est ce qui se sait sans se savoir*] (201). And because it is here that Henry, forever a prodigal son of phenomenology, also shows himself to be a prodigal son of Christian theology, if not returning from the Gnosticism of a distant land to the orthodoxy of home, then at least beginning to take some steps in that direction in the writing of *Paroles du Christ*.

Before I turn to the parable of the prodigal son, though, it will be useful to put to one side in what other ways the word "parable" might be pertinent in Henry's thought. I therefore distinguish between the parables that Henry examines, parables of his thought, and of what his philosophy might be a parable. We can think, for example, of Henry's novels as parables of his philosophy. *Le Fils du roi* (1981), for instance, shows how characters in a mental institution glimpse their salvation in an intuition of life. In a central passage we hear,

> Comme les larmes qui sourdent sous mes paupières, je sens la vie qui passe à travers moi et me soulève doucement. C'est une force têtue qui ne me demande pas mon avis et n'a cure de mon découragement. Son movement en moi ne s'interrompt pas. Je l'éprouve tout étonné et m'abandonne à son irruption. Ô mon père! Ô sang royale qui fuse à travers moi et me rend à la certitude de ma condition premiere![77]

---

[74]   See Henry, *Paroles du Christ*, 11.

[75]   See Origen, *Commentarium in evangelium Matthaei*, 14.7.10 and 14.7.17.

[76]   Henry, *Paroles du Christ*, 116.

[77]   Henry, *Le Fils du roi* (Paris: Gallimard, 1981), 199–200.

[As the tears that well forth under my eyelids, I feel the life that passes through me and gently lifts me. It is an obstinate force that does not ask my view and does not regard my discouragement. Its movement in me does not stop. I experience it, astonished, and it gives me over to its triumphal irruption. O my father! O royal blood that fuses through me and returns me to the certainty of my first condition!]

José, who is in the mental institution because he believes himself to be a son of the King, is indeed of royal blood, since his true father, the King, is Life. We might think of Henry's thought as a parable not only of Christ's message but also of Marx's. For Marx, as Henry reads him, proposes a messianic conception of history, one that leads to the Kingdom. The revolution is, as he says, a "fantasy of life."[78] And Henry's *Marx* (1976) ends with the sentence, "Marx's thought places us before the profound question: What is life?" (306).

It will be objected with good reason that in an important sense Henry's writings are resolutely non-parabolic. There is only a formal distinction between my life and the divine Life, as he sees it, and in the absence of all analogical relations between the human and the divine there can be no parabolic discourse. Nor can there be faith, as Christians usually understand it, which for Henry is no more than life's immediate knowledge of living, and which is therefore a gnosis and not faith.[79] Yet there is a real distinction between life and world for Henry, and this is precisely what enables him to speak of parables in the fourth gospel and not to find them — at least not at first — in the synoptics where they would seem to him to be revelations to the world. To regard the parables in this way is perhaps to ignore the manner in which they allow the *basileia* to reveal itself in the very act of their narrative performance. They give us, as Eberhard Jüngel rightly says, a "taste" of the *basileia*, a felt sense of what it is to be in harmony with God.[80] For Henry, though, parables will turn on an analogy of world and life, and will give us a taste of invisible life as we might concretely live it. So his philosophy might be seen as a parable itself, a dark saying, since it speaks endlessly of the darkness of the subject, wherein God abides, prior to the light of the world.

***

Let us turn to the parable of the Prodigal Son. Luke tells the story in Chapter 15 of his gospel:

---

[78]   Henry, *Marx: A Philosophy of Human Reality*, trans. Kathleen McLaughlin (Bloomington: Indiana University Press, 1983), 79.

[79]   Henry, "Speech and Religion," 227.

[80]   See Eberhard Jüngel, "The World as Possibility and Actuality. The Ontology of the Doctrine of Justification," *Theological Essays*, ed. and trans. J.B. Webster (Edinburgh: T&T Clark, 1989), 121.

11 Jesus continued: There was a man who had two sons. **12** The younger one said to his father, "Father, give me my share of the estate" [*pater dos moi to epiballon meros tes ousias*]. So he divided his property between them [*ho de dieilen autois ton bion*] **13** Not long after that, the younger son got together all he had, set off for a distant country and there squandered his wealth in wild living [*dieskorpisen ten ousian autou zon asotos*]. **14** After he had spent everything, there was a severe famine in that whole country, and he began to be in need. **15** So he went and hired himself out to a citizen of that country, who sent him to his fields to feed pigs. **16** He longed to fill his stomach with the pods that the pigs were eating, but no one gave him anything. **17** When he came to his senses, he said, "How many of my father's hired men have food to spare, and here I am starving to death! **18** I will set out and go back to my father and say to him: Father, I have sinned against heaven and against you. **19** I am no longer worthy to be called your son; make me like one of your hired men." **20** So he got up and went to his father. But while he was still a long way off, his father saw him and was filled with compassion for him; he ran to his son, threw his arms around him and kissed him. **21** The son said to him, "Father, I have sinned against heaven and against you. I am no longer worthy to be called your son." **22** But the father said to his servants, "Quick! Bring the best robe and put it on him. Put a ring on his finger and sandals on his feet. **23** Bring the fattened calf and kill it. Let's have a feast and celebrate. **24** For this son of mine was dead and is alive again; he was lost and is found." So they began to celebrate. **25** Meanwhile, the older son was in the field. When he came near the house, he heard music and dancing. **26** So he called one of the servants and asked him what was going on. **27** "Your brother has come," he replied, "and your father has killed the fattened calf because he has him back safe and sound." **28** The older brother became angry and refused to go in. So his father went out and pleaded with him. **29** But he answered his father, "Look! All these years I've been slaving for you and never disobeyed your orders. Yet you never gave me even a young goat so I could celebrate with my friends. **30** But when this son of yours who has squandered your property with prostitutes comes home, you kill the fattened calf for him!" **31** "My son," the father said, "you are always with me, and everything I have is yours. **32** But we had to celebrate and be glad, because this brother of yours was dead and is alive again; he was lost and is found."

Taking their cue from Sts Athanasius and Ambrose, most exegetes read this parable as a story of conversion, of a passage from death to life.[81] Some see a tension between the Jews (the elder brother) and the Christians (the younger brother); others regard the parable by way of the graciousness of the Father, while still

---

[81]   See St. Athanasius, *The Resurrection Letters*, paraphrased and intro. Jack N. Sparks (Nashville: Thomas Nelson, 1979), 123, and St. Ambrose, *Exposition of the Holy Gospel According to Saint Luke with Fragments on the Prophecy of Isaias*, trans. T. Tomkinson (Etna, CA: Center for Traditionalist Orthodox Studies, 1998), 317–18.

others — Barth, for instance — find a Christological thread woven carefully into the text.[82] Of all the parables in the gospels, though, this one attracts philosophical, as well as theological, interpretation, and that is because it is the one place in the New Testament where the Greek philosophical word *ousia* occurs. Jean-Luc Marion allows himself to be guided by this word, even while admitting that it is not used in a philosophical sense; and following his reading of the parable for a little way will help us get Henry's quite different interpretation into focus.

Ousia, as Marion points out, is used here in a pre-philosophical sense, as possession or property, and it is tied behind the text, as it were, to the more properly philosophical meaning.[83] Heidegger draws attention to the two senses of the word in his lectures of the summer of 1927. "Disposable possessions and goods, property, are beings; they are quite simply that which is, the Greek *ousia*. In Aristotle's time, when it already had a firm terminological meaning philosophically and theoretically, the expression *ousia* was still synonymous with property, possessions, means, wealth. The pre-philosophical proper meaning of *ousia* carried through to the end."[84] The parable, Marion says, addresses only "the entrance of *ousia* into the logic of possession" (97). The son has already been able to enjoy the possession of the *ousia* but, in asking for it, he deprives himself of its quality as a gift from his Father. He asks for bare *ousia*, right of disposal as well as right of possession, which is tantamount to asking not to have a Father.[85] This is later acknowledged by the son when he says, "I am no longer worthy to be called your son." And the Father gives back to the son exactly what he rejected, the gift dimension of *ousia* and filiation. Unlike both his sons, the Father is not beholden to *ousia*; it marks for him "the play of donation, abandon, and pardon that make of it the currency of an entirely *other* exchange than of beings" (100). For the Father is given to us as love, not being.

Turning to Henry's reading of the parable in *C'est moi la vérité* (1996), it is striking that the word *ousia* plays no role whatsoever in his exegesis. Where Marion finds an iconic moment in the parable, in which we who hear it become the object of an eternal gaze that questions us in our innermost recesses, Henry finds only a steadfast iconoclasm. Indeed, for Henry reading the parable serves to answer the question that preys around his philosophy of Christianity, namely if one is always and already in life how can one lose it and then regain it? Put more theologically, how is salvation possible according to Henry? Notice that the

---

[82]   The tradition of regarding the elder brother as representing the Jews was called into question as early as Tertullian in his *De pudicitia*, ch. 7. See Barth, *Church Dogmatics*, IV: 2, ed. G.W. Bromiley and T.F. Torrance (Edinburgh: T&T Clark, 1958), 21–5.

[83]   See Marion, *God without Being: Hors-Texte*, trans. Thomas A. Carlson, foreword David Tracy (Chicago: University of Chicago Press, 1991), 95–102.

[84]   Heidegger, *The Basic Problems of Phenomenology*, rev. ed. trans., intro. and lexicon Albert Hofstadter (Bloomington: Indiana University Press, 1988), 108.

[85]   See Joachim Jeremias, *The Parables of Jesus*, rev. ed., trans. S.H. Hooke (London: SCM Press, 1963), 129

problem is not posed within the usual eschatological frame. It is not "How does one pass from death to life?" but "How does one return from the world to life?" (In general, it must be said, Henry gives insufficient weighting to human finitude.) And it is not concerned with a relation between the individual and the community but solely with the individual. For Henry, the son must be born of Life — be a son — in order to lose Life and regain it. The condition of living, he says, "refers back to its own precondition, to the absolute-Before of Life from which the living person takes his living quality" (163). Inevitably, the parable is interpreted by way of John: "And if we know that he hear us, whatsoever we ask, we know that we have the petitions that we desired of him" (1 John 5:15). The son loses his relation to the Father in the first place only by passing from life to the world, from the sphere of immanence to the sphere of representation. There is no path to God if one begins in the world, no more so than there is an argument from the world to God (as in Aquinas's "five ways"); there is only worldly pleasure. Salvation occurs when one realizes this fact; it is the self-transformation that takes place when one affirms oneself to be a child of Life.

For Henry, then, Life cannot be forgotten; it is strictly immemorial. We pass from life to Life by extinguishing the "light of appearing," by forgetting ourselves as egos, each one becoming a "Self without Self" [*Soi sans Soi*].[86] Being born again, for Henry, is properly understood in Johannine terms as a spiritual rebirth, not tied to the uniqueness of biological birth, and indeed in terms kin to those of Meister Eckhart. "I am my own cause according to my becoming, which is temporal. Therefore I am unborn, and according to my unborn mode I can never die. According to my unborn mode I have eternally been, am now and shall eternally remain."[87] Marion's reading of the parable underlines the power of love given in verse 20: "But while he was still a long way off, his father saw him and was filled with compassion for him [*esplagchnisthe*]; he ran to his son, threw his arms around him and kissed him." Yet Henry has no resources in his account of either Life to account for this compassion, this love. Henry may say that "Life is love," and may object to the Kantian reduction of love to duty, but life is non-intentional and love, including divine love, is radically intentional.[88] And without love it is impossible for Henry to lay the ground for the ethics he believes to square with Christianity.

Henry's philosophy of Christianity is resolutely Christocentric, yet because his notion of the divine life is without any *telos* his Christology is deprived of any plan of salvation in the divine economy, and in particular the soteriological significance of the Passion. The Passion is the very place where divine love is proclaimed in all its startling difference from human conceptions of love, and Henry is unable to reflect deeply on the centrality of the Passion because, on a

---

[86]   Henry, "Speech and Religion," 229, 231.

[87]   Meister Eckhart, *Sermons and Treatises*, II, 275. Henry quotes from *Traité et sermons*, trans. F.A. and J.M., intro. Maurice de Gandillac (Paris: Aubier, 1942), 258.

[88]   Henry, *I am the Truth*, 186.

non-intentional phenomenology, he cannot establish an account of love. His philosophy of Christianity is an eschatology that excludes the hope that is rooted in the Resurrection of Christ precisely because it is radically under-realized, and it is under-realized with respect to the future precisely because it is over-realized with respect to the immemorial past and the present. Eschatology, for Henry, is primarily an event in the subject, not in Christ, and so the *basileia* is life but never redeemed life. There is, to be a sure, a significant sense in which Henry can say, with the monastic theologians of the middle ages, *ipsa philosophia Christus*; but Christ for him marks a philosophy that is a form of insight or wisdom, the gaze that separates being from knowledge, and then figures being wholly in terms of life, and codes the immediacy of life as faith.[89] A believer, for Henry, is indeed *alter Christus*, but not because he or she accepts in all humility the scandal of the Cross but because he or she affirms the endless play of life. Yet to be *alter Christus* is to show the love that Jesus exemplified to the point of death. Only a phenomenology that accords weight to intentionality, and to the counter-intentionality of the divine gaze, is one that can give an adequate account of Christianity.

---

[89]   See, for instance, Henry, *The Essence of Manifestation*, 405–6.

Appendix[*]

The Present and the Gift

Jean-Luc Marion

To explain the Eucharist — a multiform, inevitable, and instructive naïveté. In another sense, a decisive moment of theological thought.

Inevitable, since the sacrament that completes what all the others aim at, in corporally assimilating us to Christ, the sacrament that brings the logic of the incarnation to its most obviously paradoxical term, the sacrament that visibly gathers men to "form the Church," becomes like the obligatory site where every somewhat consistent theological attempt must come in the end to be tested. For the moment, we will retain in this summons only the challenge thrown out to every theology by the most concrete and least intelligible mystery of faith in Christian life. The Eucharist thus becomes the test of every theological systematization, because, in gathering all, it poses the greatest challenge to thought.

Naïveté above all. Why? What indeed does it mean here "to explain"? Undoubtedly something like giving the reason for a mystery of charity on the basis of a preliminary group of reasons, supposed in their turn to be founded in reason, hence on reason itself. Explanation, even theological, always seems to end up in a "eucharistic physics" (we will see that it matters little if for *physics* one substitutes, e.g., *semiotics*), that is, by an attempt to reabsorb the eucharistic mystery of charity in a rational conceptual system. In the case of failure, such an effort appears either useless (if it limits itself, through theological concern, to recognizing a pure and simple "miracle" in the succession of physical or linguistic events) or else insufficient (if it imputes its conceptual insufficiency to a mystery that it has not even approached, by an infracritical and terroristic subjectivism). But in case of apparent success, this effort is open no less — and here the essential appears — to two other suspicions: does one not contradict oneself by seeking, in principle to reinforce credibility, to frame and then to reabsorb the liturgical fact and the mystery of charity in a system (physical, semiotic, etc.), at the risk, here again, of attaining only a conceptual idol? Do transubstantiation, transfinalization, and transsignification allow one to reach the Eucharist? Or do they substitute themselves for it? Above all, what relevance are we to acknowledge in the enterprise that,

---

[*]   [Editors' Note] We publish here, with the kind permission of University of Chicago Press, the sixth chapter of Jean-Luc Marion's *God Without Being: Hors-Texte*, translated by Thomas A. Carlson and with a foreword by David Tracy (Chicago: University of Chicago Press, 1991), as a classic example of the convergence between phenomenological analysis and eucharistic eschatology.

in order "to explain," would attempt, voluntarily or not, to consider as self-evident the equivalence between the gift that Christ makes of his body and a conceptually retraced transmutation? A gift, and this one above all, does not require first that one explain it, but indeed that one receive it. Does not the haste to explain disclose an inability to receive and hence the loss of a primordial theological reflex?

Instructive nevertheless. For the inevitable naïveté does not suffice to disqualify every effort of meditation on the eucharistic presence. On the contrary, it incites one to consider thoroughly the conditions in which this effort will not remain vain. If "explanation"[1] there must be, we will understand it in the sense of delinquents or, if one prefers, in the sense that Jacob had, at the ford Jabbok, an "explanation" with the angel: in such an "explanation," it is a question not so much of speaking as of struggling; each adversary demands of the other, first, avowal or "blessing," hence recognition. Here, explanation would have to admit reciprocity: it is a question less of knowing whether a particular explanation can account for the eucharistic presence than of seeing whether the theoretical apparatus will let itself be criticized by that of which it is a question, to reach the dignity of what is at stake. Language, if properly theological, must therefore let itself be taken up again on the basis of the epistemological, or rather mystical, demands of that to which it pertains (and which has precisely nothing like an *object,* theology having none of the characteristics of scientificity, and especially not its objectivity).[2] This rule is valid in all matters and all manners — for the mystery of G~d, to be sure, but even for the paradoxical figures of his advent in Christ or finally in the eucharistic Christ. In a sense, the eucharistic presence of Christ constitutes the case *par excellence* where this demand becomes unavoidable: in the two other cases, in fact, a theology that transgresses it condemns itself to idolatry or to heresy but can conceal the one and attempt to exculpate itself from the other; on the contrary, before the eucharistic presence, the sanction cannot be avoided: if theological language refuses "explanation," then that to which it pertains — eucharistic presence — is dissolved. The Eucharist requires of whoever approaches it a radical conceptual self-critique and charges him with renewing his norms of thought. We will attempt to show this with regard to one precise and fundamental case: the application to the Eucharist of the concept of "presence."

---

[1]   "[E]xplication," which in the French indicates not only an explanation of or for something, but also a discussion, argument, or fight — Trans.

[2]   Theology has nothing in common with scientificity and its processes of objectivation. See M. Heidegger, *Phänomenologie und Theologie, Wegmarken, G.A.,* pp. 68–77, trans. Hart and Maraldo, pp. 22–30. In another style, see L. Bouyer, "Situation de la théologie," in *Revue catholique internationale Communio,* 1/1 (Paris, 1975).

One or the Other Idolatry

Let us take a look, then, at the usual and ceaselessly repeated critique of the
theology of transubstantiation. It is most often reproached, among other things, for
using concepts — substance, accidents, species, transubstantiation — stemming
from a historically defined metaphysics, that of Aristotle (to which one boldly
likens Thomistic theology). But the "good news of Jesus Christ" exceeds every
metaphysic. Therefore, becoming conscious of the historical relativity of a
eucharistic theology of transubstantiation, one would have to renounce it (while
saluting it from a distance as "legitimate in its time") and attempt to "invent"
a new eucharistic theology, founded on a more modern philosophical thought.
This critique, one must recall, relies on summary or inexact reflections. For in the
end, *substantia* is introduced in eucharistic theology independently of the reading
of Aristotle;³ *transsubstantiatio* is validated by the Council of Trent only as an
equivalent of the *conversio*, that is to say of the *metabole* of the Greek Fathers;⁴
rather than the Thomistic explanation (which, of course, modifies Aristotle quite a
bit, since it inverts his terms, going so far as to speak of a permanence of accidents
and of a substitution of substances) acting as the foundation of the dogmatic texts,
the latter precede the former (*transsubstantiare* appears as early as 1202, and
transsubstantiatio as early as 1215)⁵ or correct it (substituting species for accidents,
during the Council of Trent, etc.). The equivalence of the Tridentine doctrine with
Thomistic theology therefore is not self-evident.⁶ As to recognizing the essen-

---

³   Besides the translation of *ousia* (in Luke 15:35–6) by *substantia* (see *God Without
Being: Hors-Texte*, chap. 3, sec. 4, text at note 78), one should bear in mind Fauste of Riez
(452–78) (Pseudo-Saint Jerome, *Ep.* XXXVIII, P.L. 30, 272b). "Visibilis sacerdos visibiles
creaturas in substantiam corporis et sanguinis sui, verbo suo secreta potestate convertit,
ita dicens …"; the confession imposed by the Sixth Council of Rome, in 1079, on Beren-
ger: "Panem et vinum … substantialiter converti in veram et propriam ac vivificatricem
carnem et sanguinem Jesu Christi … non tantum per signum et virtutem sacramenti sed in
proprietate naturae et veritate substantiae" (Mansi, *Collectio* XX, 524; Denz. 355), etc.

⁴   Council of Trent, Session 13, e.4 (*Denz.* 877 and 884). *Metabolē:* Cyril of Jerusalem,
Mystagogical Catecheses, IV, 2, and V, 7 (P.G. 33, 1097b and 1116a); Justin, *First Apology*,
66,2 (P.G. 6, 429a), etc.

⁵   Respectively, the *Letter* of Innocent III to the Bishop of Lyon, 1202 (*Denz.* 414) and
the Fourth Lateran Council, 1215 (*Denz.* 430; Mansi XXII, 982s).

⁶   See J.R. Armogathe, *Theologia Cartesiana. L'explication physique de l'Eucharistie
chez Descartes et dom Desgabets* (The Hague, 1977), in particular pp. 6, 8, 11, 31–2, etc. It
is important to underline, even more than does J.R. Armogathe, that Saint Thomas and Duns
Scotus (*a fortiori* the Fathers) propose no explanation or "eucharistic physics" that would
claim to take up the mystery of the body of Christ within a non-theological theoretical
corpus. Only Descartes and Leibniz will take this step. This is why the equivalence of
the logics of the Eucharist that J. Guitton assumes ("Logique de L'Eucharistie," in *Revue
catholique internationale Communio*, II, 5, 1977) seems disputable. For there is an obvious

tial of Aristotle's metaphysics in the latter, one needs as little philosophical as theological sense to try to do so.

All the same, the critique will not yield. It can now only generalize an objection, which it cannot assure in detail. One can say: even if the theology of transubstantiation is not reducible to a particular theme imported from a particular metaphysic, in any case, it exposes itself to an otherwise serious danger. Indeed, the transposition of one substance into another (that of the bread and that of the body of Christ) leads one to recognize the traits of a person under the appearances (species) of a substance; the substantial presence therefore fixes and freezes the person in an available, permanent, handy, and delimited thing. Hence the imposture of an idolatry that imagines itself to honor "God" when it heaps praises on his pathetic "canned" substitute (the reservation of the Eucharist), exhibited as an attraction (display of the Holy Sacrament), brandished like a banner (processions), and so on. In this sense, profanation would increase with the bustle of a too obviously "political" worship: political in the profound sense that the community would seek to place "God" at its disposition like a thing, its thing, to reassure its identity and strengthen its determination in that thing. Of this "God" made thing, one would expect precisely nothing but *real* presence: presence reduced to the dimensions of a thing, a thing that is as much disposed to "honor by its presence" the liturgies where the community celebrates its own power, as emptied of all significance capable of contesting, in the name of G~d, the collective self-satisfaction.[7] Real presence: "God" made thing, a hostage without significance, powerful because mute, tutelary because without titularity, a thing *"denuded of all signification except that of presence"* (Mallarmé).[8]

He who pretends to go beyond a metaphysic must produce thereby another *thought*. And he who pretends to go beyond all metaphysics most often risks taking up again, without being conscious of it, its basic characteristic. Here exactly, it would be a matter of going beyond, with real presence, the idolatrous reduction of "God" to a mute thing, a vainly impotent presence. This operation is usually effected by mobilizing the explanatory models of transignification. But these

---

unevenness and an obvious original displacement of the discourse: from contemplation, it passes to explanation.

[7]   The liturgy thus would honor the eucharistic presence as the Third Estate would honor Louis XVI on the holiday of the Federation: the king, mute, sanctions by his real presence a fraternity sure of itself, and which, in acclaiming him, comprehends that it holds him in its power, that he lives only by that fraternity. Thus Talleyrand was able alone to celebrate a Eucharist even more profane than profaned.

[8]   S. Mallarmé, *Igitur ou la folie d'Elbehnon*, I, Le Minuit, *Oeuvres complètes*, Pleiade (Paris, 1945), p. 435, trans. Wooley, p. 155. One will be surprised to see Mallarmé cited here only if one underestimates certain eucharistic texts that would merit a thorough theological reading: *Catholicisme*, in *Variations sur un sujet,* loc. cit., pp. 390–95, which contains a sequence as remarkable as theologically correct, p. 394. E. Pousset denounced this risk in measured and precise terms: "L'Eucharistie, présence réelle et transsubstantiation," in *Recherches de Sciences Religieuses*, 1966, 2.

remain neutral: they can perfectly be integrated within the perspective of transubstantiation, which ballasts them, so to speak, with reality, while they themselves give to it all of the "existential" dimension required by the mystery of charity.[9] These models, therefore, taken in their legitimate usage, constitute no break with the preceding model — on the contrary. What decision or anterior condition will therefore render them polemical? The true debate obviously bears on the determination of new meanings and goals, or, more exactly, on the instance that determines them. Either it is still Christ, the priest *in persona Christi*,[10] who gives to the community the new meanings and goals of the bread and wine, precisely because the community does not produce them, does not have them at its disposal, or perform them; then this gift will be welcomed as such by a community that, receiving it, will find itself nourished and brought together by it. Or else, on the contrary, it comes back to the community, on the basis of the meanings and goals ("evangelical values," "human values," etc.) whose experiences ("struggles," "progressions," "searches," etc.) enriched it, to establish the liturgical novelty of the bread and of the wine. Among these meanings and goals, "God" will recognize his own! But He will be content with recognizing them therein, far from taking the initiative "from above" to consecrate (Himself) in a thing distinct from the community. Bread and wine will become the mediations less of the presence of G~d in the community than of the becoming aware, of "God" and of itself, by a community that *"seeks the face, the face of the Lord."* And precisely at the moment of receiving the sacrament, the community still seeks it, and has found nothing more of it than what its collective consciousness, at a given moment in its "progression," had been able to secure.[11] Presence is no longer measured by

---

[9] To reintegrate transsignification and transfinalization in transubstantiation in order to consolidate them was the effort of J. de Baciocchi ("Présence eucharistique et Transsubstantiation," in *Irenikon*, 1959 and *L'Eucharistie* (Tournai, 1964); E. Pousset, loc. cit., F.-X. Durrwell, *L'Eucharistie, présence du Christ* (Paris, 1971); and J.H. Nicolas, "Présence réelle eucharistique et transsignification," *Revue Thomiste*, 1981. We had taken up this aim, whose recent theological evolution no doubt has shown its limits, in "Présence et distance," *Resurrection*, 43/44 (Paris, 1974).

[10] *In Persona Christi*, see John-Paul II, *Dominicae Cenae*, II, 8: "The priest offers the holy sacrifice 'in persona Christi,' which means more than 'in the name' or 'in place' of Christ. 'In persona': that is to say in the specific, sacramental identification to the 'great priest of the eternal Covenant,' who is the author and the principal subject of his own sacrifice, in which he cannot be replaced by anyone." Fr. trans. *Sur le mystère et le culte de la sainte eucharistie* (Paris, 1980), p. 28.

[11] We can understand then why celebrating Eucharists on condition became inevitable: the unanimity of the community is no longer here a fruit of communion but, as collective consciousness of self, its condition. All the schismatic "fundamental communities," on one side and the other, have this common trait: the eucharistic celebration reflects first the determination of the group; it is celebrated *against* an adversary. Political pruritus does not rot certain eucharists to the same extent that, on the contrary, a distorted theology of the Eucharist delivers these communities to political pruritus.

the excessiveness of an irreducibly other gift, as far as assuming the corporally distinct appearance of an irreducible thing. No doubt there remains an irreducible presence of Christ, but it is displaced from the thing to the community: "One must pass from Jesus present in the host to Jesus present to a people whose eucharistic action manifests reality under the sacramental form."

> The heart of this mystery is that communion with God passes by way of the communion of men among themselves. It is for this reason that the sign of communion with God is the sharing between men. ... It must not be forgotten that the Eucharist is before all else a meal, the sharing of which is the sign of the communion of those who participate in it. And the community of those who share it is in its turn the sign of communion with God. It is like a ricochet: there is a reality which is the sign of something that, in its turn, is the sign of something else.[12]

That one might pray against (despite the theological non-sense of the expression) is what is undertaken by some of the "eucharistic prayers" collected by H. Oosterhuis in *Autour de la table*, Fr. trans. (Paris, 1974), p. 109. That one should say in them: "We pray to you against ourselves / against our preference not to know / against the laziness of our economic politics ..." does not diminish the aggressiveness of the request but on the contrary reinforces it, by interiorizing the accusation — so far as to illustrate emblematically the reactive comportment analyzed in the *Genealogy of Morals* I, secs. 10–11 and II, secs. 11–12. All hatred begins with self-hatred. See R. Brague, "Si ce n'est ton frère, c'est donc toi," *Revue catholique internationale Communio*, II/4, 1977.

[12]   Respectively, L. Charlot, "Jésus est-il dans la hostie?" in *Foi à l'epreuve*, no. 5, CRER (Angers, 1977), p. 20, and R. Berset, *De commencement en commencant, Itineraire d'une déviance* (Paris: Seuil, 1976), pp. 176 and 179. Despite the simultaneously unpolished and loose writing, one will have recognized, in this text, the doctrine of *res/sacramentum*, but strictly inverted: here the species become *res*, the sacramental communion becomes *res/sacramentum*, the communion with "God" (and not with Christ, a detail of some importance!), *sacramentum tantum*. And thus, the body that makes the Church (here, the deviant community) gives consistency, through the sacramental body, to the glorious (and hence historically risen) body: taken up again, inverted, from the doctrine of the *corpus triforme*.

At an entirely other level of seriousness and competence, C. Duquoe: "La notion de presence risque d'évacuer le substrat humain en lequel elle se realise: le repas ou le pain partagé," in *Revue des Sciences philosophiques et theologiques* (Paris, 1969/3), p. 427. But precisely: (a) Is it a question of a human substratum? Is it not a question, even more than of the shared meal or bread, of the gift of the Christ, free and independent of our substrata? (b) Is it indeed a question of a *substratum*? Do not presence and substratum (*substratum*, *hupokeimenon*) coincide, sometimes even as early as Aristotle, so that from one to the other there is no progression, but indeed strict equivalence? See R. Boehm, *La Metaphysique d'Aristote, Le Fondamental et l'Essential* (Paris, 1976); Fr. trans., original edition (The Hague, 1965).

We immediately note an essential point. Even if the theology of transubstantiation has lost its legitimacy and, with it, real presence, the very notion of presence remains. It is simply displaced from the eucharistic "thing" (real presence) to the community; or, more exactly, the present consciousness of the collective self is substituted for the concentration of the present of "God" under the species of a thing.

In addition, this substitution does not mark an equivalence of presence or in presence so much as it accentuates the role of the present as the unique horizon for the eucharistic gift. Presence, which no thing here comes to render real, no longer remains distinct from the collective consciousness, but strictly coincides with it, hence as long as, in that consciousness, presence endures. Or even: presence is valid only in the present, and in the present of the community consciousness. Presence — ceasing to rely on a *res* — henceforth depends entirely on the consciousness of it possessed, here and now, by that community communion. This is why all sensible mediation disappears: the bread and wine serve as a simple perceptible medium for a wholly intellectual or representational process, the collective awareness of the community by itself. The concern for the "concrete" leads, as often, to a gnostic intellectualism that in fact disqualifies every liturgy. The consecrating prayer (the canon) becomes, in the extreme, as useless as its performance by the substitute of Christ (the priest). A gesture or a gaze, provided that it permit the community awareness, suffices.[13] The immediate consciousness of the collective self hence produces the first appearance of the presence of "God" to the community. The (human and representational) present commands the future of divine presence. In the same way, presence disappears as soon as the consciousness of the collective self defines itself: the insistence with which one recalls that the sacred species only constitute finally, some "leftovers," that the eucharistic reservation has little or no theological justification, even that one can throw out or burn[14] the consecrated bread, and so forth, obviously testifies that

---

[13] See B. Besret, *De commencement*, p. 46. Hence the facility, in those apparently "incarnational" theologies, in admitting that one may substitute the bread and wine with other species (rice, tea, etc.): the singularity of the historical contingency of Jesus disappears as easily as the concrete moment of *any* consecration here and now is rendered null and void.

[14] See B. Besret, op. cit., pp. 182–3. With the forgetting or the end of expectation (subjective disappearance of the present in immediate consciousness) ends the reality of the eucharistic presence in the species. Not that there is not any presence at all, but it remains subjected to the praying consciousness; it is not by chance that B. Besret speaks of *burning* the unconsumed bread after "consecration": the icon, which includes no substantial presence (but only hypostatic; see M.-H. Congourdeau, "L'oeil théologique," in *Revue catholique internationale Communio*, II, 5, 1977), had to burn when the physical medium (wood) was becoming undone or was decomposing. The consecrated bread here plays the role of the painted wood, neither less nor more. The confusion of the two presences, hypostatic (icon) or substantial (Eucharist), either likens the icon to the Eucharist iconoclasm: see Ch. von Schonborn, *L'icône du Christ* (Fribourg, 1976), in particular pp. 223–6), or else reduces the Eucharist to the icon (contemporary deviancies, idolatry of sense); in both cases one falls short of a correct understanding of the incarnation (see M.-H. Congourdeau, loc. cit.).

no thing suffices to maintain presence, once conscious attention has disappeared. The immediate consciousness of the collective self hence prompts the end of the presence of "God" to the community. The (human and representational) present determines the relegation of divine presence to the past.

Consciousness and the Immediate

A double dependency henceforth affects the eucharistic presence. Because the gift of "God" in it depends on human consciousness, and because the latter thinks time on the basis of the present, the gift of "God" still depends on the present of consciousness — on attention. Eucharistic presence is measured by what the attention of the human community presently accords to it. It is a question of a perfect inversion (perversion?) of perpetual adoration. Far, indeed, from the Eucharistic presence ceaselessly provoking the attention of men who fall ecstatically outside of the disposability of the present moment, to exceed themselves in the past and the future, and to weave, without end or beginning, a perpetuity of attention to the eucharistic gift where the presence of the Alpha and of the Omega shines — here, on the contrary, present consciousness believes itself to govern all eucharistic presence offered to the community. The intermittencies of attention provoke the interim of presence. Adoration henceforth becomes as impossible as perpetuity: everyone knows that a group cannot concentrate its attention for a long time, all the more in that here no exterior object captivates or provokes the attention. It is not a question of adoring itself perpetually, but of becoming conscious of itself ("elevating the level of group consciousness"). But, said Descartes, the cogito endures only from moment to moment, and one need not consecrate to it more than a couple of hours a year. For the collective cogito, the case will be the same: no perpetuity, but coming to consciousness according to needs and occasions. The attention of human and collective consciousness measures the eucharistic presence on the basis of the present that, here and now, dominates, organizes, and defines the common conception of time.

Having thus defined, in its characteristic traits, the conception that pretended to reject a supposed idolatry in the theology of transubstantiation, we can turn back on it the question that it itself posed. Is the danger of an idolatrous approach to eucharistic presence now averted? Obviously, far from disappearing, idolatry here knows its triumph, and all the more that it divides into two.

Let us remark finally that the deviant and reductionist interpretation of the eucharistic present (Besret, Charlot, "Dutch Catechism," etc.) give to it the function that, in the faith of earlier times, came back to the blessed bread: offered by a member of the community, this sacramental, blessed before the consecration, was distributed to all in sign of the union of the community with itself, without replacing or rivaling the eucharistic gift. Let this pious custom be reestablished if it would avoid reducing the *conversio realis* of the Bread and of the Wine!

The idolatry for which one accused, wrongly, the theology of transubstantiation bore upon the reification of eucharistic presence: in it G~d would become an idol, in the strict sense of a material, inert, and available representation. For the moment, let us not criticize this summary criticism. Let us remark simply that the thing has at least an immense advantage over immediate consciousness of (and as) presence: it *exists*, in other words, poses itself outside of the intermittencies of attention, and mediates the relation of consciousness to presence. In becoming conscious of the thing where eucharistic presence is embodied, the believing community does not become conscious of itself, but of another, of the Other *par excellence*. It thus avoids — even at the risk of an eventual material idolatry — the supreme as well as subtly dissimulated idolatry, the spiritual idolatry where consciousness becomes to itself the idol of Christ. In fact, community consciousness, if it "realizes" what animates it, becomes the only veritable "real" presence, without any thing any longer having to mediate its relation to the Eucharistic presence. Then consciousness claims to be immediately the presence of Christ: the idol no longer stems from any representation whatsoever, but from the representational consciousness of self. Thus any gap between self consciousness and the consciousness/knowledge of Christ among us, between revelation and manifestation, is abolished. The absence of a represented object hence does not eliminate idolatry but establishes the coming to immediate consciousness of eucharistic presence as the insurmountable idol.

Hegel saw precisely in this eucharistic consciousness without real mediation the great superiority of Lutheranism over Catholicism. Hence nothing better than his reproach can allow us to understand, *a contrario*, how real presence (guaranteed by a thing independent of consciousness) alone avoids the highest idolatry: "And yet in Catholicism this spirit of all truth [that is to say, God] is in actuality set in rigid opposition to the self-conscious spirit. And, first of all, God is in the 'host' presented to religious adoration as an *external thing*. (In the Lutheran Church, on the contrary, the host as such is not at first consecrated, but in the moment *of enjoyment*, i.e. in the annihilation of its externality, and in the act of *faith*, i.e. in the free self-certain spirit: only then is it consecrated and exalted to be present God.)"[15] What the consecrated host imposes, or rather permits, is the irreducible

---

[15]   Hegel, *Encyclopaedia*, sec. 552, trans. Wallace and Miller, pp. 284–5. As replacement for the Catholic host, morality will become the highest divine presence but comprehended in the present of consciousness: "The ethical life (*Sittlichkeit*) is the divine spirit as indwelling in self-consciousness, as it is actually present (*wirklicher, Gegenwart*) in a nation and its individual members," ibid., trans., p. 283. One would have to give all the Hegelian parallels to this text, which make it much more than one incident. In the *Lectures on the Philosophy of History* (IV, II, 1), Hegel notes that the host forbids that "the presence of Christ [should be] essentially established in representation and spirit" (*Jubilaumsausgabe*, II, p. 480) and that "for the Catholic, the process does not take place in the spirit, but by the intermediary of the thingness that mediates it," ibid. Likewise, in the *Lectures on the Philosophy of Religion* (III, III, 3), he underlines remarkably that "this exteriority is the foundation of the whole Catholic religion" (16, p. 339, trans. Brown, Hodgson, and Stewart, p. 480). See also the *Lectures on the History of Philosophy* (III, II, II, B; 19, p. 146). See, from

exteriority of the present that Christ makes us of himself in this thing that to him becomes sacramental body. That this exteriority, far from forbidding intimacy, renders it possible in sparing it from foundering in idolatry, can be misunderstood only by those who do not want to open themselves to *distance*. Only distance, in maintaining a distinct separation of terms (of persons), renders communion possible, and immediately mediates the relation. Here again, between the idol and distance, one must choose.

Metaphysical or Christic Temporality

But idolatry, here, is not exhausted with this first inadequacy. Indeed, the reduction of the eucharistic presence to the immediate consciousness that the (community) consciousness has of it plays its reductionist function only as long as consciousness itself is grasped as a self-presence of thought. Or better, as a thought in the present, which measures the future and the past of presence — and of eucharistic presence in particular — starting from the present time, from time as present. Eucharistic presence is valid here only as long as the present of consciousness measures it and imparts the present to it starting from the consciousness of the present. But, to think time starting from the present constitutes the function, stake, and characteristic not of a specific metaphysic, but of metaphysics as a whole, from Aristotle to Hegel (and Nietzsche) — if at least one admits the initial thought of Heidegger, hence first if one accedes to it. According to *Sein und Zeit*, in fact, metaphysics deploys an "ordinary conception of time," whose inaugurally Aristotelian formulation is found again, term for term, in Hegel.[16] Time is deployed in Hegel in favor and on the basis of the present, itself understood as the *here and now* by which consciousness assures itself, or rather whereby consciousness assures itself of being. For, through metaphysics, being is deployed in its Being only as long as its handy and assured availability endures. The presence available in the present — as the *here and now* — *guarantees* the permanence where spirit maintains a hold on being. The present not only determines the only visible, assured, measurable mode of time but also thereby delivers to the disposition of consciousness each being

---

the same perspective, Feuerbach, *The Essence of Christianity*, II, 7. One must certainly recognize that Catholicism attempts to preserve this gap, criticized by Hegel to the benefit of Lutheranism and in view of absolute knowledge; indeed we attempt nothing other, here, under the name of "distance."

[16] *Sein und Zeit,* Secs. 81–2, from which the famous note 1, pp. 432–3, trans. Macquarrie and Robinson, pp. 483–4, but previously paragraphs 6 and 65. Obviously it is not by chance that Hegel completes the metaphysical ("ordinary") conception of time *and* rejects the Catholic real presence; this presence, at a distance from consciousness (of self and of time), disqualifies by its independence and its great perpetuity the two fundamental characteristics of the "ordinary concept of time": the primacy of the *here and now* and the reduction of time to the perception of it that consciousness experiences.

that can become an object to it. The present assures an objective possession of that which *is* (in the) present. This ontological overdetermination of a primacy of the present leads to a double reduction of the future and of the past: the past finishes and the future begins as soon as the present begins or finishes. Their respective temporalities count only negatively, as a double nonpresent, even a double nontime. Above all, this negative definition prohibits them from producing the available and assured hold over being that only the present confers. It appears that eucharistic presence never finds itself so much submitted to metaphysics as in the conception that criticizes the theology of transubstantiation as metaphysical: in this conception the primacy of the present (as the *here and now* of an ontic disposability) and that of the human consciousness of time act in the open and in full. The norms that metaphysics imposes on every being, starting from its conception of time, thus exert themselves even on the eucharistic presence, without exception or compromise. Idolatry finds its metaphysical completion in the very enterprise that claimed to criticize an apparently metaphysical eucharistic theology. Which proves, once again, that to surpass metaphysics, it does not suffice, even in theology, to forget or to ignore it.

It therefore remains to attempt to think eucharistic presence without yielding to idolatry — whether it be that, supposed, of the transubstantial thing, that, obvious, of (collective) selfconsciousness, or that, metaphysical, of the "ordinary conception of time." Is it a question, for all that, of resuming the slogan of a "theology without metaphysics"? Obviously not, for the overcoming of metaphysics — besides that far from implying the least scorn for conceptual thought, it redoubles the demand for it — is not the concern of theology, but only of philosophical thought, on condition that it accede to the nonmetaphysical essence of metaphysics. Our task here remains theological. It amounts to a precise question: can the eucharistic presence of Christ as consecrated bread and wine determine, starting from itself and itself alone, the conditions of its reality, the dimensions of its temporality and the dispositions of its approach?[17] Does eucharistic presence suffice for its own comprehension? And, first, of what presence is it a question? Not first of a privileged temporalization of time (the *here and now* of the present) but *of the present, that is to say of the gift*. Eucharistic presence must be understood starting most certainly from the present, but the present must be understood first as a gift that is given. One must measure the dimensions of eucharistic presence against the fullness of this gift. The principal weakness of reductionist interpretations stems precisely from

---

[17] One must neither maximize nor minimize that Heidegger should have begun to envisage an alternative to the "ordinary conception of time" after the privileged reading of the Letters of Saint Paul, particularly of 1 Thessalonians 4 and 5 and of 2 Corinthians 12:1–10. See O. Pöggeler, *La pensée de Heidegger* (Paris, 1967), p. 43f. Fr. trans., citing a still unpublished course from 1921–22. One might consult Y. de Andia, *Présence et eschatologie dans la pensée de Martin Heidegger*, PUL (Lille/Paris, 1965), as well as K. Lehmann, "Christliche Geschichtserfahrung und ontologische Frage beim jungen Heidegger," in *Philosophisches Jarbuch der Gorresgesellschaft* (1966), 74/1.

their exclusively anthropological, hence metaphysical, treatment of the Eucharist. They never undertake to think presence starting from the gift that, theologically, constitutes presence in the present. For the dimensions of the gift can be determined, at least in outline, according to a strictly theological approach. The rigor of the gift must order the dimensions of the temporality where the present is made gift. Now it happens that the eucharistic gift, which Christ makes of himself under the species of the consecrated Bread and Wine, includes the fundamental terms of a temporality of the gift. This temporality is in no way added here by the artifice of an indiscreetly apologetic zeal. It springs from the most concrete analyses that exegesis can give us. The present of the eucharistic gift is not at all temporalized starting from the *here and now* but as memorial (temporalization starting from the past), then as eschatological announcement (temporalization starting from the future), and finally, only finally, as dailyness and viaticum (temporalization starting from the present). As opposed to the metaphysical concept of time, the present here does not order the analysis of temporality as a whole, but results from it. This reversal, which remains for us to retrace, implies that we will understand the Eucharistic presence less in the way of an available permanence than as a new sort of advent.

The Memorial

Temporalization starting from the past: the Christian Eucharist takes the memorial up again from the Jewish blessing, not, to be sure, in order to recall to the subjective memory of the community a past fact that would be defined by its nonpresence, by the cessation of the presence concerning it.[18] It is not at all

---

[18]   See J. Jeremias, *La dernière cène, les Paroles de Jesus*, Fr. trans. Paris, 1972, pp. 283–304; L. Bouyer, *Eucharistie* (Paris, 1966), pp. 87–8, 107, etc.; *Le Fils eternel* (Paris, 1973), pp. 140–52; and "Liturgie juive et Liturgie chretienne," *Istina*, 1973/2. Inversely, *L'Introduction à la foi chretienne* ("Dutch Catechism") (Paris, 1968): "the essential reason for which the Church itself does what the Lord did. It does it in memory of Him, to think of Him" (p. 429); and B. Besret, op. cit., p. 50. On the contrary, the *Memorial* of Pascal spontaneously *obeys* theological requirements: certainly, Pascal always keeps it to himself, "to retain the memory of a thing that he always wanted present to his eyes and his mind" (note by P. Guerrier, in the 3rd collection, cited in Pascal, *Oeuvres completes*, ed. L. Lafuma (Paris, 1963), p. 618). But this subjective memory concerns an absolutely real fact of salvation (union with God which reaches him in the very midst of separation), which radically determines the present instant of recollection (the "little parchment" maintains fidelity) and aims at an eternal completion: "Eternally in joy for a day of exercise on earth. *Non obliviscar sermones tuos.* Amen." One could find a definition of the memorial such as it culminates with the eucharistic present in the Pascalian approach to hope, hence to Christian temporality: "The Christian's hope of possessing an infinite good is mingled with actual enjoyment as well as with fear, for, unlike people hoping for a kingdom of which they will have no part because they are subjects, Christians hope for holiness, and to be freed

a question of commemorating a dead person to spare him the second death of oblivion. In this case, the past still remains radically thought in view of the present (to maintain a second order presence, immortality in the memory of men: idolatry through the collective consciousness), and starting from it (as a nonpresence in the *here and now*). It is a question of making an appeal, in the name of a past event, to G~d, in order that he recall an engagement (a covenant) that determines the instant presently given to the believing community. Whether it be a question of the crossing of the Red Sea or of the conquest of the Promised Land, "the memorial of the Messiah, son of David your servant, and the memorial of your people,"[19] the event remains less a past fact than a pledge given in the past in order, today still, to appeal to a future — an advent, that of the Messiah — that does not cease to govern *this* today from beginning to end. The Christian Eucharist does not recall to memory the death and the resurrection of Christ — would we be "Christians" if we had forgotten them? — it relies on an event whose past reality has not disappeared in our day (the Ascension belongs intrinsically to the death and resurrection), in order to ask with insistence — eschatological impatience — that Christ return, hence also that his presence govern the future as much as it is rooted in the past. Thus far from the past being defined as a nonpresent, or as an accomplished actuality, it orders through its irreducibly anterior and definitively accomplished "deal"[20] a today that, without it, would remain insignificant, indifferent, in a word null and void — unreal. The memorial makes of the past a decisive reality for the present, because "if Christ is not risen, our faith is vain, and you are still presently (*eti*) in your sins … For if it is only for this life [present, *taute*] that we hope in Christ, we are the most miserable men of all" (1 Cor. 15:17–18). The present no longer opposes its clear and conscious self-sufficiency to an immemorial past. On the contrary, the memorial, because a real and past event, renders this day tenable. The past determines the reality of the present — better, the present is understood as a today to which alone the memorial, as an actual pledge, gives meaning and reality.

Epektasis

Immediately, one sees how the temporalization of the today, by its past, intimately refers to an even more essential temporalization — by the future. For the memorial itself is valid only as a support in order that prayer may implore of the Father the innovation and completion of an eschatological advent. The memorial aims at the

---

from unrighteousness, and some part of this is already theirs" (*Pensées*, Br. sec. 540, L. sec. 917), trans., Krailsheimer, p. 312.

19   Jewish prayer on the eve of Passover, cited by J. Jeremias, *La dernière cène*, pp. 300–301, and L. Bouyer, *Eucharistie*, p. 87, after B. Italiener, A. Freimann, A.L. Mayer, A. Schmidt, *Die Darmstädter Passach Haggadab* (Leipzig, 1928), fol. 32b–33a.

20   "[D]onne"; a deal or distribution, in the sense of a hand of cards — Trans.

Parousia: "You shall do this in memory of me" (Luke 22:17), "until he comes" (1 Cor. 11:26). Moreover, this is a question not only of a future period that will be unveiled in waiting for Christ to come (again), but indeed — as the exegetes agree — of a call that asks for and, in a sense, hastens the return of Christ: "so that he return," one almost would have to translate.[21] The presence to come does not define the horizon of a simple possibility, tangential utopia or historical term, as if it were a question of a simple nonpresence that would remain to bring, finally, to presence. On the contrary, the future determines the reality of the present in the very mode of the advent. The eucharistic gift relies, so to speak, on the tension that raises it since and for the future. The future *as future*, governs, runs through, and polarizes the eucharistic gift, thus "straining [*epekteinomenos*] toward that which is coming to it" (Phil. 3:13). The pledge, which the memorial sets into operation, now anticipates the future, so that the present itself occurs entirely as this anticipation concretely lived. The eschatological *epektasis* that temporalizes the eucharistic present through the future is expressed in many ways in the Christian tradition. We will say that the Eucharist constitutes the first fragment of the new creation, the pledge (*pignus*) that Christ gives us through his resurrected body, sacramentally present.[22] We will even say that the Eucharist, body of the Living *par excellence*, leads to eternal life, since it "is the remedy of immortality, the antidote that saves us from dying, makes us live in the Christ Jesus in all."[23] We might also say that, in the Eucharist, we find ourselves figured. It is generally and quite naturally supposed that the Eucharist lacks something to manifest the corporal presence of Christ, that the evidence is concealed to avid or curious gaze; it envisages, hopes for, or imagines "eucharistic miracles"; in fact, by itself, the absolute gift, whose perfection anticipates our mode of presence, surpasses our attention, dazzles our gaze, and discourages our lucidity The Eucharist anticipates what we will be, will see, will love: *figura nostra*, the figure of what we will be, but above all ourselves, facing the gift that we cannot yet welcome, so, in the strict sense, that we cannot yet figure it. In this way, "sometimes the future lives in us without our knowing it" (Proust).[24]

---

[21]   See J. Jeremias, op. cit., pp. 301–5.

[22]   John of Damascus: "This bread offers the first-fruits of the bread to come, which is *epiousion. Epiousion* means either that which is to come, the time to come, or that which we do to safeguard our being"; *De la foi orthodoxe*, IV, 13; see Fr. trans. by E. Ponsoye (Paris, 1966), p. 175. Ambrose understands the bread "of this day" as bread "that is coming": "The Latin names *daily* this bread that the Greeks say is to come (*advenientem*)"; *De Sacramentis*, V, 4. G. Martelet developed this theme with vigor and rigor in *Resurrection, Eucharistie, Genese de l'homme* (Paris, 1972).

[23]   Ignatius of Antioch, in *Die Apostolischen Vater*, ed. J.A. Fischer, (Darmstadt, 1956), pp. 158–61. See Cyril of Jerusalem, *Catecheses mystagogique*, V, 15, "Sources Chretiennes" 126 (Paris, 1966), pp. 162–3.

[24]   M. Proust, *A la recherche du temps perdu*, Pleiade, 2 (Paris, 1954), p. 639.

From Day to Day

The memorial and *epektasis*, therefore, traverse the present from end to end. Far from being defined as two absences or blackouts of the *here and now*, their two absolutely originary temporalizations determine, as such, this simple interspace that we habitually privilege under the name of the present. Henceforth what, exactly, becomes of the present? The initial demand — to think presence as a present, and the present as a gift — now finds an infinitely more concrete content. Presence must be received as the present, namely, as the gift that is governed by the memorial and *epektasis*. Each instant of the present must befall us as a gift: the day, the hour, the instant, are imparted by charity. This applies to the present time (gift given) as to manna: one must gather it each day, without ever being able to store it up or to amass it as far as to dispense with receiving it as a gift. The manna of time thus becomes daily for us. "Time is of a literal precision and entirely merciful" (Hölderlin).[25] The Christian names his bread "daily bread," first because he receives the daily itself as a bread, a food whose daily reception — as a gift — no reserve will spare. The daily quality of the bread given at each instant, of a gift that renders it (a) present, culminates in the request of the Pater: "Give us this day our daily bread," our bread of this day and which this day alone can give us, at the same time that this very day is given to us. The daily character of the bread constitutes it as a definitively provisory gift, always to be repeated and taken up again; it insures against any taking possession of the present: "really confining this bread to a single day, so that, because of the one who revealed this prayer to us, we will not have the audacity to extend our request to a second day" (Maximus Confessor).[26] Of time in the present, it can well be said that one must receive it as a present, in the sense of a gift. But this implies also that we should receive this present of the consecrated Bread as the gift, at each instant, of union with Christ.[27]

The eucharistic presence comes to us, at each instant, as the gift of that very instant, and, in it, of the body of the Christ in whom one must be incorporated. The temporal present during which the eucharistic present endures resembles it: as a glory haloes an iconic apparition, time is made a present gift to let us receive in it the eucharistically given present. Time and the eucharistic present endure in an apparent continuity only as long as in our myopic gaze the instants given and the instantaneous gifts are confused. Or rather, the consecrated Bread and Wine seem to us to borrow their indisputable permanence from a permanent present (according to the model of the *here and now*) because our charity does

---

[25]   Hölderlin, *Letter to his mother*, no. 307, *G.A.*, 6, 1, p. 467.

[26]   Maximus Confessor, *Expositio orationis dominicae*, P.G. 90, 900c–d.

[27]   Saint Cyprian: "And this is why we ask that we be given each day *our* bread, that is to say the Christ, in order that we who live by Christ and reside in Him should not regress far from his sanctification and from his body" (*De dominica oratione*, XVIII, P.L. 4, 531a).

not have enough lucidity to deconstruct this subsisting present into a present gift, ceaselessly abandoned and taken up again, gone beyond and founded, thrown and projected between the memorial (temporalization by the past) and *epektasis* (temporalization by the future). The eucharistic present thus organizes in it, as the condition of its reception, the properly Christian temporality, and this because the eucharistic gift constitutes the ultimate paradigm of every present.

This interpretation presupposes a dispossession of the *here and now*, hence a critique of its primacy in the "*ordinary conception of time.*" This critique rests in turn on the reinterpretation of the present on the basis of the memorial that gives it as a pledge and of the eschatological call that provokes its accomplishment. In addition, the importance of the memorial which renders present (given) time always anterior to itself depends on the irrepressible eschatological *epektasis*: we may say that temporalization by the future determines all, here as well.[28] This is a temporality where the present, always already anterior to and in anticipation of itself, is received to the extent that the past and the future, in the name of the Alpha and the Omega, give it. Which means: what is named (and wrongly criticized) under the name of "real presence" founders in the metaphysical idolatry of the *here and now* or else must be received according to the properly Christian. temporality.

The Gift of Presence

Can the gap between this demand and our spontaneously idolatrous approach be overcome? In such an effort, would the theology of transubstantiation merit a privileged attentiveness? The first question will find the beginning of a response if prayer can transform our approach to the eucharistic present. But, before outlining in what sense this could be realized, one must satisfy a preliminary condition. I may transform my approach to the eucharistic present — and model myself by its dimensions — only if the eucharistic present itself is distinguished from me and from the consciousness that I have of myself (that we have of ourselves) on its occasion. One must admit a distance in order that the other may deploy in it the conditions of my union with him. Now; the theology of transubstantiation alone offers the possibility of distance, since it strictly separates my consciousness from Him who summons it. In the distance thus arranged, the Other summons, by his absolutely concrete sacramental body, my attention and my prayer. The response to the first question thus implies the second, settled in favor of the theology of

---

28   See Heidegger, *Sein und Zeit*, sec. 65: "The primary phenomenon of primordial and authentic temporality is the future" [trans., p. 378]. We obviously do not claim here to maintain the least agreement. However, it is certainly not by chance that the Catholic theology of the eucharistic present leads, in its break with the metaphysical conception of time, to taking a path not unknown to the "destruction of the history of ontology." But the influence is not necessarily exerted here in a unilateral manner.

transubstantiation. In order to advance, we must better understand the aporia, and, in a sense, construct it. The eucharistic present persists, according to the theology of transubstantiation, beyond our conscious attention, and yet this persistence is not amenable to the interpretation of time according to the (metaphysical) primacy of the *here and now*. Therefore one would have to conceive the factual irreducibility — this bread and this wine as Body and Blood — without for all that having recourse to the perdurability of the present. Would it be found as a deduction (in the Kantian sense) of the eucharistic persistence on the basis of the logic of charity (hence of the Cross), with neither borrowing nor detour? Perhaps. Let us outline it in three parts.

First, the Body and Blood persist in an otherness that goes as far as the species and the appearance of the bread and wine, most certainly not to assure any (idolatrous and imperialist) permanence — G~d "does not assure permanence," even that of History — but to continue to give themselves without return. The Son took on the body of humanity only in order to play humanly the trinitarian game of love; for this reason also, he loved "to the end" (John 13:1), that is, to the Cross; in order that the irrefutable demonstration of the death and resurrection not cease to provoke us, he gives himself with insistence in a body and a blood that persist in each day that time imparts to us.

He consecrates this wine as his blood only inasmuch as this blood is "shed for you" (Luke 22:20; see Matt. 26, 28; Mark14:24). He consecrates this bread as his body only inasmuch as this body is "given for you" (Luke 22:20).[29] The commitment of Christ as far as the bread and wine, the risk thus run of blasphemy or of idolatry (which, in a sense, amount to the same), are uniquely the concern, as the whole of *kenosis*, of condescension and trinitarian "philanthropy." It is not a question of some "safety" that permanence would assure for man, but of the irrevocable commitment of the love that "endures all" (1 Cor. 13:1). In the eucharistic present, all presence is deduced from the charity of the gift; all the rest in it becomes appearance for a gaze without charity: the perceptible species, the metaphysical conception of time, the reduction to consciousness, all are degraded to one figure (or caricature) of charity: "Everything which does not lead to charity is figurative. The sole object of Scripture is charity. Everything that does not lead to this sole good is figurative" (Pascal).[30] The consecrated bread and wine become

---

[29] I Corinthians 11:24 gives, according to the variations, "body broken/crushed/given/delivered." Delivered, or even betrayed: the Christ gave his body for us, in the sense that a traitor, who represented us all, "gave" him away. The liturgy of Saint Basil says: "This is my body, which is broken for you in remission of sins", see A. Hamman, *Prières eucharistiques des premiers siecles à nos jours*, coll. "Foi Vivante" (Paris, 1969), p. 20. Canons II, III and IV (in this way more traditional than the "Roman" canon I) all mention the "body delivered for you" (ibid., pp. 120, 125, 132).

[30] Pascal, *Pensées*, Br. sec. 670, L. Sect. 270, trans. Krailsheimer, p. 112 (see Br. sec. 665, L. sec. 849), trans., p. 292). On the commitment of charity in the present, see John of Damascus: "The bread and the wine are not the symbol of the body and the blood (far from

the ultimate aspect in which charity delivers itself body and soul. If we remain incapable of recognizing in it the ultimate advance of love, the fault is not its responsibility — love gives itself, even if "his own did not receive him" (John 1:11); love accomplishes the gift entirely, even if we scorn this gift: the fault returns to us, as the symptom of our impotence to read love, in other words, to love. Hence our tendency to reduce the eucharistic present to everything except to the love that ultimately assumes a body in it. Christ endures taking a sacramental body, venturing into the *here and now* that could blaspheme and/or idolize him, because already, he took a physical body, to the point of "not resisting, not recoiling ..., not withdrawing (his) face from insults ..., rendering (his) face hard as stone" (Isaiah 50:5–7). The sacramental body completes the oblation of the body, oblation that incarnates the Trinitarian oblation — "you wanted neither sacrifice, nor oblation, but you fashioned me a body" (Psalms 40:7 according to the LXX, taken up again in Hebrews 10:5–10). In short, *the eucharistic present is deduced from the commitment of charity*.

The Urgency of Contemplation

Second, the eucharistic present does not persistently drive itself into the repeated interstices of our days to reside passively in them but rather to transform us, from glory to glory. For this bread — the contemporary deviancies are somewhat right to insist on this — is given only in order to feed; it is made present only to permit its consumption. But these same deviancies miss what to feed means here. In consuming this food, we do not assimilate the Christ — to our person or to our "social body," or whatever — like the food that finds in us its end and sole justification. On the contrary, we become assimilated through the sacramental body of the Christ to his ecclesiastical body. He who takes communion worthily "will not be transforming Christ into himself, but instead will be passing over into the mystical body of Christ."[31] The materiality that transubstantiation provokes aims only at uniting us, through the Spirit that brings it about, with the spiritual body of

---

me!); it is the very body of the deified Lord" (loc. cit.), and Theodore of Mopsuestia: "It was not said: 'This is the symbol of my body, this is the symbol of my blood,' but indeed: 'this is my body and my blood'" (*Fragments on Matthew* 26, P.G. 66, 713b).

[31]   Saint Bonaventure, *Breviloquium*, VI, 9, 6, trans. de Vinck, p. 256. This text echoes the famous one of Saint Augustine: "Cibus sum grandium: cresce et manducabis me, nee tu me in mutabis sicut cibum carnis tuae, sed tu mutaberis in me" (*Confessions*, VII, 10, 16) ["I am the food of full-grown men. Grow and you shall feed on me. But you shall not change me into your own substance, as you do with the food of your body. Instead you shall be changed into me"; trans. Pine-Coffin, p. 147. See also Guillaume de Saint-Thierry, *De Natura et Dignitate Amoris*, XIII, 38 (P.L. 184, 403); Richard of Saint-Victor, *Declarationes .... ad B. Bernardum* (PL. 196, 262), etc.: and the texts cited by H. Lubac, *Corpus Mysticum*, 2nd ed. (Paris, 1949), pp. 200–202.

Christ constituted by the Church. A spiritual body, in other words a body infinitely more united, more coherent, more consistent — in a word, more real — than any physical body. The condescension of Christ as far as the materiality of the *here and now*, even at the risk of reification, aims at the spiritual incorporation *par excellence*: incorporation with the completed Body, this body which the Church permits us to "complete" (Col. 1:24) by the conformity, which it bestows on us, of our will to that of Christ accomplishing the design of the Father. The detour through the materiality of the eucharistic present plays a very precise role: as we spontaneously conceive it, the union called "spiritual" constrains us to less seriousness, fidelity, and commitment than "material" union; thus, by the violent and insurpassable fact of the eucharistic body — "this discourse is too hard!" a remark that reacts to the *Discourse on the Bread of Life* (John 6:60) — Christ indicates to us a spiritual communion that is not less but even more close than any union that is, in our sense, "spiritual." The bread and the wine must be consumed, to be sure, but so that our definitive union with the Father may be consummated in them, through communion with the ecclesiastical body of his Son. *The eucharistic present is deduced from the real edification of the ecclesiastical body of Christ.*

Finally, the eucharistic present can be accommodated, under the double relation of sacramental commitment and of ecclesiastical edification, only when understood as mystical body. In its most traditional acceptation, in fact, the locution "mystical *body*" concerns the eucharistic body of the Christ — as opposed to his *corpus verum*, the ecclesiastical body. Modern semantics has transferred the first adjective to the second substantive.[32] Indeed, we, who privilege the point of view of the *here and now* as the preeminent dimension of time and hence of (the) Being (of being), can hardly attribute reality but to an available and permanent thing. Or rather, we can hardly conceive that a reality should unfold outside of the available and permanent *here and now*. On the contrary, a properly theological gaze considers the eucharistic present as mystical, without this being a question of a reduction of its reality to some vague "mysticism"; the mystical character of the eucharistic present implies a full reality; thus one can speak of "the true manducation of the mystical flesh of Christ" (Anastasia the Sinaïte):[33] the flesh, though becoming mystical, remains nonetheless really edible. More, the mystical character of the eucharistic present not only does not destroy its reality, but carries it to a completion above suspicion, before which the reality of the *here and now* itself becomes a simple relay and support; common reality becomes mystagogy for the true reality, that of the eucharistic present as gift that itself is given as mystical. It is necessary to revive here the doctrine, common though fallen into disuse, of the couple *res et sacramentum*.[34] The bread and wine consecrated and

---

[32] See the demonstration given by H. de Lubac, op. cit., p. 55.

[33] *In Hexameron*, XII (P.G. 89, 1069c), cited in H. de Lubac, op. cit., p. 55.

[34] See the *Letter* of Innocent III to the Bishop of Lyon (*Denz.* 415); Saint Thomas, *Summa Theologica*, I IIa, q.73, a.3, *ad. resp.*; a.6, *ad. resp.* Lucid explanations in H. de Lubac, op. cit., p. 189f.; and *Catholicisme* (Paris, 1938), pp. 63–5.

transubstantiated into the Body and Blood are valid as *res* — *Christ* really given in the eucharistic present but, at the same time, they still remain a *sacramentum* with respect to the ecclesiastical body of Christ, the Church, which they aim at and construct; only this ecclesiastical Body should be called purely *res*. What are we to understand if not that, from the point of view of the *here and now*, the distribution of the terms *res et sacramentum* would be radically inverted? For our naturally blind gaze, the bread and wine *are* real, the consecrated bread and wine *are* real as bread and wine, sacramental ("mystical" in the ordinary sense) as Body and Blood of Christ, whereas the ecclesiastical body remains purely sacramental ("mystical body," according to a modern acceptation). But only the inverse has a correct theological meaning. The real is exclusively "that which the eye has not seen, that which the ear has not heard, that which has not risen to the heart of man," but that "God revealed to us by the Spirit" (1 Cor. 2:9) — all the rest has only a sacramental and indicative function. The real is exclusively that which seems "mystical" to the ordinary gaze — the Body of the Christ and his ecclesiastical body. Whoever fears that an idolatry of presence according to the *here and now* might ensue from the theology of transubstantiation admits by this very fact that he does not see that only the eucharistic present touches, in the consecrated host, the "real," and that what he fears as overvalued only plays there the role of *sacramentum*. In a word, the common objection can be raised only from the most radically nontheological point of view; the only one on the basis of which one can, even for a single moment, imagine that the theology of transubstantiation is interested in the *here and now* of the species, whereas through the species it attempts to approach the mystical *res* of the Body and of the blood. *The eucharistic present is deduced from theological, mystical "reality" alone.*

This triple deduction of the eucharistic present demonstrates, at least in outline, that its presence depends on charity, aims at the ecclesiastical body, and is amenable to a mystical reality. We thus rediscover the three temporalizations (kenotic commitment, anterior pledge of the Incarnation and Resurrection; mystical reality, *epektasis* of eschatological glory; ecclesiastical body, the daily gift of our days). The fundamental elements that permit the conjoining of our subjective approach with the objective demands of the eucharistic present reproduce in their turn the dimensions of a properly Christian temporality, so that each one of the justifications of the Eucharistic present reinforces the originality of this temporality. From this we draw, provisionally, two conclusions.

That which separates a good number of Christians from a theologically correct (if not adequate) comprehension of the eucharistic present has to do with nothing less than the *"ordinary conception of time"* and hence with the metaphysical discourse of presence. That certain objections have the theology of transubstantiation in view as "metaphysical" does not prove that it belongs to metaphysics but, on the contrary, reveals criticisms so filled by the essence and the destiny of metaphysics that they cannot stop themselves from reducing a discourse even as radically theological as that of the eucharistic present/gift. There is nothing surprising in this: here, as in other less decisive but more visible domains (politics, epistemology, etc.),

Christians confront, consciously or not, the test of the end of metaphysics. And as salvation does not cease to come first to them, the danger also increases first for them. Theological thought undoubtedly never experienced in such an imperative way the duty of formulating its own radically *theological* logic (which especially does not mean "dialectical theology," etc.); undoubtedly its responsibility never appeared as great with respect to all thought in expectation of a "new beginning"; but theological thought undoubtedly never stole away with so much fear from its theological task. The conversion of theological (and hence ecclesiastical) thought to its task and, here, to the meditation of the eucharistic present first requires prayer. In this sense, what we understand by the term "eucharistic contemplation" here assumes its true meaning: summoned to distance by the eucharistic present, the one who prays undertakes to let his gaze be converted in it — thus, in addition, to modify his thought in it. In prayer, only an "explanation" becomes possible, in other words, a struggle between human impotence to receive and the insistent humility of God to fulfill. And without defeat in this combat, thought will never carry the least speculative victory. Eucharistic contemplation, in this sense, would become an urgency: "Not only do we not sin by adoring Him, but we sin by not adoring Him" (Saint Augustine).[35]

---

[35] Saint Augustine, *Commentary on Psalm* 98.9 (P.L. 37, 1264).

Index